Cutting edge

Cutting edge

A Cook's Californian Inspiration

Richard Whittington

with drawings by Brian Ma Siy

Conran Octopus

Dedication

To all my Californian friends and most particularly Sybil Robson, Jeffrey and Cindy Marmelzat, Shelly and Deborah Berger and Tony Griffiths, without whom this book would not have been possible.

And for my children Sam, Olivia and Catherine.

Metric, imperial and American volume measures are given. In each recipe, use all metric, all imperial or all volume, as the three are not necessarily interchangeable.

Commissioning Editor: Louise Simpson
Editor & Project Manager: Lewis Esson
In-house Senior Editor: Catriona Woodburn
Art Director: Helen Lewis
Art Editor: Paul Welti
Production: Jill Beed
Editorial Assistant: Penny David
Americanizer: Norma Macmillan

First published in 1996 by
Conran Octopus Limited,
37 Shelton Street,
London WC2H 9HN

Cataloguing in Publication Data: a catalogue record for this book is available from the British Library.

ISBN 1 85029 772 X

Typeset by Peter Howard
Printed in Hong Kong, produced by Mandarin Offset

Contents

The early morning sky is a uniform pale blue...

… powdered around the edges with the faintest wisps of high cloud that will burn off long before the day heats up. A single condensation trail rules itself from left to right, so far up and so fast it must be a military aircraft. The weather report this May morning warns of 80 degrees and bad air as high pressure slams a lid on the city, allowing the fumes and ozone to bubble to a miasmic rolling boil. Asthmatics are told to stay indoors while even the health fanatics should avoid intense physical activity, not that this will deter the roller-bladers and runners who are already making their swift style statements in the parks. We are cautioned that unprotected skin at noon will burn in 35 minutes, and are reminded with unseemly relish that melanoma kills.

Even such grim intimations of mortality cannot spoil the joy of the day and with it the knowledge that the markets are bursting with beautiful produce just crying out to be cooked, and lush Californian wines to be opened, appraised and drunk. The sun is a constant reminder that its foods are to be enjoyed every day.

You would be forgiven for thinking all this describes Los Angeles but today I am writing about London. While England revels in an early summer, the temperature in Los Angeles today is in the 50s and the majority of that city's inhabitants will be thrilled by the fact. The sun which enchants those of more temperate climates is not such a big deal when you have it all year round. The only people who sport suntans along the Pacific Rim are Hispanic gardeners, the pool maintenance people and old hippie surfers whose legacy of beach exposure is to look like boot-polished scrotums with eyes. Today most kids know better and are zip-locked from head to toe in clinging neoprene wet suits, while the facial look on Rodeo Drive is as white as driven cocaine.

In the air-conditioned cafés, grills and restaurants only the food is hot, the people and their drinks remaining determinedly cool. Anyway, when the food is this good you come inside to enjoy it. Giant rectangular Santa Barbara umbrellas shade the al fresco lunch-time crowd, but there is nothing which

demands that Californian cooking be eaten only when it is hot or outdoors. This is not Greece on holiday where the taverna terrace is a mandatory part of the experience – indeed the essential enhancement to make the limited food enjoyable – but a centre of culinary excellence where you expect to eat as well as you once did in France, and not just in the Michelin- and Gault-Millaut-starred firmament.

California today is what France once was, a place where you find affordable excellence around every corner, where bakers produce wonderful bread and drinkable wine is to be had for $5 a bottle. It is a place where the emphasis will always be on pristine ingredients and where people do not automatically buy their fruit and vegetables drenched in pesticides and packed in plastic from supermarkets.

For the visitor who is a keen cook or discerning eater California delivers some of the best food to be had in the world today and from which we can all take inspiration. One could spend a lifetime learning from California's finest chefs – Alice Water's seminal work at Chez Panisse in Berkeley, the Mexican influences of Susan Feniger and Mary Sue Milliken at the Border Grill and City Restaurant, Barbara Tropp's reworking of Chinese classics at China Moon Café, the new fast-food restaurant as redefined by Cindy Pawlcyn at Fog City Diner in San Francisco, the trailblazing cooking of Jeremiah Tower at Stars and John Sedlar in Santa Monica, the remarkable achievements of Wolfgang Puck – we have a food revolution to explore and embrace.

This book is concerned, however, not with individual achievements in detail but with their collective inspiration and culinary energy. It is not a travelogue of restaurants the majority of readers will never visit but about the ideas they offer us as private cooks, a truly international process and one that can help us create vividly different meals at home wherever we live. California has been inspirational and has taken cooking forward, but it constantly absorbs new themes and directions. When we go there we take with us things like our own ways of working and enthusiasms. The process is therefore dynamic and open-ended.

More than 25 million people live in this vast state of 158,000 square miles – its coastline stretching northwards 840 miles from the Mexican border – and the great majority are to be found in the 40-mile-wide coastal strip which embraces the cities of San Diego, Los Angeles and San Francisco, with only Sacramento and Fresno further inland. Outside of the metropolitan areas there is space to lose yourself in some of the most stunning country in the world. Nobody who has ever driven the coastal road through Big Sur from Santa Lucia to Point Lobos by Carmel can ever forget it. Best actually to be driven, otherwise craning your neck to look up at the precipitous hills that tumble down to the road while negotiating the tight bends of the cliff edge can be less than relaxing. North of San Francisco the wine areas of Napa and Sonoma are entrancing.

It is a land of magic mountains, from the soaring spectacle of the High Sierras to the looming presence of the coastal foothills. Yosemite National Park and Death Valley are here, as different in character as San Francisco is from Anaheim. This is not one climate but many micro-climates. You can find everything from desert through sub-tropical to temperate, lush valleys, wooded hills, rolling grasslands and rocky mountains. It is more a nation state than a state of the union. Ranked in economic terms against countries, California's GNP is eighth in the world, its agricultural production seventh largest, its population growing faster than any other in the USA.

A frequent visitor for the past 20 years, I have eaten in its most famous and glamorous restaurants, from Beverly Hills to the Napa Valley, as well as in Mexican pit barbecue joints and chilli bars, simple cafés and diners, both traditional and reworked. I have shopped in local markets and cooked for my friends in the cities and in the country. California cooking is defined by the best fresh ingredients, simple preparation and its unique mix of influences. There is a lot of grilling and a lot of dry pan-searing. There is a lot of fish and fowl, vegetables and salads. There is superb beef to be had too and a qualified amount of pork, but the contemporary emphasis eschews saturated fat. This is no bad thing, although the vehemence of the new disapproval is sometimes rather alarming.

Asking a Californian friend what she would like for a dinner party I suggested a daube of beef and was doing fine on the marketing – 'slow simmered in wine and perfumed with garlic' – when I inadvertently mentioned the word shin. 'Yech. Shin! What next, faces?' The sale was dead and the situation not negotiable. We settled on roast chicken after I had painted a picture of the rural idyll in which it had been nurtured, scratching in a farmyard straight out of *Little House on the Prairie*. The only thing missing was 'Shall We Gather at the River' on the soundtrack, and I glossed over the death-house scene.

This book does not set out to be a comprehensive gazetteer and is inevitably personal in what is included and what left out. It focuses more on the south than the north because that is where I have spent most time and where my heart, however perversely, resides. My mission is to communicate not only what I learned on my travels but some of the pleasure I had acquiring that knowledge. Led by California's chefs, the contemporary professional kitchen is turning more and more to a style of cooking which is essentially simple but which embraces rich multi-cultural references. Current Californian cuisine has been as much influenced by Mexican cooking as by the peasant Italian dishes of the Southern Mediterranean and by the culinary maelstrom of South-east Asia, where Thai, Vietnamese, Cambodian, Malay and Indonesian styles mix so delightfully. These are the references that underpin a new wave of exciting cooking, where Japan can meet France in one bowl, where Italy and China unite on the same plate.

If a Mexican influence predominates in this book, then this is entirely appropriate. Historically Mexico was a Spanish colony, as was California, which was nominally governed from Mexico. It was not a case of Mexican food *per se* being imported across a border. Precisely the same foods were grown and eaten. The Spanish colonists embraced local produce such as turkeys, beans, corn, avocados, chillies, tomatilloes, tomatoes, potatoes, guavas, cumin and coriander [cilantro], while introducing beef, pork and chickens. With hindsight it seems a pretty poor exchange. It was not until the Gold Rush of 1849 that California experienced a second colonization, this time by Americans, bringing with them different Northern European cultural antecedents. A third, and much larger, flood of immigrants seized the opportunity of cheap travel provided by the railway price wars of the 1880s, which brought hundreds of thousands of people from the East to the golden coast. California has always been seen as a land of opportunity, a dream place where the sun continues to shine long after the dreams have died.

California is the originator of an imaginative cooking which vigorously mixes styles and ingredients from the global kitchen. Where California cooks have already gone, the rest of the world will surely follow. One can see in the work of French Michelin-starred chefs like Alain Ducasse that a new lightness and freshness are beginning to impact even in the notoriously reactionary temples of classic French gastronomy. In a recent television interview, the great Paul Bocuse said that he goes regularly to California for inspiration.

This inspiration, with its emphasis on simplicity and balance, unquestionably defines the food of tomorrow, driven partly by health considerations and partly by changing perceptions of how imaginatively a menu can be structured. But the food of California also has clear historical and cultural roots in its early Spanish/Mexican lineage. This century has seen a succession of influences which have brought with them new opportunities in terms of both ingredients and cooking styles, as we will see in the recurring national themes which simmer in contemporary Californian cuisine. It is the ultimate culinary melting pot.

Some restaurant critics who are only happy when eating dishes from the French bourgeois tradition sneer at what they invariably refer to as 'fusion food' or 'eclectic cooking'. Both terms are overused and frequently misapplied, their implication usually pejorative. In reality, Californian food is characterized more by elegant simplicity than by pretension, though pastry chefs are producing some ludicrous desserts that look like three-dimensional abstractions which are just plain silly, the sort of food that only needs one prod of a fork to collapse into visual garbage. It is also fashionable to build high on the plate, which is just as irritating. Like all such trends, however, it will pass. This excess is not, anyway, purely a Californian phenomenon but one that has seemingly overnight permeated America's restaurants from coast to coast, an unfortunate trend that will undoubtedly be felt all over the world. And yes, you can find restaurants where the ingredients don't sit happily together on the plate but clash and bang up against each other in awkward disharmony, but in California these are exceptions rather than the rule.

There are those fortunate people who live nominally in Los Angeles but who spend their weekends far north of that sprawling city in quiet adobe towns like Santa Barbara or on ranches in the Santa Ynez valley, feeling safe there to drive their Porsches without the threat of them being taken away at stop lights by disadvantaged slum-dwellers with guns. The locals include songwriter Bernie Taupin – whose brother Kit has a beautifully simple Mexican-based restaurant in the small town of Santa Ynez called Una Mas Café – and Whoopie Goldberg and Michael Jackson, not that you ever see them. People are very private, behind their electric gates.

One day, lying out by the pool on just such a weekend escape, with the mountains shimmering far away under a cloudless sky, my host propped himself up on his elbow and took a sip from a glass of chilled Chardonnay produced just a few miles away across the valley. He scanned around his property and watched his girlfriend Cindy putting her paint Chile Pepper through its dressage paces in the corral under the critical eye of Jesus, the ranch hand, then slumped back with a satisfied sigh. 'Another shitty day in paradise, right Richard?' I grunted. Not a lot you can say to a line like that. There was a pause while I checked out the wine, aromatic and smokily complex, figured I'd finish it and have something more appropriate like a vodka and freshly squeezed grapefruit juice. Aah, decisions. 'I'm hungry.' He is always hungry. 'What are you cooking for lunch?' I thought hard. A 10-minute drive away between Los Olivos and Solvang in the middle of nowhere is a food market that is nothing short of wonderful. Really fresh seafood, locally grown fruit and vegetables, an extraordinary butcher, aisles of fresh tortillas, acres of cold beers, thousands of bottles of local wines. They do bizarre promotions. Sometimes you enter past an Elvis look-alike who sings loudly in a jumbo jump-suit of lights but, alas, not remotely like Elvis. At weekends they have a big, open-air pit barbecue with great hunks of tri-tip beef smoking gently, filling the air with an irresistible aroma. I squinted against the sun and looked at him, a substantial presence sprawled on a white wood lounger.

'That's a hard question, Jeffrey. We've got the whole of California to choose from. Let's decide when we see what looks best in the market.' A turkey vulture soared high overhead on a thermal, its wings motionless, inspecting us. It looked hungry too.

'The whole of California to choose from,' he mused. 'You should write a book about it. You loving being here and cooking and stuff.'

So I have.

Introduction to the Recipes

Agriculturally generous in its climate and topography, California is astonishingly fertile. More than 300 different fruits and vegetables grow in just three valleys – the Central, Salinas and Imperial. Indeed, there is almost nothing that won't grow here, unless you exclude fully tropical fruits. The peripatetic visitor keeps doing double-takes – are those really melons, lemons, limes, oranges, pomegranates, tomatilloes, chillies and artichokes in the fields? For those who rarely see such things in their natural state, it is a joyous abundance that unfolds beside the road. Better still, you are rarely far from the sea. The Pacific Ocean is a rich source of fish, while close inland California's ranches raise some of the best beef cattle in the world. The state's vineyards also produce diverse and extraordinary wines that have redefined our appreciation of the grape's most revered product.

Think of California as the best supermarket you could ever visit, then consider the market where you do your weekly food shop. In many ways it is a microcosm of the same generous diversity. For at certain times of the year much of what it sells comes from California. The avocados, peaches, cherries, citrus fruits, mange-tout peas, asparagus and strawberries may well have been grown there. All the foods that have helped shape Californian cooking are available to us, excluding (at the time of writing) tomatilloes – a sharper-flavoured and more fashionable relative of the tomato.

While there are still areas for improvement, these are more in terms of quality than in matters of choice. As California was colonized by people from all over the world, so in culinary terms were we British. If the supermarket does not stock it then an Asian or Oriental market will. Availability is no longer a restricting factor, and today we are only limited by our imagination and our willingness to try new things and explore different worlds.

Chillies are very much a case in point. You can buy them fresh in most British supermarkets and we are starting to see them sold as specific types – Anaheim, serrano, jalapeño, habanero, and so on. You will find more than one kind of avocado: the Haas type with thicker, darker skin, and others with smooth skins. There is not one dried pulse or bean on the shelves, but dozens. You can specify, and get, a range of potatoes. If you want one that is floury and another that is waxy, all you have to do is ask. Limes, once a rarity, are now available all year round and, as more people eat them, their price goes down.

You should have no problem obtaining any of the ingredients used in the recipes that follow. Where substitution is possible it says so, but as a general rule it is not a good idea. Obviously when Kikkoman soy sauce, say, is specified you can use a different brand, though none will be as good. However, a shallot is not the same thing as an onion, and lime juice is very different from lemon juice. South-east-Asian fish sauce bears no resemblance to anchovy essence. Saffron is not turmeric and vice versa. None of the ingredients demanded should be difficult to source, unless you live on the Outer Hebrides or are wholly dependent on the local mini-market, as we have learned to call Mr Patel's invaluable corner shop.

How to Use this Book

From a practical point of view and while cross-referencing between recipes is kept to a minimum, I have gathered together a 'basics' section consisting of those elements which crop up frequently throughout the book. Thus you will find there pastry, stock and sauce recipes, etc. The most vexing matter is assumption of prior knowledge on the part of the reader. While a few will groan at the prospect of a detailed piece on making chicken stock, this is so much a key to achieving the desired result in so many of the recipes that it is essential to include it. We all go about things differently, and the pastry section is very much food-processor-driven, just as the bread-making section uses an electric mixer extensively.

There is no vegetarian section as such. I cook a lot of dishes that contain neither meat nor fish, notably my versions of Indian food, but this seems natural enough in an omnivore and the vegetarian area is covered more fully by numerous other writers. A vegetarian diet is not what Californian cooking is all about. Vegetarianism is certainly on the increase there, but for the time being people still eat meat – though, it has to be said, a great deal less than they used to.

Healthy Eating

On a daily basis, the message about diet must be that less is more, both in terms of fish and meat, and most certainly so far as saturated fat is concerned. The flavoured butters called for in the recipes never involve using more than 15g/½oz [1tbsp] per serving. If this sounds excessive, then perhaps one of those 'Ankle and Buttock Diet' cookbooks is what you are after. The use of butter in this book is restricted, not only because it is now viewed as deeply unhealthy in California but because it is unnecessary with olive oil to hand. Butter is used in pastry, of course, but its wider application is carefully controlled. Butter in excess is the cheap trick of the professional kitchen, a sort of chef's sleight-of-hand.

Current medical thinking suggests that balance is the key to a healthy diet, that monounsaturated fats are better than polyunsaturates and that oily fish eaten at least twice a week offers significant cardiovascular benefits. In richer and more sinful food areas it is not a case of never, but of exactly how much and how often.

The current recommended maximum drinking quota of half a bottle of red wine a day seems depressingly low, but perhaps the powers that be forgot to say that this is to be taken with meals and should be multiplied by three.

Ingredients

There is a number of basic ingredients to consider:

The quality of tomatoes available in supermarkets is at last improving and you can now buy vine-ripened ones seasonally if you are prepared to pay a premium for them. It is normally best to buy imported plum tomatoes, which generally have a better flavour and texture than our British home-grown product. All tomatoes are sold unripe and should not therefore be stored in the refrigerator but laid in a single layer on a wire rack to ripen at room temperature, which usually takes three or four days.

Red sweet peppers are ready to eat on purchase and, since they are invariably roasted as a necessary preliminary to their inclusion in any of the recipes in this book, it is a good idea to do this as soon after purchase as possible. The peppers are then peeled and stored in oil in jars in the fridge, ready at a moment's notice when needed.

Onions, garlic and *potatoes* are bought weekly, as are fresh herbs, some now available growing in pots. *Coriander [cilantro], chives, lemon grass* and *flat-leaf parsley* should be kept in the salad box in the fridge. Herbs like basil, which deteriorate rapidly, should be bought on the day they are to be used.

Perishable dairy products, including *yogurt, crème fraîche, feta, goat's cheese, mozzarella* and *mascarpone* are all items for the weekly shop. *Reggiano Parmesan* and farmhouse *Cheddar* are bought as required. A premium dark *chocolate* is kept in the fridge.

Store-cupboard staples include *canned tomatoes, anchovies, clam juice, Worcestershire sauce, Kikkoman soy sauce, Thai fish sauce, hoi-sin sauce, oyster sauce* and *good-quality tomato ketchup*. Your pantry should ideally also contain *long-grain, fragrant* and *risotto rice, dried pasta, high-* and *low-protein wheat flours, polenta* and/or *cornmeal, flageolets, haricots blancs* or *other dried white beans, Puy lentils* and *red lentils (masoor dal)*. Dried *ceps* or *porcini* and a mixture of *ceps, trompettes* and *pleurottes*, the so-called *forestière* mixture, are always

useful, and since you only need a few to deliver a tremendous amount of flavour or to augment fresh cultivated mushrooms, they are not as expensive as their price by weight implies.

Extra-virgin olive oil is specified in many recipes. There is a view that it should never be cooked, but I believe it contributes unique flavour when it is. Again, its usage is moderate because, while olive oil is low in saturated fats, it remains highly calorific.

For shallow- and deep-frying, use *sunflower oil* and in mayonnaise use a mixture of sunflower and olive oils in equal proportions. A favourite oil is Colonna, one of the finest examples of Italian estate-bottled extra-virgin oil. On this subject it is not safe to assume that an Italian label means that the oil originated in Italy, a country which imports vast amounts of Greek and Spanish oils but does not see the necessity of passing this information to the consumer when it re-exports it. There is nothing therefore intrinsically superior about Italian olive oil. Spain has always produced superb big-flavoured olive oil and you pay less for it. Much of the fashionable obsession with premium brands is mere snobbery. Supermarket own-label olive oils are generally excellent. Buy small bottles initially and decide what you like best before going on to buying in larger quantities.

Much is made these days of commercially flavoured oils, but they are overvalued. Some, like lemon-flavoured oil, taste to me like cheap soap. Fresh lemon juice mixed with good oil gives a much fresher result.

The salt of choice is *Maldon sea salt*, one of the best in the world. Generally use *black peppercorns*, since the use of white is purely a matter of aesthetics. The ready-made mixture of black and green peppercorns with tiny red pimentos gives a different aromatic finish. Peppercorns are always ground at the point when they are used. As a general rule, never buy ground spices. You will always get more from a whole spice, like cumin seeds, when you first roast them and then grind them only minutes before incorporating them in a dish. A coffee grinder dedicated to this task is a handy piece of kitchen kit.

Saffron is used in a number of recipes. The best comes from Spain where its quality is measured by the length of the dried threads – the stigmas of the crocus *sativus* – and by the levels of the volatile and aromatic oils that give the deep vermilion colour and strong flavour. The best saffron is still produced by small family businesses in the La Mancha region of southern Castile during the 10-day harvest period that straddles October and November. Before use, saffron threads need to be soaked in hot liquid, usually water but possibly wine, milk or stock. How much to use and when to add during cooking are difficult questions. For the dishes in this book, which are almost all for four people, a pinch of saffron (or about 20 threads) is enough for a risotto of 350g/12oz [1½ cups] of uncooked rice. In a risotto, broth or potato dish, it is better to add the saffron towards the end of cooking as its power is diminished by lengthy exposure to heat.

Preparation

As a cook you have to do something a number of times to know every angle and to ensure consistent delivery, but my assumption is that you are not a professional chef, or rather, this is not a book written for such chefs but for amateurs.

In French, *amateur* does not mean 'dilettante' or 'neophyte' in this context, but 'enthusiast'. Let our ambition always be to cook for fun and to give pleasure doing so. This does not invariably mean, as the current fashion suggests, fast preparation. Some things do take all day and there are no shortcuts but, of course, there are lots of dishes that take only minutes to prepare. You decide what to cook based on what is available and that applies to time just as much as ingredients.

The single most important lesson that the professional kitchen has to offer the private cook is the concept of *mise en place*. This means strategic planning mixed with common sense and is designed to reduce pressure on the cook and, by definition, everybody else. Whatever you can do ahead of time to make getting the food on the table in good shape and on time should be done. The start point is defined by working backwards from the time when you plan to serve the food. In many of the recipes this means beginning the day before, infrequently even sooner.

You probably think you do this already, but whenever I go somewhere to dinner and the food arrives an hour late it is because the cook either has failed to cook within his or her abilities or, most often, has just left too much to the last minute. Saying, 'look, I've got a proper job all day,' is not an acceptable excuse; this is true for a lot of people. Cook the first course and dessert the night before. Have only one hot dish. Buy in some items ready-made. There are lots of ways around the problem.

The French say that you never grow old at the table. It is an encouraging thought. Good food is for every day and every one. It is neither exclusive nor is it the privileged territory of the rich and famous. Good food does not necessarily mean expensive food, and this is where it begins and ends. Every time we cook something we should try to do it a bit better than the last time and we should always be our own toughest critic. Incremental improvement is what it is all about, just like making anything work better over a period of time, because you can always learn something new every day. This is not a revolutionary philosophy, simply one that strives for excellence in everything, whether it is boiling an egg or making a sabayon. If you care, then that shines through your food. In the end, however, good food is about life and laughter, not plaudits, for cooking is not a competition but a celebration.

Equipment

There is a number of items of kit you will need if you are to cook everything in the book. A *ridged grill pan* is used extensively in preference to a charcoal grill. I have an ancient pan found many years ago on a market stall in Honfleur. It is very heavy; its ridges are thin and stand proud from the base by a good half centimetre. Grill pans that have wide, shallow ridges are worse than useless and are really defective frying pans, but a heavy flat metal grill that covers the width of two burners is very useful for grilling things on skewers. A hibachi-type barbecue makes a pleasant change in the summer but the grill pan gives you better control and is there all year round.

Heavy *non-stick Le Creuset pans* are also much used, though they are not without their problems. All non-stick pans need to be heated gently if you are

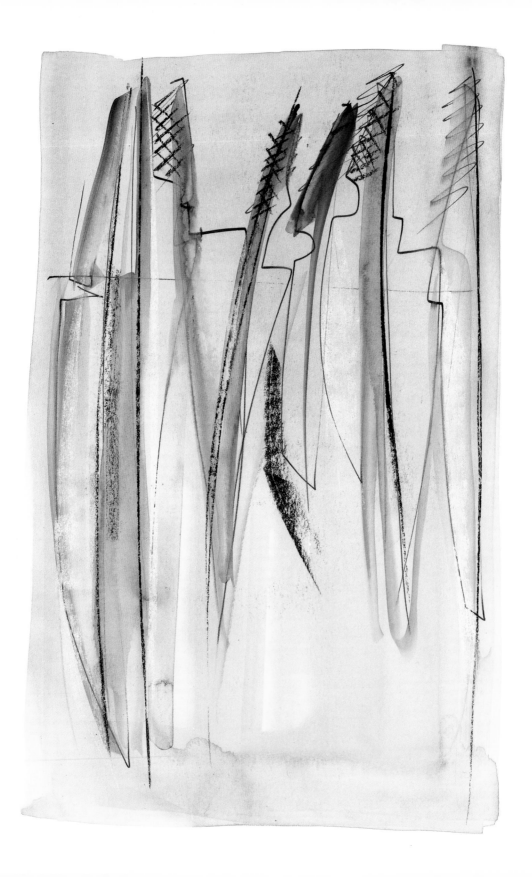

cooking dry. Exposure of a cold non-stick pan to high heat either on the hob or in the oven will rapidly damage the coating. A good range of *casserole dishes* and *saucepans* and of *ovenproof dishes* is obviously necessary.

You can never have too many *mixing bowls, sieves, pudding basins, plastic boxes* with airtight lids, *wooden spoons, whisks, ladles* and – very important – several pairs of different-sized sprung *tongs*. Heavy-duty *Swiss-roll [jelly-roll] pans* have myriad uses. A *blanching basket* that allows you to plunge vegetables or pasta in and out of boiling water is very useful, as are a *salad spinner* and a *grilling basket* that allows you to turn fish or vegetables easily.

You don't need lots of *knives*, but you do need a minimum of three: a small knife, a large chef's knife and a heavy-duty serrated knife. A heavy *chopper* and good pairs of *scissors* and *poultry shears* are also helpful if not actually essential. Scalpels with disposable blades are also useful. Keeping knives and other bladed instruments sharp is vital and this cannot be achieved with a butcher's steel alone. Whet stones are the best means of sharpening blades at home. Itinerant knife grinders are generally not a good idea.

Essential machines are a *food mixer* and a *food processor*. God knows how we all managed before they were invented. I have an *ice-cream maker, a juice extractor, a hand-held electric mixer* and a small *blowtorch* for brûlées. I also possess a hand-cranked *pasta machine* but this is not used in this book, the whole thing about home-made pasta having been done to death elsewhere. As a general rule the *freezer* is only used for ice-making, ice-cream and sorbet setting and for the storage of won-ton wrappers, Chinese pancakes, pitta breads, filo and puff pastry. It also contains reduced stocks frozen in cubes.

On Vegetables and Side Dishes

In every cookbook a decision must be made whether vegetables should be dealt with separately or in conjunction with the dishes they best complement. Having chosen the latter course in this book, I should still say that these are only suggestions. Specifying a particular side dish with a given dish does not preclude the reader from choosing something different. But never, please, three or four vegetables with a meat or fish course. One side dish is usually best, two at most – or, following the restaurant lead, none at all. Multiple vegetables are typical of all that goes wrong in the British kitchen. They reflect a generosity of spirit but an inappropriate clash of flavours and textures. As Escoffier said, 'keep it simple'.

When cooking green vegetables, use the restaurant technique of blanching and refreshing; that is, an initial cooking in boiling salted water followed by a brief immersion in very cold water to stop the cooking process. Just before serving return them to the boiling water for a few seconds to heat them through. This is a very helpful trick which gets things to the table hot, cooked to perfection and with the minimum amount of aggravation.

Basics, Sauces and Accompaniments

Stocks

Stocks are an essential part of good cooking. Stock or bouillon cubes may be getting better, but they will never be as good as the real thing. I never use veal stock – which the majority of restaurants cannot function without – because it is too strongly flavoured. A good chicken stock, when reduced, will give you all the depth of flavour you need for any meat or poultry dish.

Every time you roast a chicken, the carcass and bones provide the basis for a stock, but one carcass has obvious limitations in the amount of stock it can produce. Your butcher will give you carcasses if you are a regular customer. Chicken wings will also produce excellent results once roasted to a good colour in the oven. Chicken giblets are now rarely obtainable because of government rulings which forbid the sale of undrawn poultry. Also, large-scale producers can make money selling them to manufacturers of bouillon and pet-food.

Variations on the theme are always welcome. Wood pigeons, for example, have a terrific flavour and are quite cheap. Buy them and use the breasts only in a salade tiède, as in the Warm Pigeon Salad with Borlotti Beans and Sugar-snaps on page 176, then brown the rest of the birds in a hot oven and use to make stock, either on their own or augmenting a standard chicken stock. With meat and poultry stocks, always leave the skins on the onions. This gives a depth of colour to the finished product.

Meat stocks should be made with long slow simmering. The professional view is that this should never be for more than eight hours, but this is more to do with the constraints of service than the issue of flavour. The water is only brought to the boil initially and the heat lowered immediately after skimming. Boiling forces albumen and calcium from the bones and gives the stock a nasty gluey taste and a cloudy finish. Meat and poultry stocks can be simmered for several hours and this can be done overnight or for as long as 24 hours, replenishing the water from time to time. You then strain them through a muslin- or cheesecloth-lined sieve and then boil them to reduce and intensify flavour. Produced in this way you will have a golden-coloured broth which is

absolutely clear, a consommé without all that aggravation with egg whites. Taken down to an extreme reduction, stocks can be frozen in ice trays, and the cubes bagged and kept in the freezer. A few cubes added to the pan after deglazing will give you an instant sauce with lots of flavour.

Fish and vegetable stocks do not benefit from long cooking. After 20 minutes you will have extracted all the flavour there is to be had and after 30 minutes fish stock gets bitter.

Chicken Stock

1.8 kg / 4 lb raw chicken wings, cooked carcasses or bones
3 onions, halved but unpeeled
3 leeks, split and rinsed
4 celery stalks
3 carrots, peeled
sprig of thyme
handful of parsley
2 bay leaves
1 tbsp black peppercorns, lightly crushed

Preheat the oven to 250°C/475°F/gas9. Put the chicken wings, carcasses etc in a roasting pan and brown in the oven for 30 minutes, turning frequently.

Transfer the bones to a large pan and cover with 4 litres / 8 pt [4 qt] of cold water. Bring to the boil and skim the scum from the surface, then add the vegetables and aromatics. Return to the boil, skim again, then reduce the heat to a bare simmer and cook for a minimum of 4 hours, replenishing the water from time to time. A stock can be simmered like this overnight or even longer.

Pass through a muslin- or cheesecloth-lined sieve to give a light stock; or put the strained stock into a clean pan, return to a fast boil and reduce by about two-thirds for a stronger result. Alternatively, take the reduction further, leave to cool and freeze as cubes.

Vegetable Stock

2 each carrots, leeks, onions, fennel bulbs
4 celery stalks, plus leaves
1 head of garlic
3 tbsp olive oil
450 g / 1 lb canned chopped [crushed] tomatoes
3 tbsp gin
handful of spring onion [scallion] green parts
2 bay leaves
handful of tarragon
handful of parsley
1 star anise
300 ml / 1/2 pt [1 1/4 cups] dry white wine

Because there are no bones to exude unpleasantness, vegetable stocks are the exception to the gentle simmer rule and can be boiled hard.

Cut all the fresh vegetables into 2 cm / 3/4 in dice and sweat gently in the olive oil in a saucepan until soft but not coloured.

Add the tomatoes and gin. Turn up the heat and flame the gin, then add the spring onion greens, herbs and star anise and pour in the white wine with 2 litres / 3 1/2 pt [2 qt] water. Boil vigorously to reduce by half. Strain before use.

Fish Stock

1 kg / 2¼ lb white fish heads
   and bones
1 live hen crab or shells of
   crabs and lobsters (optional)
450 g / 1 lb onions
4 celery stalks
6 garlic cloves
450 g / 1 lb leeks
2 carrots
2 fennel bulbs
125 ml / 4 fl oz [½ cup] olive oil
450 g / 1 lb canned chopped
   [crushed] tomatoes
sprig of thyme
bunch of parsley
2 bay leaves
strip of dried orange peel
1 bottle of dry white wine
   (vinegary rubbish or left-over
   is fine)

It is good practice to keep white fish heads and bones in the freezer so that you can make fish stock from time to time. Always rinse the bones well and cut out the gills before freezing, as it is much more difficult to do so afterwards, and this way you can use them straight from the freezer. Most fishmongers will give you heads and bones for nothing.

Any white fish – like sole, turbot, brill, cod, conger eel, monkfish and whiting – are good for stock. Oily fish, like mackerel, salmon or herring, are unsuitable. Any shellfish heads and shells are excellent additions. Otherwise, buy a hen crab and smash it with a hammer, making the first strike between the eyes.

Dice the onions, celery, garlic, leeks, carrots and fennel. In a large heavy saucepan, sweat the vegetables in the olive oil until translucent, being careful not to brown them as this would ruin the flavour.

If using a live crab, send it to its maker now with a hammer, smashing it into small bits and scraping all the gunk into the pot. If you have prawn or shrimp shells or any shellfish shells from another dish, then add them with the fish heads and bones. Add all the other ingredients with 3 litres / 5 pt [3 qt] of water and bring to the boil. Skim, lower the heat to a simmer and cook gently for 30 minutes. Strain through a sieve into a clean saucepan, pressing with a wooden spoon to extract all the juices. Taste and season with salt and pepper.

This is a basic fish soup in its own right, needing only the addition of some pieces of skinned boned fish, some saffron and a touch of Pastis to give you something close to a bouillabaisse (see page 84).

Shellfish Fumet

Make as above, but add as many prawns, shrimp or shellfish shells as you can to the fish trimmings.

Some Notes on Important Ingredients

Home-dried Tomatoes

Cut the tomatoes in halves and scoop out the pulp and seeds. Sit them, cut side up, in trays, sprinkle with a little salt and caster sugar [US granulated sugar], then drizzle with olive oil.

Cook slowly in an oven at 150°C/300°F/gas2 until most of the moisture has evaporated from them. Depending on how many you are drying at a time, this can take anything from two hours upwards. It also depends on how dry you want to make them. All ovens have hot spots so move the tomatoes on the tray from time to time to give an even result and to avoid burning any.

Remove and, when cool, pack tightly in jars and cover with olive oil. They are fabulous in salads, as a relish with cold meats or cheese, and on pizzas and open tarts.

Roasted Peppers

Roasted and peeled red sweet peppers are demanded for many of the recipes in this book. The preliminary cooking changes both the flavour and the texture markedly and, once done, the peppers will keep in jars, filmed with olive oil to keep out the air for as long as you let them.

You have five choices when roasting red peppers:

1 Over an open flame. This delivers the most profound flavour enhancement and can be done one pepper at a time, which is painfully slow, or several can be held in a grilling basket – either one of those Aga toast-makers or, better, the hinged contraptions for putting fish on a charcoal grill or under a grill [broiler], that allow you to turn it without damage to the skin. You actually want to blacken and blister the skins completely. This does not, surprisingly,

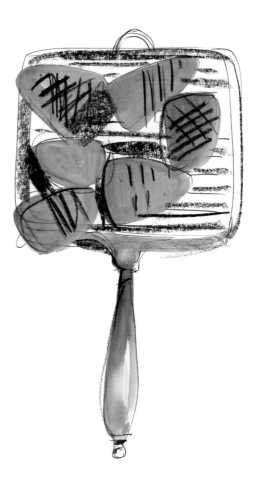

result in a bitter or burnt flavour in the flesh, but rather it gives a sweetness and intensity that is very pleasing. Transfer the blackened peppers to a bowl, cover the top with plastic film (or put them in a zip-lock bag) and leave for 15 minutes to generate steam, which loosens the skins and makes them very easy to peel.

2 Under an overhead grill [broiler], turning frequently.

3 On a dry ridged grill pan over a high heat, turning frequently.

4 Cut in halves, brushed with olive oil and roasted in a pan in the oven at 220°C/425°F/gas7 for about 30-40 minutes.

5 Roasted whole, standing upright, without oil, in a hot oven until blistered. Then cover and leave to steam for 10 minutes. This is the most effective preliminary method for easy peeling.

Try all the methods and note the differences each gives you.

Red-hot Chilli Peppers

How hot is hot? It is like that old saw about how long is a piece of string. The chilli (or, more correctly, chile) came originally from South America and was taken to Europe in the 16th century by Spaniards; in due course it was exported on to India and South-east Asia. Used fresh, the chilli is a vegetable like a sweet pepper. When dried it is used as you would a spice, and people in the countries where chillies are grown value it in its dried form just as much as when it is fresh.

All chillies are of the genus *Capsicum*, and are therefore relatives of sweet peppers. Their vast diversity makes the subject confusing and there is no way to tell how hot chillies are just by looking at them. The usual colour rule of red being hot and green cool does not apply, for chillies vary in size, appearance and intensity. There are dozens of different chillies including arbol, ancho, cascabel, guajillo, jalapeño, mulato, pasilla, poblano and serrano, all of which have individual flavours and heat intensity. As a general rule, the smaller they are – like the deceptively innocent-looking and tiny Thai green chilli – the more vicious, but this is not a safe way of judging either. The pretty lantern-like Scotch bonnet or habanero is arguably the hottest.

The heat of the chilli is concentrated in the white placenta or seed cluster. You can calm the hottest varieties by soaking them for 30-40 minutes in 300 ml / ½ pt [1 ¼ cups] of water mixed with a tablespoon of vinegar and two teaspoons of salt. Ultimately the only way to test heat is to put a tiny piece on your tongue. The more you explore chillies, the more you will become aware of their complexity and the range of flavours. Just be circumspect.

Capsaicin, the heat-producing element in chillies, is measured in Scoville units, which range from zero for a sweet pepper to 300,000 for the habanero. Most of the capsaicin is contained in the seeds and the connecting membrane, and when you remove these you make the chilli milder, though in the case of the habanero mild is an adjective you could never use. On a scale of 1 to 10, the habanero is an undisputed 10. If you try the habanero rashly and screech with pain, treat your tongue with spoonfuls of yogurt. Sugar also helps, water or beer does not. People do go on excessively about the care needed in handling chillies and many books call for rubber gloves. This is silly. Just concentrate on dealing with them, then immediately wash your hands without going to the bathroom first - in the American sense of, 'Mommy, look at the puppy going to the bathroom on the sidewalk'. When you do go, because we all get side-tracked by a telephone call or our daily units or whatever, it will help focus you wonderfully effectively for the next chilli-chopping session.

In California the most common chilli is the New Mexican or Anaheim type. They are about 16 cm / 6½ in long, 2-3 cm / ¾–1 ¼ in across at the stem end and tapering to a point. They are of a medium heat intensity. Jalapeño and serrano are the most frequently used in Mexican cooking. Both are hotter than the Anaheim.

However, thinking of chilli only in terms of heat misses the point. They have an incredible range of flavours and add a great new taste dimension to everyday foods like soups, sauces, stews, salsas – and even ice-cream, as suggested by chilli-importer and distributor Dodie Miller (I wait to be convinced about that). We all owe a debt of gratitude to Dodie who has pretty much single-handedly brought fresh and dried chillies to the aisles of Britain's major supermarkets.

When using dried chillies, like ancho and chipotle, soak them in just-boiled water for 20 minutes, scrape out the seeds and pulp, then purée them in some of the soaking liquid before adding by the spoonful to whatever you are cooking, tasting after each addition to control the amount of heat. Larger, meaty dried chillies, like the ancho or mulato, can be stuffed after a preliminary soaking. Dried chillies can also be soaked and then cut into thin strips to add to stir-fries, or marinated in olive oil and vinegar for salads.

Smoked dried chillies, like the chipotle, are integral to Mexican cooking and provide a complex flavouring that is elusive yet strangely reminiscent of bacon in cooked dishes. There are few recipe references to smoked chillies in this book because I don't like them. *Droit de seigneur.*

In the California of 100 years ago apparently all fresh chillies were prepared *asada*: grilled and blistered over flame so the skins could be removed. This is really only what we have now learned to do with sweet peppers (see page 26), called 'bull-nose peppers' in old California and 'bell peppers' throughout the USA today. While we are now encouraged to blacken and burn peppers, chillies should not be taken as far. Restrained grilling softens the chilli's heat while imbuing it with a trace of smoke, a mellowing process. It is worth the effort and can be put to good use in many of the recipes in this book. Burn the skin, however, and they will become unpleasantly bitter. After grilling, treat them like sweet peppers and put them in a covered bowl or into a zip-lock bag to steam. This loosens the skins, making them easier to remove.

We still don't have a vast choice of chillies in British supermarkets at the time of writing, though things are improving rapidly. Since types of chillies go by different names in different countries, this is not such a big problem. Our individual perception of heat varies from person to person to person. What one finds mild, another may find intolerably hot. The more chillies you eat, the more your tolerance grows. This can be problematic for the cook. Your ability to tolerate heat is not a measure of your machismo, though tell that to the weekend post-pub, lager-and-curry brigade.

Keep in mind that eating very chilli-hot food can lead to catastrophic upsets in untrained stomachs; so, unless you know where your guests rate on the capsaicin stakes, tread warily and err on the mild side. Put julienned raw chillies and chilli relishes on the table along with a bottle of Salsa Picante (page 39) for those of cast-iron mouths and stomachs to augment the fire on their plates. Cooling salads like cacik (cucumber and yogurt) are also good to calm the inflamed palate, together with bowls of mint, basil and coriander [cilantro] leaves. This is something they do a lot in South-east Asia and it is as delicious as it is effective.

Beans, Bountiful Beans

The bean-eating sequence in Blazing Saddles, as the cowboys grew increasingly flatulent around the camp-fire, made me cry with laughter. Well it was 20 years ago and at 27 I knew no better. Beans and cowboys have always gone together and all our lives would have been the poorer without canned baked beans. No self-respecting student in Britain in the 'Sixties could have lived without Mr Heinz and hashish.

Black beans, borlotti, coco, canellini, flageolet and black-eyed peas, mung, pinto, butter and kidney, the list is long but perhaps visually and texturally more varied and interesting than the base flavour. They are the blank canvas upon which we paint as our imagination dictates. Beans can be extravagantly sauced or served as a plain oil-and-lemon-dressed counterpoint with something expensive and rich, like lobster or sautéed tiger prawns. Or you can enjoy them pretty much au nature, with nothing more than a squeeze of lemon, some extra-virgin olive oil and salt and pepper.

Since they are usually dried, they are always to hand in the store cupboard, needing nothing more than an extended bath to bring them back to life. They are cheap and cheerful without being as grim as that description usually implies. Should you boil them too long, all you need do is purée them briefly in a food processor, serving the purée instead of mashed potatoes or pasta. You can fire them up with spices and chilli or make them into a delicious spread for toast or fried bread. (Sorry, bruschetta or crostini.) Beans are at the very heart of Central-American cooking. No refried beans, no meal. In the contemporary kitchen they are high in proteins and fibre, low in fat. Of course, Californians love them.

All dried beans need the same basic preparation. Soak them overnight in lots of cold water, bring them to the boil next day, boil hard for three to five minutes then throw this water away and replenish with fresh. Most beans then take roughly an hour to cook at a gentle simmer; some, if they have been hanging around a few years, may take a little longer. You could almost certainly rehydrate beans from an Aztec tomb and nobody save the Sun God would be any the wiser.

As you simmer, flavour as you like: onions, garlic, bay leaves, lime leaves, celery, chilli and herbs. Break this flavouring into two stages, discarding the initial aromatics and adding cooked elements after the beans are cooked. Make them pungent with briefly fried garlic, sweet with crisped shallots, fresh with herbs. Add astringency with citrus zest and juice or make them aromatic with vinegar. Toast Middle Eastern spices, then fry them and toss the beans in them. Dress them in a tomato sauce. There are no rules save that beans should be salted towards the end of cooking rather than at the beginning otherwise the skins toughen. In your flavouring, seek natural balance. It is as simple as that.

Baked Beans

FOR 6

450 g / 1 lb haricot beans [2¹/2 cups dried navy beans]
900 g / 2 lb canned plum tomatoes
170 g / 6 oz pancetta (in a piece)
350 g / 12 oz [2 cups] onions, diced
2 garlic cloves, chopped
4 tbsp Heinz tomato ketchup
30 g / 1 oz demerara sugar [2¹/2 tbsp brown sugar]
1 tbsp dried oregano
2 bay leaves
1 tbsp Colman's mustard powder
1 very hot fresh red chilli
1 tbsp black treacle or molasses
1 tsp salt
2 tsp black pepper
1 glass of dry white wine

There are some commercial products which defy domestic imitation and one of them is Heinz baked beans. Precisely what mix the company uses is secret but you can bet there is salt and sugar and tomato in there. The following recipe sits somewhere between Boston and San Diego, pace Mr Heinz. These beans are great with a grilled pork chop, with sausages or bacon and eggs.

Soak the beans overnight in cold water, then bring to the boil, boil for 3 minutes and discard the water.

Preheat the oven to 130°C/275°F/gas1.

Put the beans in an ovenproof casserole. Put the tomatoes and their juice in a food processor and blitz to a purée. Add to the beans with the pancetta, the onions, garlic, tomato ketchup, sugar, oregano, bay leaves, mustard powder, chilli, treacle, salt and pepper. Stir to mix, pour over the wine and cover with water.

Bring to the boil on the hob, then put on a lid and place in the oven to cook for 8 hours. Check from time to time, adding more water if it starts to dry out. Remove the bay leaves, chilli and pancetta before serving. (The bacon is edible, but keep it for a sandwich.) Once cooked the beans will keep in the fridge for a week.

Refried Black Beans

Refried beans are not really fried but mashed, traditionally with lard but here with olive oil. The usual beans for this dish are pink or pinto beans, but try black beans, which look more interesting when mashed than either. Put that another way: your average refried beans taste great but look ghastly, like something scraped off a shoe.

Serve refried black beans on the side with Flank Steak Fire Chilli (page 199), with Chicken Fajitas (page 180) or with grated cheese – either Cheddar or Parmesan – and Wheat-flour Tortillas (page 57).

FOR 6

450 g / 1 lb [2¹/₂ cups] dried black beans
1 onion, diced
3 garlic cloves, smashed and chopped
1 tbsp hot chilli powder
2 bay leaves
2 dried hot red chillies
1 tsp salt (or more)
2 tsp cumin seeds
1 tsp black peppercorns
150 ml / ¹/₄ pt [²/₃ cup] olive oil
4 spring onions [scallions]
1 fresh hot green chilli
handful of flat-leaf parsley

Cover the beans with cold water by at least 6 cm / 2¹/₂ in and leave to soak overnight. Alternatively, bring to the boil and boil hard for 5 minutes, then remove from the heat and soak for 1 hour before proceeding.

Bring the beans to the boil, boil hard for 5 minutes (a second time in the case of the fast-preparation option) and then drain. Rinse under running water. Rinse the pan, removing any scum adhering to the sides. Return the beans to the pan, cover with fresh cold water, return to the boil for 5 minutes, then lower the heat to a simmer.

Put the onion, 2 of the garlic cloves and the chilli powder in with the beans. Add the bay leaves and dried chillies, stir in and cook until the beans are just done. This will take about an hour, but start tasting after 50 minutes. Stir in salt to taste at this point, cooking in for 2-3 minutes. With any pulses, always season towards the end of cooking, not at the beginning.

You can eat the beans immediately, just as they are, or allow them to cool and then have them as a bean salad, dressed with a vinaigrette or with Gremolata (see page 92). Alternatively you can make Black Bean Soup with Chicken Albondigas (page 80).

You can now hold the beans for a day or two in the fridge before finishing. To do so, discard the bay leaves and dried chillies. Put the cumin and peppercorns in a dry pan and toast over a low heat for 2-3 minutes, stirring, to release their aromas. Grind in a coffee grinder. Put the olive oil in a pan over a medium heat and add the spice mix and remaining garlic clove. Stir and cook for 2 minutes. Lower the heat and stir in the beans, then mash with a potato masher to a coarse purée.

Spoon into a serving bowl. Shred the spring onions and scatter on the top. Cut the fresh chilli across into the thinnest rings possible, discarding the seeds, and scatter the chilli rings over the beans with some torn parsley leaves.

Some Sauces and Dressings

Roasted Tomato Chilli Sauce

The difference between oven-dried tomatoes (see page 26) and roasted tomatoes is purely one of degree. Roasting is done at a higher temperature: you will get the edges blackening and the flavour is markedly different.

MAKES ABOUT 600 ML / 21 FL OZ [2¹/2 CUPS]

900 g / 2 lb ripe plum tomatoes
2 tsp salt
1 tsp black pepper
about 2 tsp sugar
5 tbsp olive oil
225 g / 8 oz onion
4 garlic cloves
1 fresh jalapeño-type (very hot) chilli
4 sprigs of thyme

Preheat the oven to 220°C/425°F/gas7, and lightly oil a roasting pan. Fill the pan with halved tomatoes, cut side up and tightly packed, then sprinkle them with salt, pepper and a little sugar. Dress them with a little olive oil and roast for 20 minutes. Turn the oven down to 180°C/350°F/gas4.

Dice the onion, garlic and chilli and scatter over the tomatoes. Toss the thyme sprigs on top. Dress with more oil and return to the oven to roast for 30-45 minutes, when the tomatoes will have shrunk and the onions browned. During this second roasting period, check at regular intervals that the tomatoes are not burning. If you allow them to burn you will make the sauce bitter and unpleasant.

Remove the pan from the oven and discard the thyme sprigs. When cool, purée the tomatoes and flavourings and press through a sieve. Pack in screw-top jars and film the surface with oil to store. If you ensure your jars and their lids are sterile and that the contents are not exposed to the air, the sauce should should keep for months.

Variation
You can ring all kinds of changes to your sauce at the puréeing stage. Try adding anchovies or pitted black olives or basil.

Quick Tomato Sauce

Canned tomatoes are one of the greatest gifts the cook has to hand in the store cupboard and should not be thought of as invariably inferior to fresh tomatoes. On one level, that of the raw ripe tomato for a salad, only those starving in a lifeboat could substitute canned. In a lot of sauces, however, they deliver a superior result because before being canned, they were vine-ripened perfection. Somebody else went to the trouble of nurturing them for you, picking them, peeling them and then conveniently packing them so they cannot deteriorate. Use them lavishly for they are cheap and available all year round, and with very little effort they can be converted into a range of fabulous sauces which don't taste remotely of cans. And these are sauces which can be made well in advance and kept in jars in the fridge for a week.

Don't be embarrassed about including some tomato ketchup. Good-quality ketchups contain nothing but reduced tomato, spirit vinegar, salt and sugar. A few tablespoons will intensify your sauce splendidly but will not be discernible as ketchup.

MAKES ABOUT 600 ML / 21 FL OZ [2 1/2 CUPS]

900 g / 2 lb canned Italian plum tomatoes
170 g / 6 oz Spanish or Bermuda onion
4 tbsp olive oil
2 garlic cloves
4 tbsp tomato ketchup
2 tsp dried oregano
1 bay leaf
salt and pepper

Slice and then dice the onion. Put in a pan with the olive oil over a low heat and fry until soft and translucent. Smash and chop the garlic and stir in.

Pour in the tomatoes, complete with the juice from the can. Add the ketchup, oregano and bay leaf. Turn up the heat and bring to the boil. Lower to a gentle bubble and cook, stirring from time to time, until you have a thick sauce. Taste and add some coarsely ground pepper, but add salt only if you think it needs it. Remove the bay leaf and discard. Transfer to a food processor or blender and blitz to a smooth purée.

Use immediately or store in a lidded container in the fridge. Always reheat gently. If the sauce becomes too thick, simply add a little water.

Variation

For a chilli version of this sauce add several shredded fresh hot chillies with the tomatoes. You must yourself decide how much chilli to use and you can only make that decision by tasting a tiny piece of the chilli, otherwise how can you qualify your judgement? Often you can judge by touching to your tongue the knife blade with which you have sliced the chilli. Those who like things hot should leave the seeds in.

Roasted Tomato, Pepper and Chilli Coriander Sauce

Fresh ripe tomatoes and red sweet peppers are roasted until they start to blacken and are then finished in a saucepan on top of the stove, spiced with chilli and coriander seeds and finally scented with coriander leaves. As in the previous recipe, you must decide how many chillies are appropriate since this will depend on how hot they are and how spicy you want the sauce to be.

MAKES ABOUT 600ML/21 FL OZ [2 1/2 CUPS]

900 g / 2 lb ripe plum tomatoes
4 red sweet peppers
150 ml / 1/4 pt [2/3 cup] olive oil
170 g / 6 oz red onion(s)
2 garlic cloves
4-6 fresh hot green chillies (see above)
4 tbsp tomato ketchup
1 tbsp coriander seeds
1 tsp black peppercorns
handful of coriander leaves [cilantro], to serve

Preheat the oven to 250°C/475°F/gas9. Prick the tomatoes in several places with a pin. Put half the oil in a bowl and toss the tomatoes and red peppers in this to coat. Put them in a pan and roast for about 30 minutes, shaking every 10 minutes to expose different surfaces. You want them to blacken markedly and collapse.

Towards the end of their cooking, slice the onions and fry gently in the remaining oil until soft. Then turn up the heat and brown them, stirring constantly to prevent sticking.

Thinly slice the garlic. Remove the stems from the chillies and chop coarsely. Peel the skin off the sweet peppers, halve, deseed and chop the flesh coarsely. Add the garlic, chillies and sweet pepper flesh to the onions, together with the tomatoes and the ketchup. Lower the heat and simmer, breaking up the tomatoes with a spoon. Cook until thick.

In a dry frying pan, toast the coriander seeds and black peppercorns over a low heat for 2-3 minutes to release their aroma. Grind in a coffee grinder and add to the pan. Stir in and continue to cook for 5 minutes. Transfer to a food processor or blender and blitz to a smooth purée. Push through a sieve with a wooden spoon.

Use at once, in which case warm through in a clean pan, or store in a screw-top jar in the fridge for up to a week. Pick the coriander leaves off the stems, chop coarsely and stir in just before serving.

Chilli Balsamic Vinaigrette

MAKES ABOUT 175 ML / 6 FL OZ
[³/₄ CUP]

1 fresh hot red chilli
1 large fresh, mild green chilli
2 tbsp balsamic vinegar
¹/₂ tsp salt
¹/₄ tsp pepper
5 tbsp extra-virgin olive oil
1 tbsp chopped coriander
   leaves [cilantro]

Cut the stem end off the chillies and slide them on to skewers. Roast over a flame until just blistered. If you do not have gas, do them on a metal tray under the grill [broiler]. Put the chillies in a zip-lock bag or in a covered bowl to steam for 5 minutes. Remove, rub off the skin, cut in half and scrape out the seeds. Cut the flesh into small dice.

Put this into a bowl with the vinegar, salt and pepper and stir until the salt has dissolved. Stir in the oil and add the coriander only just before serving.

Salsas

Mexican in origin, salsas are the most versatile cold sauces and their fresh and forceful flavours find a wide application in the contemporary kitchen. Invariably consisting of uncooked ingredients, the classic salsa is a mixture of tomato, onion, chillies and fresh coriander or cilantro.

The ripeness of the tomatoes used is a vital consideration and unless you have the good fortune to be picking your own vine-ripened tomatoes at the point of perfection, imported ripe plum tomatoes generally seem to have the best flavour.

Tomato salsa will keep in a screw-top jar in the fridge for up to a week, during which time the flavours actually develop markedly. When you watch somebody from Mexico or Central America making salsa you will see an interesting technique where the cut face of an onion is repeatedly chopped with a sharp knife at different angles so that an interconnecting network of shallow cuts is incised into the surface. This is then shaved off, producing a myriad of tiny pieces. The smallness of these pieces is what differentiates the hand-made salsa from the machine-made, which is a coarse thing by comparison. The painstaking cutting and the uniform smallness of the component pieces produces quite a lot of liquid and while tomatoes are vital in the mix they do not dominate. Indeed, in appearance the colour is as much green as red, for fresh coriander is cheap and plentiful and is used not simply as a herbal flavouring agent but as a salad green.

Commercially produced salsas tend to be tomato-heavy and consequently are bright red and overly sweet. If, when making them at home, time considerations force you to the food processor, the result will never be as good. Careful chopping by hand will deliver a uniformity of constituent elements which have individual definition. The processor smashes and batters, tearing as much as chopping and exuding far too much water.

Although most frequently served in this raw state, salsas are perfect in cooking. The addition of olive oil in a pan and a brief bubble through on the hob and you have a fresh spicy sauce to serve with poached or grilled fish and meats. Drain off excess liquid, stir a spoonful into scrambled eggs and you have a simple version of Huevos en Rabo de Mestiza (see page 135).

There is no absolute recipe for salsa as the following variations demonstrate. It has different names, 'salsa', 'salsa cruda' and 'salsa fresca' all describing the same thing. You can make it heavily fragrant with a high percentage of fresh coriander or push up the chilli content to make it fiery-hot. Those who dislike coriander can substitute flat-leaf parsley wholly or in part. The onion balance is critically important and, while white Spanish-style onions are most commonly used, the emphasis may be altered by using red onion or spring onions [scallions] to give a milder result. A further variation includes a little garlic. The salsa is invariably seasoned with salt and finished with lime juice, lemon juice or vinegar. It makes a great dip for tortilla chips.

Basic Salsa Cruda

Although there is no rule, I think salsas benefit from the tomatoes being skinned and most of the seeds and pulp removed.

FOR 6

225 g / 8 oz Spanish or
*   Bermuda onion(s)*
450 g / 1 lb ripe plum tomatoes
2 fresh hot green chillies
bunch of coriander [cilantro]
1 tsp salt
1-2 tsp lime or lemon juice

Slice the onion(s) across into 2 mm / $^{1}/_{12}$ in thick discs, then cut these into dice and put into a bowl.

Dip the tomatoes in boiling water for 30 seconds, refresh in cold water and peel. Cut into quarters, scoop out the pulp and seeds, and discard. Chop into 2 mm / $^{1}/_{12}$ in dice and scrape into the bowl.

Remove the stems from the chillies and split them. Discard the seeds if you are of a sensitive disposition, but this is unnecessarily refined. You should gauge the heat of a chilli, including its seeds which is where the capsaicin resides (see page 28). Cut into thin strips, then into 2 mm / $^{1}/_{12}$ in dice and add to the bowl.

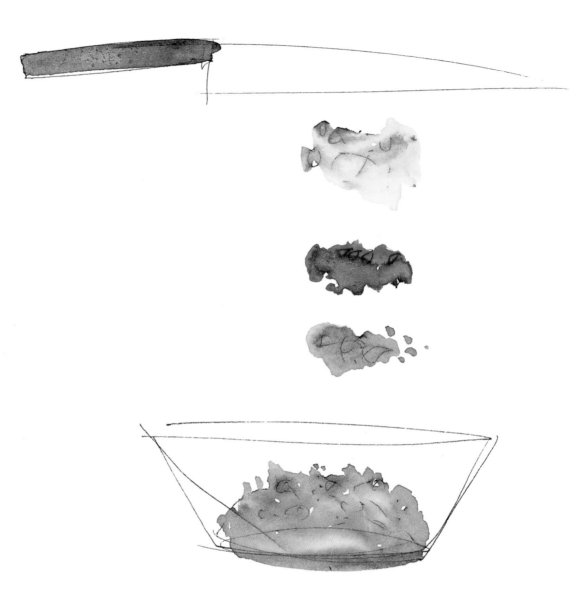

Take the coriander leaves off the stems, chop into tiny pieces and stir in. Stir in the salt and lime or lemon juice. Leave for 1 hour at room temperature before serving. If using salsa that has been refrigerated, allow to come to room temperature before serving.

Techno Salsa

(Make this quick version of Basic Salsa Cruda when no traditionalist Guatemalans are in the kitchen.) Plunge the tomatoes into boiling water for 30 seconds, refresh in cold water and peel. Cut into quarters, strip out the pulp and seeds, and put into a food processor. Shred the chillies and add. Dice the onion and add with the citrus juice, salt and pepper. Chop the coriander finely – including the stems – and add. Blitz for 60 seconds.

This is very good with any grilled fish or chicken. It also makes a nice dip for blue corn chips to go with your Margarita (see page 62).

Variations

Substitute a red onion for the Spanish onion.

Substitute 8 thinly sliced spring onions [scallions] for the Spanish onion.

Add 1 garlic clove, smashed and finely chopped, and use red wine vinegar instead of citrus juice.

Use double the amount of tomatoes and substitute super-hot habanero (Scotch bonnet) chillies for what you thought were hot chillies – that is, until you tasted the habanero.

Add a green sweet pepper, cut into 2 mm / $^1/_{12}$ in dice.

Salsa Picante

This is a delicious Mexican version of Tabasco. Keep a jar of it in the fridge, topping up a Kikkoman soy bottle so you can dispense it a few drops at a time, a necessary precaution because this little mother will help redefine your perceptions of hot. Unlike Tabasco, which is made exclusively from hot chillies and vinegar, salsa picante is further flavoured with garlic, cumin, sesame, coriander, pumpkin seeds, cloves and allspice. Use any hot dried chillies, the hotter the better.

Once made there is no known organism that will make it go off. Most primitive organisms are too scared to go anywhere near it and the vinegar in any case is an anti-bacterial agent. You should still sterilize the jar and the bottle you use before proceeding.

This sauce is based on a recipe by Rick Bayless and Dean Groen Bayless who first thought of adding sesame and pumpkin seeds. Given the dominant fire, their flavour makes a surprising difference to the finished product. Their book, Authentic Mexican *(Morrow), remains the best book ever written on regional Mexican cooking.*

Put the sesame seeds in a small dry, heavy frying pan and toast over a low heat

2 tbsp sesame seeds

2 tbsp pumpkin seeds

1/2 tsp coriander seeds

1 tsp cumin seeds

1 tsp black peppercorns

3 cloves

1/4 tsp ground allspice

1/2 tsp dried oregano

2 tsp salt

115 g/4 oz dried hot red
    chillies

575 ml/1 pt [2 1/3 cups] white
    wine vinegar

3 garlic cloves

until they turn golden brown and the odd seed pops. Scrape the seeds into a coffee grinder.

Repeat with the pumpkin seeds, adding at the same time the coriander seeds, cumin seeds, peppercorns and cloves. Stir until the pumpkin seeds start to pop, then put into the coffee grinder. Add the allspice, oregano and salt. Remove the stems from the chillies and discard. Cut them open and extract the seeds. This is best done on a plate. Reserve the chillies and put the seeds into the coffee grinder.

Grind to a smooth powder. Transfer to a large screw-top jar. Now grind half the dried chillies to a coarse powder and add to the jar. Pour in the vinegar. Smash and chop the garlic very finely, and add. Put on the lid and leave at room temperature for 5-7 days, shaking from time to time.

Strain through a fine sieve into a jug, pressing down on the residue and squeezing as much through the mesh as you can. Put the remaining chilli pieces into a bottle with a pouring spout and pour the sauce from the jug through a funnel into the bottle. Top up with bottled water, adding about 300 ml/ 1/2 pt [1 1/4 cups]. Leave for 2 weeks before using

Chilli Oil

Chilli oil is the most useful of flavoured oils and is made by heating equal parts olive oil and sunflower oil with lots of hot red chillies to 110°C/230°F, and keeping it simmering at 100°C/212°F for 20 minutes, then leaving it to cool before bottling with the chillies in the bottle. This way it keeps getting hotter and can be topped up with fresh oil. The risk of bacterial contamination is also greatly reduced.

The possible growth of botulism – a deadly anaerobic nerve toxin – in flavoured oils, has been flagged in the USA, where a few cases have been ascribed to home-made garlic oil. The higher the acid level of what you are flavouring the oil with, the less prone it is to bacterial contamination. An initial lengthy soaking in vinegar or lemon juice of items like uncooked garlic or herb leaves is therefore a sound practice.

Savoury Butters

Savoury butters are the best way to make the maximum use of a small amount, because a 15 g/ ¹/₂ oz [1 tbsp] disc of chilled flavoured butter on a piece of grilled meat or fish is often all the sauce you need. You can make several different sorts, roll them in foil and freeze them, and they will keep for as long as you like. Then when you want to give a lift to a simple dish you have a wealth of flavour seconds away.

The following are suggestions rather than recipes. Perhaps you grow herbs and have a favourite – try flavouring a butter with it. All butters can be spiced with fresh hot chilli. Whatever the chosen flavouring, always use unsalted butter as the base.

You can make smaller amounts, but 225 g/8 oz [1 cup] packs are ideal. Think of each pack as 16 servings, and the idea becomes less painful to the arteries. Cutting everything by hand before processing will eliminate any large pieces, delivering a more uniform mixture, while pulse-chopping in the processor helps retain a flecked appearance.

Use the butters straight from the freezer. If the foil sticks, hold the package briefly over steam. To avoid temper tantrums down the line, label the packages before freezing. All the following butters are just as beneficial to vegetables and are nice on pasta with grated Parmesan.

Coriander and Green Chilli Butter

MAKES ABOUT 250 G / 8¹/₂ OZ
[2 CUPS]

handful of coriander leaves
    [cilantro]
2 fresh Anaheim-type
    (medium-hot) green chillies
1 tsp salt
¹/₂ tsp black pepper
225 g / 8 oz [1 cup] unsalted
    butter

Chop the coriander, including stems, and put in a food processor. Remove stems from the chillies. Cut in half, strip out the seeds and discard. Chop the chillies as finely as you can and add to the processor with the salt and pepper. Blitz to a mulch. Add the butter, cut into 1 cm / ¹/₂ in dice. Blitz again to cream.

Scrape out on to foil, compact with a knife and roll up into a neat cylinder, twisting at both ends to tighten. Freeze.

Use with fish, meat or vegetables.

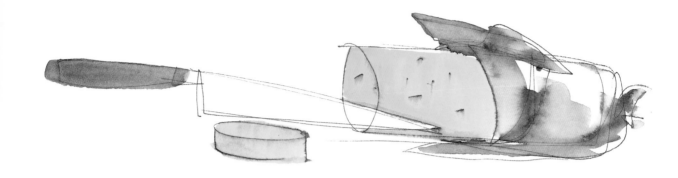

Lime, Orange and Mint Butter

MAKES ABOUT 250 G / 8¹/2 OZ
[I CUP]

I lime
I small juicy orange
6 mint leaves
I tsp salt
¹/2 tsp black pepper
225 g / 8 oz [I cup] chilled
    unsalted butter, cut into
    2 cm / ³/4 in dice

Scrub the lime and orange, rinse and dry. Grate the zest from both and put in the processor with the juice of ¹/2 the orange and ¹/2 the lime and the torn mint leaves. Add the salt and pepper and pulse-chop. Add the butter dice and process again until creamed.

Scrape on to foil and roll as above. Freeze.

Use with fish, particularly oily fish like salmon or tuna.

Parsley, Garlic and Red Chilli Butter

MAKES ABOUT 250 G / 8¹/2 OZ
[I CUP]
handful of flat-leaf parsley
2 garlic cloves
I fresh hot red chilli
I tsp salt
¹/2 tsp black pepper
225 g / 8 oz [I cup] chilled
    unsalted butter, cut into 2 cm / ³/4
    in dice

Chop the parsley, including the stems, and put in the processor. Smash and chop the garlic as finely as you can. It should be a pulp. Remove and discard stem and seeds from the chilli. Put all of these into the processor with the salt and pepper and pulse-chop to a mulch. Add the butter and work to a cream. Scrape out on to foil and roll into a cylinder. Freeze.

Use with fish or meat.

Saffron, Mustard and Pepper Butter

MAKES ABOUT 250 G / 8½ OZ
[1 CUP]
2 tbsp dry sherry
16 threads of saffron
1 tbsp Colman's mustard
*   powder*
1 tsp salt
1 tsp coarsely ground black
*   pepper*
225 g / 8 oz [1 cup] chilled
*   unsalted butter, cut into*
*   2 cm / ¾ in dice*

Heat the sherry in a small pan, remove from the heat and add the saffron threads. Leave to infuse for 30 minutes.

Stir the mustard powder to a smooth paste with the saffron liquid, adding a little water if the mixture is too thick. Add the salt and pepper. Pulse-chop with the diced butter.

Scrape out on to foil, roll into a cylinder and freeze.

Use with meat.

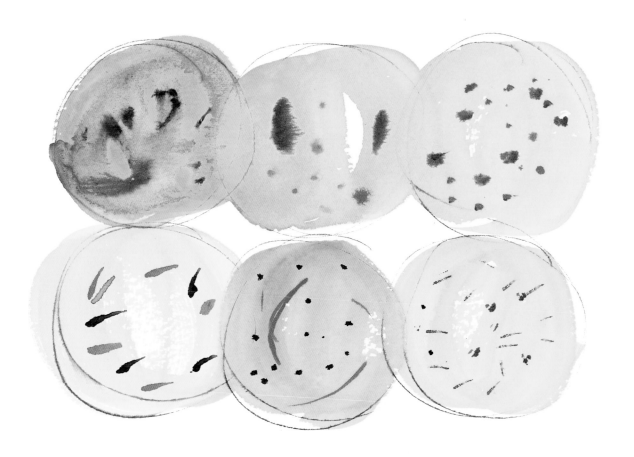

Red Onion, Cumin and Coriander Butter

MAKES ABOUT 450 G / I LB
[2 CUPS]

170 g / 6 oz red onion

225 g / 8 oz [1 cup] chilled unsalted
  butter, cut into 2 cm / $^3/_4$ in dice

1 tsp cumin seeds

1 tsp coriander seeds

1 tsp coarsely ground black pepper

1 tsp salt

Cut the onion into 3 mm / $^1/_8$ in dice. Melt 30 g / 1 oz [2 tbsp] of the butter in a pan and sweat the onion dice in this, stirring occasionally, until the onions are soft and translucent.

Meanwhile, over a low heat, toast the cumin seeds, coriander seeds and pepper in a dry heavy frying pan, stirring, for 2-3 minutes. Grind to a powder.

Stir this into the onions and cook for 2-3 minutes. Transfer to the food processor, add the remaining butter with the salt and pulse-chop to a paste. Scrape on to foil and roll into a cylinder as before. Freeze.

Use with fish or meat. It is also very good with bitter greens like bok-choy.

Roasted Red Pepper, Chive and Parmesan Butter

MAKES ABOUT 350 G / 12 OZ
[1 $^1/_2$ CUPS]

$^1/_2$ roasted red sweet pepper,
  peeled (see page 26)

small bunch of chives

225 g / 8 oz [1 cup] unsalted
  butter, cut into 2 cm / $^3/_4$ in dice

55 g / 2 oz [$^1/_2$ cup] Reggiano
  Parmesan cheese, freshly grated

1 tsp salt

$^1/_2$ tsp black pepper

Dice the red pepper as small as you can. Chop the chives into the smallest possible pieces. Put these with the butter, Parmesan, salt and pepper into the processor and pulse-chop to a flecked cream.

Scrape out on to foil, roll into a cylinder and freeze.

Use with fish, meat or vegetables.

Basil and Lemon Butter

MAKES ABOUT 250 G / 8 $^1/_2$ OZ [1 CUP]

12-15 basil leaves

225 g / 8 oz [1 cup] chilled unsalted
  butter, cut into 2 cm / $^3/_4$ in dice

grated zest and juice of 1 lemon

1 tsp salt

$^1/_2$ tsp black pepper

Chop the basil leaves finely. Put with all the other ingredients in the processor and blitz to a uniform green.

Scrape out on to foil, roll into a cylinder and freeze.

Use with fish or vegetables.

Mayonnaise and Variations on a Rémoulade Theme

Mayonnaise is as important in the cold larder as béchamel is in the creation of hot dishes. The purity of a classic mayonnaise defies improvement. Variations are not therefore improvements but enhancements.

For the record, a basic recipe is included here because we all have our idiosyncrasies and heresies. I was taught to make mayonnaise in a stone mortar, stirring with a wooden spoon. Now I use an electric beater and a glass bowl. Don't make mayonnaise in a food processor or blender; it is never as good for some reason.

Purists use white peppercorns so as not to distract from the golden yellow sheen of the sauce. This seems immaterial. I like a little mustard in the mix, and use champagne vinegar.

It is important to have all the ingredients at room temperature and initially to add the oil very slowly. A neat way to ensure this is to have a Kikkoman soy sauce bottle filled with olive oil. This will produce the thinnest of pouring streams and by the time you have incorporated half the bottle you will have a very thick base which will not split.

In the unlikely event that it does, start again with a single yolk and pour from the soy bottle rather than trying to incorporate the separated mayonnaise as is usually suggested. Only start to add the split mixture after you have the thick stable base.

In *extremis*, the variations may be made using what is usually laughingly described as 'a good quality commercially produced mayonnaise'. These white gelatinous substances have more in common with genital lubricants than mayonnaise but, if you are without shame, go ahead.

These days we have to mention the matter of salmonella and raw eggs. There, it's been mentioned.

Basic Mayonnaise

MAKES ABOUT 575ML/1PT [2¹/₃ CUPS]

2 egg yolks
1 tsp Colman's mustard powder
1 tsp salt
¹/₂ tsp freshly ground pepper
300 ml / ¹/₂ pt [1 ¹/₄ cups]
  sunflower oil
2 tbsp champagne vinegar
300 ml / ¹/₂ pt [1 ¹/₄ cups] extra-
  virgin olive oil

In a glass or pottery mixing bowl, put the egg yolks with the mustard powder, salt and pepper. Whisk to amalgamate, then, pouring from the Kikkoman bottle (see above) add sunflower oil in a steady stream, continuing to whisk until you have a very thick homogenized base.

Add 2-3 teaspoons of the vinegar, which will cause the thick threads to soften to a creamier texture. Now add the olive oil in a faster stream, alternating with the remaining sunflower oil and, as it becomes thick, the remaining vinegar a teaspoonful at a time.

When all is incorporated, taste and adjust the seasoning, adding more salt and pepper as you like. If very thick, add 2-3 tablespoons of hot water, a teaspoon at a time, until you achieve the consistency of double [heavy] cream. If the mayonnaise is to be one of the variations that follow, do not add water as the additional ingredients will have a thinning effect.

Green Chilli Mayonnaise

2 fresh hot green chillies
575 ml / 1 pt [2¹/₃ cups] thick
  Mayonnaise (see above)
handful of coriander [cilantro]
small bunch of chives

Remove stems from the chillies and cut in half lengthwise. Scrape out the seeds and discard. Shred the chillies as finely as you can, then cut across into the tiniest dice you can manage. Stir into the mayonnaise.

Pick the leaves off the coriander stems and chop very small, using a rocking and chopping motion, until you have a green paste. (A mezzaluna can be brought into play for this job if you have one handy.) Scrape into the mayonnaise and stir in, then repeat with the chives.

Leave covered in the fridge for 2-4 hours to let the flavours develop.

Red Pepper Mayonnaise

2 roasted red sweet pepper
  halves, peeled (see page
  26)
575 ml / 1 pt [2¹/₃ cups] thick
  Mayonnaise (see above)
2 tbsp tomato ketchup
2-4 tsp (or to taste) Tabasco
  sauce or Salsa Picante
  (page 39)

Purée the red peppers in a food processor and push through a fine sieve. Stir into the mayonnaise with the ketchup, then add hot sauce to taste.

Saffron Mustard Mayonnaise

1 tbsp almost-boiling water
   (90°C/195°F)
16-20 threads of saffron
1 tbsp Dijon mustard
575 ml / 1 pt [2⅓ cups] thick
   Mayonnaise (see left)

Pour the almost-boiling water over the saffron and leave to infuse for 15 minutes. Mix with the mustard, then whisk into the mayonnaise.

Caper and Green Peppercorn Mayonnaise

1½ tbsp fresh green
   peppercorns
2 tbsp salt-packed capers
handful of flat-leaf parsley
575 ml / 1 pt [2⅓ cups] thick
   Mayonnaise (see left)

Buy fresh green peppercorns all year round in Asian markets. Try to get hold of salted capers; rinse them under the tap before using. They are superior to capers sold brined in jars.

Coarsely chop the peppercorns and capers. Finely chop the parsley leaves and stems. Stir all of these into the mayonnaise.

Mayonnaise Tartare

55 g / 2 oz [⅓ cup] capers
55 g / 2 oz small gherkins or
   cornichons
575 ml / 1 pt [2⅓ cups] thick
   Mayonnaise (see left)
2 tbsp chopped flat-leaf parsley
2 tbsp chopped chervil
2 tbsp chopped chives

Leave the capers whole, but chop the gherkins. Add to the mayonnaise with the herbs.

Focaccia, Ciabatta and Bread, Glorious Bread

The breads baked by the Il Fornaio bakeries in San Francisco and Los Angeles are remarkable. Il fornaio means 'the baker' in Italian, forno means 'oven'. Il Fornaio started in San Francisco in 1980 and now has bakeries throughout California. They have completely changed people's expectations of what good bread should be. Their influence, and that of other bakers like La Brea, can be felt in more and more of the state's restaurants, many of which now make a proud point of baking their own breads. One used to expect great bread as a right in France. That alas is no longer true. Today the assumption is more safely made in California.

A traditional baker uses a wooden peel, a long-handled paddle, to transfer the risen dough into the oven and the finished bread out of it. Pizzas and many breads benefit from being baked in direct contact with heated stone, which is what gives them their inimitable base crust. You can buy baking stones to go into domestic ovens but if you do, you will then have to work out a technique for sliding the dough on to them, as the baker does with a peel. While the result will never be quite as good as the bread baked in direct contact with hot stone, heavy carbon-steel baking sheets will give good results. I use good-quality Swiss-roll [shallow baking] pans or trays but you need to buy the best. Cheap, thin metal sheets and pans warp and buckle.

The more you bake bread, the better you get at doing it. Looking back at what I was producing five years ago, I shudder with embarrassment because, by comparison with my bread today, the results were crude and heavy-handed. A number of factors have contributed to the improvement.

First, the flour. Discovering 14% imported Canadian wheat flour made an astonishing difference, the elasticity given by the higher than usual gluten content trapping more air and delivering a lighter loaf with a terrific crust. Second, I now use an electric mixer with a dough hook to knead, but do so at the lowest speed. Third, I use water at 40°C/105°F — hand-warm rather than hot. Fourth, I include of a piece of starter dough to change the taste and character of the bread. Fifth, I leave the dough to rise at a cooler ambient temperature than I had previously thought desirable. The slower the rise, the greater the resilience and, in the case of focaccia and ciabatta, the larger the air-holes. I discovered by accident that putting knocked-down dough into zip-lock bags and leaving them in the fridge for 24 hours before allowing them to return to room temperature and rise again delivers an even lighter result. If the dough is left in the fridge for three days, the holes are larger still and you get perfect ciabatta. It is what a baker, working in a more usual idiom and wanting to produce a uniform inner texture, would regard as spoiled. Sixth, I throw water into the very hot oven just prior to baking in order to generate steam.

No single element works a miracle but, in combination, the difference is miraculous. If there is a general rule, then it is to be gentle but firm, as true in the kitchen as it is in any other room in the house.

A great baker like Franco Galli of Il Fornaio says that you should first make bread by hand, a sort of elemental 'getting in tune with the life flow of the dough' type of thing. I defer to his skill and his wisdom, but would point out that it is hard work, particularly if you are kneading the minimum quantity of high-protein bread flour recommended in the following recipes.

There is little point in making less, since the dough sits happily in the fridge for three days, and experience suggests that working with larger amounts delivers a better loaf or loaves. Secondly, commercial bakers machine-knead. They touch and smell the dough to assess it and handle it to make individual loaves. So far as getting in any closer, I prefer to leave that to the crystals and channelling folk.

Bread dough can be made with a food processor, though the results will not be as light. The blade of a processor is really too rough and the dough reacts to brutal battering by refusing to rise properly. If you do want to try anyway, put all the dry ingredients into the processor bowl first; then, while working at full speed, add the olive oil if required and finally the hand-warm water through the feeder tube until the dough balls. Then you need to transfer it to a floured surface and knead by hand for about 5 minutes.

The best wheat for bread-making comes from Manitoba in Canada. It contains an average 14% protein content compared to British home-grown wheat that is closer to 10%. Britain used to import a lot of Canadian flour, but restrictive EC tariffs have unfortunately put a stop to this on any significant scale because of the need to pass the cost on to shoppers.

People do not bake bread to any significant extent and do not, therefore, demand high-protein flour. As a consequence, white flour produced in the UK is much softer than it used to be. This is true even in flours which are described on the packet as 'strong for bread baking', Even though supermarkets do not stock 14% flour, let it be known to the management that you would like to buy it.

For the past 10 years I have used dried yeast. The type called 'fermipan' or 'easy-blend', which is made up of tiny uniform granules, is the best and needs no preliminary activation in liquid. Getting hold of fresh yeast is not always easy and the great thing about the dried sort is that it is there when you need it, performs in an absolutely consistent way and allows precise measurement against known quantities of flour. It does not keep forever and is therefore best bought in boxes of 6g / ¼ oz sachets. Yeast granules bought in cans soon lose their potency once the can is opened.

The basic dough recipe is incredibly versatile. Push it out on a rectangular pan to the thickness of a double pizza and dress it heavily with olive oil just before it goes in the oven and you will have focaccia. Leave the dough covered in the fridge for two or three days, pull it out gently into an oval and you will get ciabatta superior to most you can buy. Put it to rise in loaf pans and you will produce a light airy bread to slice for sandwiches. Make it into individual rolls, pagnottine, or roll it out and pan-fry it for a leavened flat bread. Mix it with differing percentages of rye and wholemeal or wholewheat flours to give a range of breads with different tastes and textures. Add plumped raisins, sugar and saffron and bake a lovely bread to have buttered for afternoon tea. The basic dough is very forgiving when baking and can be cooked successfully at 220°C/425°F/gas7, though best results are achieved if the oven is at 250°C/475°F/gas9 when the bread first goes in.

On the subject of temperatures, it is a good idea to invest in an oven thermometer, because domestic ovens are notoriously variable and what the gauge tells you is not always the true reading. When baking always resist the temptation to open the door during cooking. The temperature drops when the door is opened and the bread gets peevish.

The following recipes specify 900 g / 2 lb [8 cups] flour, though you can make them with half the amount. If you do, it is essential to halve the quantities of yeast and oil as well as flour. However, the dough works better when made in larger amounts; 900 g / 2 lb of flour is not expensive and in any case does not go all that far. It also happens to be precisely the right amount for one 6g / ¼ oz sachet of easy-blend yeast.

Once made, the dough will keep in the fridge in a zip-lock bag for 3-4 days, but needs to be allowed to return to room temperature before it is pulled or rolled out.

Two important pieces of kit are a spray bottle that will deliver a fine mist of water and a wire rack to cool the bread on. With the exception of pizza, all bread should be allowed to cool before being cut. In the case of a large loaf, the inside will still be cooking after it comes from the oven. All bread, except focaccia (which can stay in the pan in which it is baked), should be cooled on a rack which allows air to circulate under the bread. If placed hot on a flat surface the bottom crust will soften with the steam.

Starter Doughs

Starter doughs are called 'poolish' by some, biga by Italians. You find many Polish bakers throughout the USA. For some reason that nobody has been able to explain satisfactorily, Poland has always been associated with good bread. The name 'poolish' for sourdough starter comes from French bakers referring to it as Polish style. Presumably a French baker was asked in English what sourdough starter was called and 'e say, 'pooleesh', making some suitably Gallic gesture with an upraised finger.

Sourdough loaves are made using a starter activated initially by wild yeasts, the tiny organisms which float about in the air, a piece of the previous risen dough being incorporated into the next batch of dough and so on ad infinitum. This type of starter is temperamental, hates tap water and may not work. It is easier to make a starter with some commercial yeast. The dough takes on a characteristic nutty quality once risen and then used as part of the ongoing process.

Starter doughs will keep in zip-lock bags in the fridge for two weeks or can be divided into smaller pieces and frozen. Baking nutters beg pieces of starter from ancient bakeries, take them home and add them to their own – the origin of the Starter Bore: 'This starter comes from my great-great-grandfather's cousin's bakery in Lodz and was first grown in 1840. We drove 300 miles across Poland to get it.' You: 'Fascinating.' Your teeth lock into the bread and stick. Amazingly resilient things, yeasts.

6 g / 1 1/4 oz sachet of easy-blend yeast
350 ml / 12 fl oz [1 1/2 cups] hand-warm water (40°C/105°F)
450 g / 1 lb [4 cups] strong bread flour

Mix the yeast, water and flour to a sticky batter. Cover and refrigerate for 24 hours before using. Pull off a handful and add it to the next batch of dough when it is being machine-kneaded, for a distinct improvement to taste and texture. This is not, however, obligatory. The basic dough recipe will give you a good loaf without it.

Basic Bread Dough

CAUTION: High-protein flour will push the average domestic mixer to the limit. Check the manufacturer's instructions for maximum duration of usage. My Philips machine says eight minutes. After that you risk burning out the motor. The manual will always err on the side of safety and I frequently run mine for 10-12 minutes, but at that point it feels hot to the touch and makes a rather agonized noise.

575 ml / 1 pt [2⅓ cups] hand-
    warm water, plus 1-2 tbsp
    more water if required
6 g / ¼ oz sachet of instant easy-
    blend yeast
1 tsp sea salt
1 tsp caster sugar [US
    granulated sugar]
1 tbsp olive oil, plus more for
    brushing
900 g / 2 lb [8 cups] strong
    wheat bread flour, plus
    more for dusting

Put the 575 ml / 1 pt [2⅓ cups] of hand-warm water, the yeast, salt, sugar and 1 tablespoon of oil in the mixing bowl. Using the dough hook and starting at low speed, gradually mix the flour into the liquid and work for 7 minutes. (Do it the other way around and you cover the kitchen in flour.) If the dough is not holding and is still pulling apart in strands, add more water, 1 tablespoon at a time. Increase to full speed for 1 minute, when you should have an elastic dough that is resilient to the push of a finger and which springs back when you stop pushing. If the dough is too sticky and adhering to the bowl, shake in a little more flour. If it is too resistant to the touch, or breaking up, turn on the machine again and add a last tablespoon of water, then work for a minute or so to amalgamate.

Turn on to a floured surface, knock down and shape into a ball. Brush a bowl large enough to allow the dough to treble in size with oil, put the dough in and brush the top with a little more oil. Cover the top loosely with plastic film and put to rise in a cool but draught-free place. Excessive heat should be avoided as this will force the dough too quickly and deliver a heavier result.

Leave for at least 4 hours, when the dough should have risen above the top of the bowl like a Quatermass alien. It will be very moist, sticky and elastic when you take it from the bowl. Transfer to a heavily floured surface, knock down with your fist and knead by hand for 2-3 minutes. It is now ready to shape for whatever type of bread you want to make.

Focaccia

Basic Bread Dough as above
rosemary or garlic to flavour
    (optional)
about 300 ml / ½ pt [1¼ cups]
    olive oil
coarse sea salt

This quantity of dough will make three focaccia the size of Swiss-roll [shallow-baking] pans measuring 33 x 23 cm / 13 x 9 in. Divide the dough into three and fill the pans, pushing and stretching the dough to cover the surface to a depth of 2 cm / ¾ in. You can flavour the bread with rosemary or garlic by pressing this into the dough while stretching and pushing it into the baking pans. Cover with a cloth and leave to rise again.

Preheat the oven to 250°C/475°F/gas9.

Using two fingers, gently poke impressions into the surface in parallel lines. Pour on olive oil, say about 6 tablespoons per loaf, and sprinkle with sea salt.

Open the oven door and throw an espresso cup of water on to the oven floor or spray the sides of the oven generously with water. Shut the door for 5 seconds. Open again, put in the loaf and bake for 15 minutes.

Ciabatta

MAKES 2 LOAVES

handful of Starter Dough (page 52)
900 g / 2 lb Basic Bread Dough
   (page 52)
flour, for dusting
olive oil, for brushing

Add the starter dough to the basic dough immediately after you switch on the mixer. Knock the dough down with your fist and divide in half, then brush each piece of dough with a little olive oil. Put in zip-lock bags and refrigerate for a minimum of 48 hours, maximum of 72. Remove from the fridge an hour before you want to bake.

Take the dough out of the bags, dust with flour as they will be sticky and pull gently into ovals that fit into non-stick Swiss roll [shallow baking] pans measuring 33 x 23 cm / 13 x 9 in, or heavy-duty baking sheets. Cover with cloths and leave to rise for 30-40 minutes.

Preheat the oven to 250°C/475°F/gas9.

Throw an espresso cup of water into the oven or spray the sides of the oven generously with water to generate steam. Mist the loaves with water and bake for 30-35 minutes, turning the temperature down to 220°C/ 425°F/gas7 for the last 10-15 minutes. Transfer to a rack to cool.

Your oven may be able to cope with two large loaves, but I find both my electric oven and my gas oven deliver a better result when you give them only one loaf at a time to deal with, idle, energy-inefficient sods that they are.

Pizza

MAKES 2 SIX-SLICE PIZZAS

450 g / 1 lb Basic Bread Dough
   (page 52)
300 ml / 1/2 pt [1 1/4 cups] Quick
   Tomato Sauce (see page
   34)
1 buffalo mozzarella cheese,
   cut into 6 mm / 1/4 in dice
handful of basil leaves, torn
   into shreds
olive oil, to dress

Preheat the oven to 250°C/475°F/gas9.

Push the dough thinner than for focaccia, say about 1 cm / 1/2 in in depth but slightly deeper around the edges. After its secondary rising in the pans, spread the tops thinly with tomato sauce and scatter over the cheese and basil. Keep pizza toppings sparse and always leave the rim uncovered. The aim is a thin, crisp-bottomed crust, not a doughy pie covered in too many things. The crust is really the point, the topping is its adjunct.

Dribble olive oil generously over the surface just before it goes in the oven. Toss in a cupful of water or spray the sides of the oven with water to generate steam and bake for 10-12 minutes.

Variations:

Other toppings to try include roasted, peeled red sweet peppers (see page 26) and feta cheese; home-dried tomatoes, anchovies and black olives; red onion, hot chillies and Cheddar cheese; garlic sliced wafer-thin, olive oil and salt; pancetta and shallots (before putting these on the pizza, sweat the shallots until soft and translucent and fry the pancetta, cut into lardon strips, until it starts to exude fat).

Grissini

MAKES ABOUT 30

small handful of Starter Dough
    (page 52)
450 g / 1 lb Basic Bread Dough
    (page 52)
30 g / 1 oz [2 tbsp] softened butter
olive oil, for brushing

Add the starter dough to the basic dough immediately after you switch on the mixer, and replace the oil with the butter. When the dough has risen, take half, knock it down with your fist and form into a rectangle about 23 × 15 cm / 9 × 6 in. Turn the first 2 cm / $^3/_4$ in on the long edge nearest to you over and then roll away from you into as tight a cylinder as you can contrive. Brush a non-stick pan with a little olive oil, lay the roll down the middle, brush it with oil too, and cover with a cloth. Leave to rise for 1 $^1/_2$ hours.

Preheat the oven to 220°C/425°F/gas 7.

The cylinder will now have spread and be more than doubled in size. Using a big sharp knife, cut it across into 1 cm / $^1/_2$ in slices. Roll a slice and then pick it up by both ends so it stretches into a long thin cigar about 25-30 cm / 10-12 in long. Transfer to non-stick baking pan(s), and repeat until all the dough is used up, leaving 2 cm / $^3/_4$ in between them to allow for expansion during baking.

Spray the grissini with water from the mister and spray the sides of the oven. Bake for 20 minutes, when they should be crisp inside and out. Transfer to a rack to cool.

Pan-grilled Bread

MAKES ABOUT 24

small handful of Starter Dough
    (page 52)
450 g / 1 lb Basic Bread Dough
    (page 52)
30 g / 1 oz [2 tbsp] softened butter
olive oil, for brushing

Proceed as for grissini, but roll each slice off the end of the cylinder with a rolling pin on a heavily floured surface until about 1 cm / $^1/_2$ in thick.

Cook in a hot dry frying pan for 1-2 minutes a side, pressing down with a spatula as it cooks. This encourages the breads to balloon. Wrap in a cloth and keep warm in a low oven as you cook the rest. Bring to the table in a basket.

Saffron Sultana Loaf

MAKES 2 ROUND LOAVES

$^1/_4$ tsp saffron threads
1 tbsp hot water
900 g / 2 lb Basic Bread Dough
55 g / 2 oz [4 tbsp] softened butter
115 g / 4 oz drunken sultanas
    [golden raisins] (see page 208)
55 g / 2 oz caster sugar [$^1/_4$ cup
    granulated sugar]

Put the saffron threads to soak in the hot water. Make the dough, replacing the olive oil with the butter. In the last 2 minutes of machine kneading, add the saffron and soaking liquid, sultanas and sugar. Make two round loaves, cover with cloths and leave to rise for 30 minutes.

Preheat the oven to 220°C/425°F/gas 7.

Mist the loaves with water before baking. Generate steam in the oven by throwing in an espresso cup of water before you put the loaves in, and bake for 40-45 minutes.

The loaves should sound hollow when rapped on the base, indicating they are cooked through to the centre.

Masa and Corn Tortillas

Corn tortillas crop up frequently in Californian cooking and when treated in different ways are called a bewildering variety of names: chimichanga, burrito, enchilada, quesadilla, tostada and so on. The lineage of the corn tortilla goes far back into Mexican history and remains central to that country's cooking. Nobody knows when some inquisitive spirit added powdered limestone – or possibly wood ash – while boiling corn to mush and discovered that this addition miraculously made the corn more digestible and – with the calcium and niacin it incidentally imparted – more nutritious. Today when making tortilla dough, slaked lime (calcium hydroxide) is used.

Dried white field corn, which is starchy and not at all sweet, is first brought to the boil in water with slaked lime, simmered for 15 minutes and then left to soak overnight. It is then washed under running water while being rubbed to rid it of the yellow hulls until only the white kernels remain. These are ground while still wet and then mixed with more water to give a smooth soft dough. Traditionally the tortillas are then patted out by hand into saucer-sized rounds, though most home cooks use a hinged metal tortilla press.

Fresh masa (maize dough) can be bought from tortilla factories (*tortillerias*) in California, but no such facilities exist yet outside Central and North America. Tortillas can also be made from masa harina, force-dried finely ground corn meal. Quaker Oats produces one in the USA which you find in most markets there, but don't hold your breath while looking on the shelves of even the largest British supermarket. The masa harina delivers a tortilla that is perfectly reasonable, but no better than the ones you buy ready-made and, in most cases, not nearly as nice.

I once went through the whole tedious performance of making masa by hand when staying with somebody who had a hand-cranked corn grinder with stone plates, among other never-used pieces of kitchen kit. It was not something I ever want to do again, since the washing and grinding felt interminable and the performance of laying pieces of plastic within the press plates for each tortilla gave the phrase 'labour-intensive' a whole new meaning.

The finished dough is not easy to work with since it has none of the elasticity of a yeast dough and it dries out and becomes unworkable very quickly. Maybe you could really get into making authentic corn tortillas in the same way I have with bread, but I am going to wait for another life, preferring in this one to make wheat-flour tortillas.

Wheat-flour Tortillas

As with all the most simple and basic preparations, perfect results only come from practice. The precise consistency of the dough is one that you will eventually gauge by pressing with a finger, while by repetition you will gain the experience needed to tell when the hot metal on which they are cooked is just the right temperature. It needs to be hot enough so a tortilla starts to bubble within 3 seconds of hitting the pan. The best tortillas have lard in them, and a mixture of lard and sunflower oil actually produces the most satisfactory results. Duck fat, while scarcely traditional, works well and gives a great flavour. Yet again, the food processor makes a tricky task quick and easy. The dough can be made the day before, plastic-wrapped and kept in the fridge. If using it that day, first allow it to rest, covered with a cloth, for at least 45 minutes before rolling and pan-grilling or cooking on a griddle plate.

MAKES 12 TORTILLAS

345 g / 12 oz [3 cups] 14% protein white flour (see page 48), plus more for dusting
2 tbsp lard or duck fat
3 tbsp sunflower oil
1 tsp salt
about 175 ml / 6 fl oz [³/₄ cup] hand-warm water

Put the flour, lard or duck fat, oil and salt into a processor and work at full speed to combine. While continuing to process, pour the warm water through the feeder tube in a thin stream until the dough balls. (This may take a little more water, but better to add than to start with too wet a dough.) Continue to process until you have a smooth, elastic dough.

Turn the dough out on a floured surface and divide into 12 pieces. Roll these into balls, put them on a plate, cover with plastic film and leave to rest for 45 minutes.

Heat a dry heavy frying pan or flat griddle over a medium heat. On a lightly floured surface, roll out a ball of dough, rotating, rolling and turning until you have a 17.5 cm / 7 in disc. Dust with more flour if it sticks. Place the tortilla on the hot metal. The surface will start to bubble with hot air. Turn after about 30 seconds, when the under surface will have brown blisters on it. Cook for another 30-45 seconds. Do not overcook or the tortilla will go crisp. Transfer to a thick cloth and wrap loosely to keep warm. Repeat with the rest of the dough balls.

You can reheat fresh tortillas wrapped in a slightly dampened cloth which, in turn, has been surrounded with foil, in an oven at 130°C/275°F/gas1.

Pastry

Pastry is one of those areas where a lot of fat is effectively concealed. The precise fat-to-flour ratio is very much a matter of individual preference. Basic pastry has roughly half fat to flour. As the butter content goes up, so the resulting pastry become more delicate and crumbly, friable they call it, like good earth. Where eggs are used, for example in sweet shortcrust, the pastry will be sticky and needs to be well chilled. Even then it may be too short to roll out, in which case roll into a cylinder in plastic film, refrigerate and then cut in discs, pressing them into the tart pan.

Making pastry demands precision, so always measure ingredients with accurate kitchen scales. American cooks have grown up with cups and sticks and other oddities, but weighing is the best route to successful baking.

Coming only late in life to making pastry I have no hang-ups about using machinery and all the following recipes work in a food processor if you first blitz the flour and butter to crumbs before adding the egg(s) through the feeder tube, followed by any binding liquid. The food processor gives you complete control and does the job so quickly you won't over-mix, while the pastry stays cold so, even if you have those super-hot hands that exclude you from the pâtissier's life, you can make successful pastry every time. The only thing to watch out for is that processed pastry needs less liquid than hand-made. The instant it balls, stop adding water.

Always try to make pastry with plenty of work space. Chefs insist that a marble rolling top is ideal. Doubtless they are right, but it does ultimately depend on your kitchen. They are certainly right to insist on as cool an environment as possible.

Many cooks use block margarine and lard when making flaky and puff pastry. If you do then you might as well buy the pastry ready-made. In the USA and Australia you can buy frozen butter puff pastry, which for some reason we are denied in Britain. Industrial-scale production of factory-made puff pastry delivers an excellent product, but it is all made with non-dairy fat, so while it is fine for savoury applications, it is not as nice in desserts.

Where a recipe calls for a tart shell to be baked blind, preheat the oven to 200°C/400°F/gas6. Roll out the pastry to a round 3 cm/1 1/4 in larger than the diameter of the pan (use one with a detachable base) and line the pan with it. Fold the edges back over to give a double thickness. If you don't, the pastry will shrink down the sides during cooking.

Prick the bottom of the shell all over with a fork and cover with foil. Fill with some dried beans or those ceramic beads that have the advantage of not stinking the house out like dried beans do after a few goes in the oven. (Keep the foil and beans in a plastic container as they can be used many times.) Bake for 15 minutes, then remove the foil and beans and continue to bake until the bottom is golden-coloured, which takes about another 5 minutes.

Shortcrust Pastry

MAKES ONE 23CM/9IN TART SHELL

115 g / 4 oz [$^1/_2$ cup] chilled butter
225 g / 8 oz [1 $^2/_3$ cups] flour
$^1/_2$ tsp salt
about 4 tbsp ice-cold water

BY HAND...
Cut the butter into 2.5 cm / 1 in dice and leave to soften at room temperature for 30 minutes.

Sift the flour on to a work surface and make a well in the centre. Put the butter dice in the well and add the salt. Use your fingertips to rub these in, pulling in more flour from the outside as you work. When all the flour has been combined, moisten the mixture with the water and knead with the heel of your hand, making three or four turns, when you should have a silky smooth ball of dough.

Wrap in plastic film and leave to rest in the fridge for at least 1 hour before using. (It will keep in the fridge for a week and also freezes well.)

IN A PROCESSOR...
Use the butter while still cold, and cut into 2.5 cm / 1 in dice. Put in the bowl of the processor with the flour and salt and blitz briefly to crumb. Add the water through the feeder tube, a spoonful at a time, until the dough balls. Wrap in plastic and refrigerate for 1 hour or more.

Savoury Tart Pastry

MAKES ONE 23CM/9IN TART SHELL

125 g / 4 $^1/_2$ oz [$^1/_2$ cup] butter
1 egg
250 g / 8 $^1/_2$ oz [1 $^2/_3$ cups] flour
1 tsp salt
2 tbsp water

Follow the same method as for Shortcrust Pastry above, adding the egg after the butter and the water right at the end, before the final kneading. Again, chill for at least 1 hour before rolling.

Sweet Shortcrust Pastry

MAKES ONE 23CM/9IN TART SHELL

140 g / 5 oz [10 tbsp] butter
250 g / 8 1/2 oz [1 2/3 cups] flour
55 g / 2 oz caster sugar [1/4
  cup granulated sugar]
grated zest of 1 lemon
1 egg

Follow the same procedure as for Shortcrust Pastry, but rub in the butter, sugar and zest before adding the egg.

Almond Pastry

MAKES ONE 23CM/9IN TART SHELL

115 g / 4 oz [1/2 cup] butter
225 g / 8 oz [1 2/3 cups] flour
85 g / 3 oz [1 cup] ground almonds
85 g / 3 oz caster sugar [6 1/2 tbsp
  granulated sugar]
1/2 tsp salt
1 egg
few drops of water if required

Follow the same procedure as for Sweet Shortcrust Pastry, but adding the almonds with the sugar.

Flaky Pastry

This recipe makes a very acceptable sweet flaky pastry with the minimum amount of aggravation. This is not as light as true puff pastry, but then it is so much easier to make.

MAKES ONE 23CM/9IN TART SHELL

225 g / 8 oz [1 2/3 cups] flour
1/4 tsp salt
140 g / 5 oz [10 tbsp] chilled butter
100 ml / 3 1/2 fl oz [7 tbsp] iced water

Put the flour and salt in the processor bowl. Cut the butter into four pieces; put one in with the flour and blitz to crumbs. While continuing to process at full speed, dribble in the water through the feeder tube until the dough balls.

Remove from the bowl and transfer to a floured surface. Form into a cylinder and cut into four pieces. Return them to the processor bowl in a single layer. Cut the remaining butter into 1 cm / 1/2 in dice and put between the pastry pieces. Blitz for a few seconds to recombine.

Scrape out on to a floured surface and roll out to a thickness of 5mm / 1/4 in. Fold the side closest to you to the middle and the side furthest away over the top of this. Make a half turn to the right, then roll out and fold as before. Repeat this three times. Cover with plastic film and refrigerate for at least 1 hour or overnight before using.

Cookbooks rarely mention alcohol...

... for reasons that are difficult to understand. This does not apply to wine, although that subject is too huge to do more than make the odd recommendation, as in 'don't drink it with soup'. The cocktail is, however, very pertinent. One taken before lunch or dinner gets the gastric juices flowing nicely and sets your guests up for the meal, putting them in the right frame of mind – relaxed and receptive. Cocktails too are party fuel, but when taken in quantity should always have food served with them. A meal afterwards misses the point. Nibbles are always a good idea when drink is taken. *Mezze*, which were created for drinks, can get a bit out of hand, particularly when served in an unrestrained way with aperitifs before a meal, a mistake because nobody is left with any appetite for the main event. The recipes that follow the drinks in this section could never be misconstrued as *mezze*, but are so much nicer to offer people than something out of a packet and they don't take long to prepare.

Margarita

The Margarita is indisputably the cocktail of the West Coast. A properly made Margarita is delicious, refreshing and deceptively innocuous-tasting. Most bars and many restaurants serve it by the pitcher, knowing full well that one glass leads rapidly to another and another. There is a nauseating substance sold in bottles called 'Margarita mix', which tastes of saccharine, sulphur and chemicals. You have been warned.

After years of dedicated research I have come to the opinion that the best Margaritas are shaken over ice and served straight up – that is, with no ice in the glass; but you do whatever works best for you. You can obtain a similar effect by stirring it in a jug with lots of ice and straining into glasses as you would when making a Martini. When using a shaker, the inclusion of an egg white will give you a frothy opaque version that you could call something else, for example 'frothy Rita'.

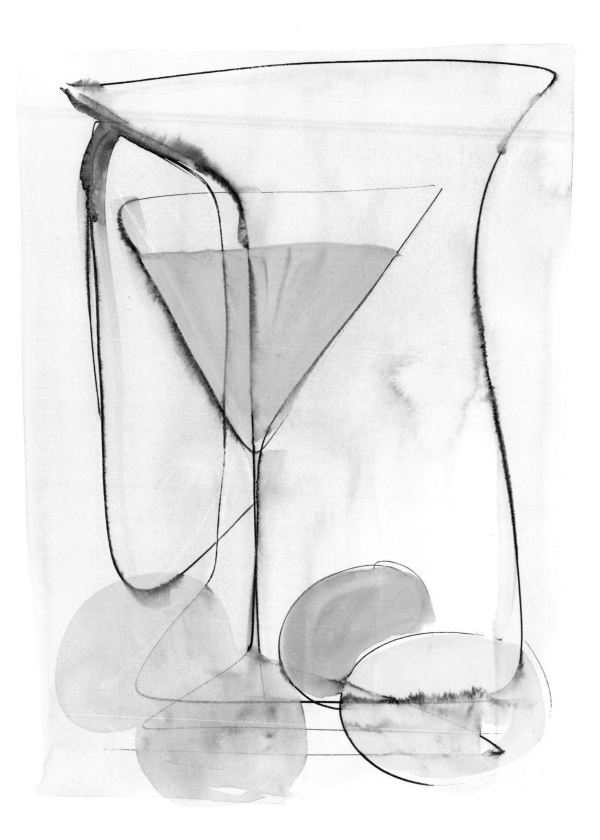

The classic Margarita is always served in a salt-rimmed glass. It is a mystery why the same Californians who blench at the thought of half a teaspoon of salt in their food will cheerfully drink half a dozen Margaritas, licking the salt crystals joyously from the glass. They are perfectly good without the salt rim, a practice which comes from the classic accompaniments to a shot of straight tequila – a lick of salt before and a quick suck on a quarter of lime after, all acquired tastes.

Margaritas are usually made with Triple Sec, but Cointreau is more subtle. Limes are the orthodox citrus, but a mixture of lemon and lime is better. The quality of the tequila is the absolute in the mix. Cuervo Gold is a favourite, but try whatever your imaginative spirit merchant has to offer. The standard mix is 2 parts tequila to 1 part Cointreau or other orange liqueur and $^1/_2$ part lime or lemon juice, or a mixture of the two.

With Mexican food, which in the main is no great respecter of wines, Margaritas can be drunk with beer chasers throughout the meal. Corona, Dos Equis and other Mexican beers are now widely available.

FOR 4

*250 ml / 8 fl oz [1 cup]
  tequila*
*125 ml / 4 fl oz [$^1/_2$ cup]
  Cointreau*
*4 tbsp lime juice, or 2 tbsp
  lemon and 2 tbsp lime*

Like a Martini, a straight-up Margarita is served in a wide-rimmed, shallow glass. Take a slice of lime and wipe around the rim of each glass with it. Put Maldon sea salt flakes on a flat plate and press the rim into it. Shake off excess. Fill a cocktail shaker with ice cubes and add the ingredients. Put on a mariachi CD. As the trumpets wail mournfully, shake vigorously with a stylish high wrist action. Pour into the glasses carefully so as not to damage the salt rim.

Margaritas are also served blended with ice and in order to drink them you need those thick straws with the flexible bit in the middle that look like leg prostheses for Barbie. Put the same mixture in a blender or food processor with 12 ice cubes and blitz to a uniform mush.

Sangrita

FOR 8

*575 ml / 1 pt [2$^1/_3$ cups]
  freshly squeezed orange
  juice (blood orange is
  nicest)*
juice of 4 limes
4 tbsp grenadine
1 tsp salt
1 tsp hot cayenne pepper

As I said before, a lot of people drink beer chasers with Margaritas, which is fine if you want to get totally slammed very fast, but a more sensible alternative is Sangrita. You chase the tequila with a chilled shot of this.

Put all the ingredients in a blender or processor and blitz briefly to mix. Refrigerate in a jug and serve in shot glasses.

Shot glasses are very difficult to buy, but neither the tequila nor the Sangrita tastes right in ordinary glasses. Too many movies, I guess.

Strawberry Daiquiri

FOR 2

125 ml / 4 fl oz [¹/₂ cup] dark rum
100 ml / 3¹/₂ fl oz [7 tbsp]
   Orange Curaçao
225 g / 8 oz hulled strawberries
1 tbsp caster sugar [US
   granulated sugar]
2 tbsp lime juice
8 ice cubes
mint leaves, for garnish

This is the drink that has the lilt of long summer afternoons. Enjoy too many of them and evening will creep up on you real fast.

Put all the ingredients into a food processor or blender (reserving 2 good-looking strawberries for decoration) and whizz to a slush. Pour into 2 stemmed glasses and stick in doll's-leg prosthesis straws. Garnish each with a whole reserved strawberry and some mint leaves.

Mulholland-driven Madness

You may never have traversed Mulholland Drive's winding length from Interstate 405 east through Hollywood, but you will know it from a hundred movies. Just a few yards from the La Brea end, near its junction with Outpost Road, is a turnout where people pause at night for the astonishing view it affords of LA's lights stretching off, multi-coloured jewel-bright to the horizon. A police helicopter clatters overhead and you are in the movie too. All you need is the right drink to take you further in and help unravel the script.

Cider in America is mostly an unappetizing, over-sweet alcohol-free children's drink so you must use hard cider. This version tastes great, is not sweet and will blow your head off.

Should you not have lemon syrup to hand (an unlikely thought), then just mix the juice of a lemon and a teaspoon of grated zest with two teaspoons of sugar and a spoonful or two of boiling water to dissolve it.

FOR 8

150 ml / ¹/₄ pt [²/₃ cup]
   Calvados (or cooking brandy)
150 ml / ¹/₄ pt [²/₃ cup] dry sherry
1.1 litres / 2 pt dry cider [5
   cups dry hard cider]
8 strips of cucumber peel
575 ml / 1 pt [2¹/₃ cups] club
   soda water

FOR THE LEMON SUGAR SYRUP:
450 g / 1 lb caster sugar [2¹/₄
   cups granulated sugar]
2 lemons

To make the lemon sugar syrup: dissolve the sugar in 500 ml / 16 fl oz [2 cups] water. Add the pared zest and juice of the lemons. Bring to the boil, turn down the heat and simmer for 10 minutes. Let cool and then refrigerate in a screw-top jar with the lemon zest. It will keep until it runs out. You can use it for all sorts of things, like sorbets and drinks.

In a jug, mix 1 tablespoon of the cool lemon sugar syrup with the Calvados or brandy and the sherry. Top up with ice-cold cider.

Put a strip of cucumber peel into each tall glass with some ice. Pour over the mix and add a squirt of soda to give it a little fizz.

Take a deep draught. Narrow your eyes. The barman looks strangely like Quentin Tarantino and that entrancing girl by the window could be Patricia Arquette. Now, is that a gun in your pocket?

'Just the One' Bloody Mary

FOR 1

50-75 ml / 2-3 fl oz
    Stolichnaya or Absolut
    vodka
25 ml / 1 fl oz dry sherry
150 ml / 1/4 pt [2/3 cup]
    tomato juice
juice of 1/2 lemon
1 tbsp Worcestershire sauce
2 tsp Tabasco sauce (or Salsa
    Picante, page 39)
pinch of celery salt
black pepper

Bloody Marys should be very spicy, include dry sherry as well as vodka, have plenty of lemon juice in them, and be shaken over ice before being served straight up. Such dogmatism will inevitably excite disapproval and disagreement, so let's put it another way. A Bloody Mary which has very little alcohol, is insipidly spiced and is served without lemon juice over ice is not worth drinking. It tastes like a poor sort of tomato soup. Nobody could confuse this drink with anything other than the very superior cocktail it is. Drink one before lunch, not restricting this aperitif just to Sunday brunch (see page 129).

The tomato juice you use is very important. Some, particularly those sold in cardboard cartons, are foul. A pleasant alternative, and a preferred option, is Clamato, the tomato and clam juice mix.

Half-fill a cocktail shaker with ice cubes. Pour over all the ingredients and shake vigorously for 20 seconds. Pour into a chilled low-ball glass, and keep the rest of the drink in a flask from which to top up.

Grown-up Rum Banana Shake

After I was weaned I refused to eat anything except bananas for two years. At one point a nurse was employed to force food into me, a procedure always undertaken behind closed doors with her emerging triumphantly perhaps an hour or so later to display a clean plate. After some weeks it was noticed that I was growing thinner while my nurse grew larger and my father's perceptive legal brain put two and two together and she was sacked. Banana sandwiches still taste good, but I am suspicious of cooked bananas in the main. Alcoholic banana milkshakes, however, are entirely acceptable. They are called Daiquiris and generally very good news. You know the shakes you get in fast-food outlets, so thick you feel your head will implode as you try to suck them up through a straw? Add white rum and you have something special. The secret is ice-cream.

FOR 4 PROPER DRINKS

4 ripe bananas, chopped
285 g / 10 oz [about 1pt]
    Vanilla Ice-cream (page 218)
250 ml / 8 fl oz [1 cup] white
    rum
575 ml / 1 pt [2 1/3 cups] milk

Put all the ingredients in a blender or processor and blitz to a thick cream. Check the consistency. If unsuckably thick, add up to 150 ml / 1/4 pt [2/3 cup] more milk and a smidgen more rum if so inclined.

Guacamole

Always use red onion in a guacamole. Spanish onions are too dominant and work against the avocado's subtle flavour. Avocados are always sold unripe, so buy them a few days ahead and leave at room temperature to soften. Ripe avocados give to gentle pressure from your thumb at the stem end, leaving a depression in the skin. It is important to peel and remove the pulp and seeds from the tomatoes or they will water the guacamole down too much.

FOR 8

4 ripe tomatoes

4 ripe avocados

1 red onion

3-4 jalapeño-type (very hot) chillies

2 handfuls of coriander [cilantro]

1 tsp salt

1/2 tsp pepper

juice of 1 lemon

juice of 1 lime

Blanch the tomatoes briefly in boiling water, refresh in cold water and peel. Cut into quarters; scrape out the pulp and seeds and discard. Chop the remaining flesh into small dice and reserve. Cut the avocados in half and remove the stones. Scoop out the flesh into a serving bowl. Mash roughly with a fork (you don't want a smooth purée).

Cut the onion into 1 cm/1/2 in dice and add. Remove stems and seeds from the chillies, shred, then cut into tiny dice and add. Chop most of the coriander, reserving a few whole leaves for garnish. Add the chopped coriander and the tomato dice to the avocado. Season with the salt and pepper, then mash and mix all together. Stir in the citrus juices. Taste, and adjust the seasoning.

Serve as soon as you can because, whatever you do, the avocado flesh will oxidize and blacken. You can slow this process by smoothing the surface and pouring the citrus juice on top, only stirring it in just before the dish is eaten. It also helps to cover the surface with plastic film. Sticking the stones of the avocado in does not help.

Serve with blue or white corn chips.

Enlivened Grissini

These are fashionable, delicious and easy to make. If not baking them yourself (see page 55), all you need is a packet of grissini – those feather-light Italian breadsticks – and some very thinly cut streaky bacon. Even better is paper-thin pancetta, which you can buy sliced to order at any good Italian food shop. When you buy a box of grissini some of them are bound to be broken, but there should be at least 30 left intact. To be on the safe side, buy two boxes, putting all the broken sticks in one to return to the shop.

2 tbsp hot chilli powder

85 g / 3 oz demerara sugar [1/2
    cup raw brown sugar]

450 g / 1 lb pancetta, thinly
    sliced

30 grissini

Preheat the oven to 180°C/350°F/gas4.

Put the chilli powder and sugar in a processor and blitz briefly to mix. Scatter this mixture in a Swiss-roll [shallow baking] pan or tray or on a sheet of greaseproof [wax] paper. Wrap a slice of pancetta around each breadstick in a spiral. Roll each of these bacon sticks in the chilli sugar to give them a light dusting, and arrange (not touching each other) on a rack set in a roasting pan. Bake for 15-20 minutes, and leave on the rack to cool. The bread will have softened, but leave it for 10 minutes and it will firm up again.

Serve at room temperature.

Anchovy Wafers

These are also very easy to make and are good as a salty nibble with a glass of dry sherry. Home-made taramasalata makes an alternative spread to top the wafers.

MAKES ABOUT 40

170 g / 6 oz [1 1/4 cups] flour

85 g / 3 oz [6 tbsp] chilled
    butter, cut into 5 mm / 1/4 in
    dice

2 egg yolks

2 tsp anchovy essence

FOR THE ANCHOVY
SPREAD:

55 g / 2 oz canned anchovy
    fillets

55 g / 2 oz [4 tbsp] butter

1 hard-boiled egg

3 tbsp crème fraîche

1 tsp cayenne pepper

red food colouring (optional)

In a food processor, blitz the flour with the butter until they crumb. Add the egg yolks and anchovy essence and process briefly, adding a little water through the feeder tube until a stiff dough is formed. Scrape out on to plastic film, roll up and refrigerate for 1 hour or overnight.

Preheat the oven to 200°C/400°F/gas6. Roll out the dough on a floured surface as thinly as you can. Use a pastry cutter to produce discs or squares, placing them on a baking sheet. Bake for 10-15 minutes until golden brown and crisp. Cool on a rack.

Make the anchovy spread: drain the anchovies and whizz them in the food processor with the remaining ingredients. If you have some red food dye (cochineal beetle extract), add a few drops to give a pinker colour if desired. If you are feeling tricky, pipe the spread on the wafers. If not, just spread it thinly with a knife.

Parmesan and Lemon Zest Crackers

These biscuits, or crackers, are easy to make. When people ask for the recipe pretend it is a family secret which cannot be divulged so they get bitter and resentful before they leave.

MAKES ABOUT 40

115 g / 4 oz [³/4 cup] flour, plus more for dusting
115 g / 4 oz [1 cup] freshly grated Parmesan cheese
55 g / 2 oz [4 tbsp] chilled butter, diced
grated zest of 1 lemon
1 tsp sea salt
2 tsp coarsely ground black pepper

Put all the ingredients in a food processor and whizz to a crumb consistency, then add 1-2 tablespoons of cold water through the feeder tube until the dough balls. Scrape out on to a lightly floured surface and roll into a cylinder. You will cut the biscuits from this, so size the roll accordingly. You should get about 40 biscuits. Wrap tightly in plastic film and refrigerate for at least 2 hours or overnight.

Preheat the oven to 190°C/375°F/gas5. Cut the dough cylinder into discs 5 mm / ¹/4 in thick and lay these on non-stick baking sheets, leaving at least 2 cm / ³/4 in between them. Bake for 10-12 minutes, and then transfer the crackers to a cake rack to cool.

Californian Potato Chips

Mandolins, fixed-blade slicing panels, are easier to control than the slicing disc on a food processor. The best are called Benriners and come from Japan with Japanese instructions. For Health and Safety warnings see page 200. If you can't be bothered to turn to these pages: these are DANGEROUS and should be called Avengers of the Rising Sun.

FOR 6-8

450 g / 1 lb floury potatoes
oil for deep-frying
sea salt

Slice the potatoes paper-thin on a mandolin (see above). Put the slices into iced water for 15 minutes, then spin-dry in a salad spinner and spread out on paper towels to get rid of as much moisture as you can. Preheat oil for deep-frying to 190°C/375°F. Fry the potato slices in small batches, removing them as they brown and draining on more paper towels.

When they are all done, put into a large serving bowl, sprinkle with flake sea salt and serve as soon as possible. You can spice them up by also sprinkling on some cayenne and paprika. A teaspoon of each to every 450 g / 1 lb of potatoes will be about the right amount.

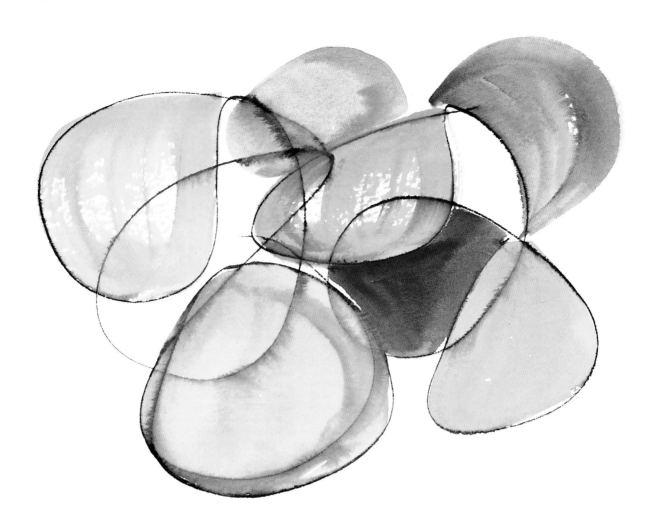

Variation:

Try preparing in the same way and deep-frying chips made from plantains, turnips, beetroots [beets] and parsnips. They are as pretty to look at as they are good to eat and go well as a nibble with drinks.

Thai-scotched Eggs

Tutti's in Montecito is the kind of simple small restaurant that encapsulates the contemporary Californian dining experience. The kitchen is open to the room and the menu leans towards Italy, with many fresh pasta dishes. There is an open fire rôtisserie on which plump chickens spin to a golden, crisp-skinned finish. It boasts a splendid and far-ranging wine list and there is also a delicatessen and food shop.

One night over dinner there, the conversation turned to London and the food people remembered fondly. Astonishingly, three out of six at the table plumped for pub Scotch eggs, a frankly bizarre choice in that setting and as far removed from the elegant simplicity of the food on the table as the imagination can stretch. Even the best pub Scotch eggs are belt-loosening fare, fashioned on the heavy side and the size of hand grenades. But this bizarre longing got me thinking, and these Thai-scotched eggs were the result. Cut into quarters and served still hot, they make ace party food. You must decide how spicy hot you make them. As always, the amount of chilli in the recipe is only a suggestion.

Use the best quality sausagemeat you can buy as the base. By the time you have added the herbs and spices this is more than adequate. Cookbooks invariably tell you to flour the boiled eggs before wrapping them in the sausagemeat. This is wholly unnecessary.

Breadcrumbs are something that you ideally make once a week, keeping them in an airtight jar. Allow bread to stale completely before blitzing it to a fine crumb in a food processor. If you don't have any to hand, dry some slices of bread in a low oven until crisp but not brown.

Mashing the sausagemeat and flavourings on a Swiss-roll [shallow baking] pan or tray is a convenient way of containing the rather sticky mess and also makes dividing into 12 easy. Never make the mistake of speeding things up by putting everything in a food processor. This will turn the mixture into an unworkable wet mess.

FOR 4

6 eggs
450 g/1 lb premium pork
*   sausagemeat*
4 spring onions [scallions]
2 serrano-type (hot) red
*   chillies*
2 Anaheim-type (medium-
*   hot) green chillies*
1 garlic clove
handful of coriander
*   [cilantro]*
black pepper
115 g/4 oz [2¹/₂ cups]
*   white breadcrumbs*
oil for deep-frying

Boil 4 of the eggs for 6 minutes, refresh in cold water, shell and reserve.

Put the sausagemeat on a large shallow baking pan and mash it into an even layer with a fork. Trim the spring onions; remove seeds from the chillies, and peel the garlic. Chop them all as finely as you can and scatter over the surface of the meat. Chop the coriander and add too. Grind over plenty of pepper. Mash all together with a fork, turning and mixing to distribute all the flavouring elements evenly. Spread out to cover the bottom of the pan.

Break the remaining eggs into a bowl and whisk. Put half the breadcrumbs in another bowl. Divide the sausagemeat into four pieces.

Take a piece of sausagemeat and flatten it in one hand. Put a boiled egg on top and pull the sausagemeat around it in an even layer. Take care that the egg does not peep through at any point. Roll in the egg wash and transfer to the crumbs. Shake and gently toss the bowl to cover the exterior. Put to one side and repeat with the remaining eggs, adding more crumbs to the bowl as you go along. When all are done, repeat to give them a second coating. This is always advisable when deep-frying a crumb coating.

You can keep the eggs in the fridge for several hours before cooking, or you can freeze them on a tray, transferring to zip-lock bags and storing for up to a month.

Preheat oil for deep-frying to 190°C/375°F. Fry the eggs for 4 minutes and drain on paper towels. Allow to rest for 2 minutes, then cut in half and serve while still hot. They will disappear like snow off a dike, an intriguing phrase in common usage long before it developed a new twist.

Variation:
Make this recipe with 12 hard-boiled (3 minutes) quail's eggs and serve these cut in half lengthwise.

Cheese Straws

MAKES 20-25

450 g / 1 lb puff pastry
flour, for dusting
2 tbsp Dijon mustard
1 tsp hot chilli flakes
black pepper
85 g / 3 oz [^{3}/$_4$ cup] Reggiano
   Parmesan cheese, freshly
   grated
1 egg
1 tbsp sesame seeds

Preheat the oven to 200°C/400°F/gas6.

Roll out the pastry on a lightly floured surface to make a neat rectangle with a thickness of about 3 mm / ^{1}/$_8$ in. Brush with the mustard, scatter over the chilli flakes and grind over some black pepper. Distribute the cheese over one long half of the pastry and fold the other half over that. Press down gently all over to seal.

Cut the pastry across into strips about 5 mm / ^{1}/$_4$ in wide. Holding the ends of each strip, twist to make them into corkscrew shapes. Lightly beat the egg in a small bowl. Brush the pastry twists with beaten egg, shake the sesame seeds over and arrange on a non-stick baking sheet. Bake for 15-20 minutes, until puffed and golden brown. Transfer to a rack to cool before serving.

Soups can be whatever you want...

… light and delicate, chilled for a summer's day or hot and thick enough to stand a spoon in and support a dark winter's night. Soup is usually a preliminary, but can as easily be a one-course meal. The Black Bean Soup with Chicken Albondigas (page 80) and Poached White Fish in an Intense Broth (page 84) are cases in point. Soup can take advantage of leftovers, but should not be seen as an automatic dumping ground for yesterday's residues. The real key to unlock the finest soup is good stock. Indeed, a consommé – clear and bright as a gem – may be its ultimate and finest expression.

Gazpacho with Shredded Lobster

You don't have to use a lot of lobster in this dish. Indeed, one 675 g / 1 $1/2$ lb lobster will provide enough meat for four. Gazpacho is a favourite cold soup that demands no further embellishment, but this combination is a genuine enhancement.

a 675 g / 1 1/2 lb lobster
4 slices of white bread,
    crusts removed
850 ml / 1 1/2 pt [3 1/2 cups]
    tomato juice
6 plum tomatoes
1 red onion
1 red sweet pepper,
    roasted and peeled (see
    page 26)
1 cucumber [English
    hothouse cucumber]
2 garlic cloves
2 tsp Salsa Picante (page 39)
    or Tabasco sauce
2 tbsp sherry vinegar
150 ml / 1/4 pt [2/3 cup] extra-
    virgin olive oil
salt and pepper
12 basil leaves

FOR THE LOBSTER DRESSING:
2 tsp lime juice
1 tbsp olive oil
1/2 tsp coarsely milled black
    pepper

Tear up 2 of the slices of bread, put them in a large bowl and cover them with the tomato juice.

Plunge the tomatoes in boiling water for 20-30 seconds, refresh in cold water and peel. Cut in quarters, strip out the seeds and the pulp and discard. Cut the tomatoes into 1 cm / 1/2 in dice and add to the bowl. Cut the onion across into 5 mm / 1/4 in slices and then into dice. Stir into the bowl. Dice the sweet pepper and add.

Using a potato peeler, peel strips from the length of the cucumber. Cut these lengthwise into 1 cm / 1/2 in slices, then into strips and finally into dice. Add to the bowl.

Smash and chop the garlic as finely as you can and stir in. Add the salsa or Tabasco and the sherry vinegar. Season with salt and pepper. Leave at room temperature for 1 hour to allow the flavours to develop, then cover the top with plastic film and refrigerate for 6 hours or overnight.

Cook the lobster in heavily salted boiling water as described on page 102. Remove, rinse under cold running water and leave to cool. Cut the lobster open as described on page 102. Remove the meat and shred. Crack the claws and cut into two lengthwise. Mix the lobster dressing ingredients, and toss the lobster meat in a bowl with the dressing.

Cut 2 discs from each of the remaining 2 slices of bread using a pastry cutter (to make 4 discs in all). Brush these on both sides with olive oil and fry in a non-stick pan over a low heat until crisp and golden brown on both sides. Reserve these croûtes.

Take the chilled gazpacho from the fridge and ladle into 4 chilled soup bowls. Zig-zag the remaining olive oil over the surface. Pile the lobster on top of the croûtes and float in the middle of each bowl. Tear the basil leaves and strew around.

Drink a Manzanilla or Fino with this, as it will destroy any white wine.

Butternut Squash and Herb Soup

Squash is an edible gourd and one of the indigenous vegetables of the West Coast. Today it is enjoying a fashionable popularity. Perhaps it is the name or the bright orange colour, because the flavour is not particularly strong. One approach is to include quite a lot of pancetta, but I think the smokiness obscures the squash to an unacceptable degree. This more sympathetic treatment uses lots of chives, watercress and parsley, which work with the squash without overpowering it. The single star anise gives only the most delicate trace of aniseed to the finished dish, so slight that it is not identifiable as such. You notice its exclusion more than its inclusion, for it makes a subtle difference to the overall effect.

FOR 6

1 kg / 2 1/4 lb butternut squash
1 onion
3 garlic cloves
2 celery stalks
30 g / 1 oz [2 tbsp] unsalted butter
bunch of watercress
bunch of chives
   bunch of flat-leaf parsley (enough to give 5 tbsp when chopped, plus 30 leaves to garnish)
1 bay leaf
1 star anise
1.5 litres / 2 1/4 pt [1 1/2 qt] Vegetable Stock (page 24)
115 g / 4 oz [1/2 cup] dry freshly mashed potato
150 ml / 1/2 pt [2/3 cup] crème fraîche
salt and pepper
3 tbsp double cream [heavy cream]

Cut the squash in half, then into quarters and run a knife around the inside of the skin to remove the flesh. Discard seeds and fibres, and chop the flesh in large chunks. Chop the onion and garlic, and cut the celery stalks across into thin strips.

Put the butter and all the vegetables in a large saucepan and sweat gently until soft, stirring from time to time. Add the watercress, most of the chives, coarsely chopped, 3 tablespoons of chopped parsley, the bay leaf and star anise. Pour in the stock and bring to the boil, then lower the heat and simmer for 20 minutes.

Add the mashed potato and 2 more tablespoons of chopped parsley, then season with salt and pepper. Return to the boil, stir and remove from the heat.

In a blender or processor, purée the soup in batches, removing the bay leaf and star anise before you do so. Return to the pan and bring back to a simmer. Stir in the crème fraîche; taste and adjust the seasoning if needed.

Ladle into bowls and zig-zag the cream on top, then garnish with the whole parsley leaves and reserved chives, cut into 5 mm / 1/4 in lengths.

Pippa's Chilled Avocado Soup

One summer, my wife and I borrowed Maxwell and Juliet Caulfield's house which looked out over the ocean near a little Mexican town called Carpinteria. The garden was a riot of bougainvillaea, fuchsias and trumpet-vines, and busy with iridescent humming birds – their wing noise surprisingly loud. At night, as the stars filled the sky, we sat on the deck and drank Margaritas and looked out to sea at the flickering flames of the oil rigs, so ugly in daylight but entrancingly romantic after dark.

The house nestled at the base of the foothills and was surrounded by avocado groves. For some reason or other this was called a ranch as opposed to a farm, though neither horses nor lassoes are involved in avocado-

FOR 6

4 ripe avocados

juice of I lemon

juice of I lime

8 spring onions [scallions]

*575 ml / I pt [2¹/3 cups] Greek-
    style yogurt or other plain
    thick yogurt*

*about 575 ml / I pt [2¹/3 cups]
    light Chicken Stock (page 24)*

3 tbsp crème fraîche

salt and pepper

small bunch of chives, to garnish

gathering. The property had two dogs, one of which had developed a passion for the fruit. She looked like a barrel on sticks, a walking reminder of how calorific avocados are.

Every morning the ranch-hand brought another pail of avocados. My wife suggested making a cold soup. It was a timely way of preparing them when the thought of guacamole finally palled.

Cut the avocados in half and remove the stones. The easiest way to do this is to sink the butt end of a chef's knife into the stone with a controlled strike. The base of the blade sticks into the stone and it can then be neatly lifted away. Scoop out the flesh into a large bowl. Add the lemon and lime juices and mash to a pulp with a fork.

Trim the spring onions, cut across into the thinnest rings and add. Whisk in the yogurt, then add just enough stock to give the texture of double [heavy] cream. Season with salt and pepper, then stir in the crème fraîche. Taste, adjusting seasoning as you think appropriate.

Cover with plastic film and refrigerate for 2-4 hours. Any longer and the soup may darken as it eventually oxidizes.

Serve garnished with chives snipped into 5 mm / ¹/4 in pieces.

Cilantro and Courgette Soup

The Spanish word for what we British know as coriander is cilantro, 'coriander' being used in California and Mexico to describe the seed of the plant. Strongly flavoured herbs like this can be used to best advantage in soup and sauces, where only a relatively small amount makes a big impact. This recipe is very Mexican so it is also very Californio, as the earliest Spanish settlers were called.

In Britain the best place to buy coriander is an Asian or Chinese market, where a huge bunch the equivalent of 20 supermarket packets costs about the same as two such packets. It also usually comes with its roots, an important flavouring element in Mexican and South-east Asian cooking.

100 g / 3 1/2 oz coriander
   [about 2 cups cilantro], with
roots
450 g / 1 lb courgettes [zucchini]
3 tbsp extra-virgin olive oil
1.5 litres/2 1/2 pt [1 1/2 qt] light
   Chicken Stock (page 24)
225 g / 8 oz onion
2 fresh hot green chillies
6 tbsp dry freshly mashed
   potatoes
150 ml / 1/2 pt [2/3 cup] crème
   fraîche
little milk (optional)
salt and pepper
blue corn tortilla chips, to
   serve (optional)

Wash the roots of the coriander. Chop them with the stems and reserve.

Trim the courgettes, cut them into quarters and then across into batons. Cook with 2 tablespoons of water and 1 tablespoon of olive oil in a covered saucepan over a medium to high heat for 4 minutes, shaking from time to time. Transfer to a blender or food processor, add the chicken stock and whizz until smooth.

Dice the onion and sauté in the remaining olive oil until soft and translucent. Remove seeds from the chillies, then slice into rings. Add these to the onion together with the dry mashed potato, the coriander roots and stems, and the courgette purée. Simmer, stirring occasionally, for 10 minutes.

Chop half the coriander leaves and stir into the soup with the crème fraîche. Season with salt and pepper and simmer for a final 2 minutes. If too thick, thin with a little milk. Serve garnished with crisp blue corn tortilla chips and the remaining whole coriander leaves. This soup may also be refrigerated and served chilled.

Black Bean Soup with Chicken Albondigas

Bean soups are popular the world over, some thick enough to stand a spoon up, others made into a creamy purée. They can be restrained and simple as a first course or dressed up to be a main course. This soup retains some whole beans but the rest are puréed, giving a nice contrast of textures.

Albondigas are meatballs, most frequently made from beef or pork or a mixture of the two, but here with herbed chicken. You could use chicken breast meat, but thighs are very easy to bone and are ideal for mincing [grinding]. If you don't have a mincer [meat grinder], cut the meat up into small pieces by hand and then pulse-chop briefly in a food processor.

The soup can, of course, be eaten without the meatballs, but the combination is particularly pleasing. The dish is enhanced by cooking the beans in chicken stock or a mixture of stock and water. Serve with crusty bread or wheat flour tortillas (page 57).

FOR 8

350 g / 12 oz [2 cups] dried
   black beans
450 g / 1 lb canned tomatoes
1.75 litres / 3 pt [7^1/2 cups]
   Chicken Stock (page 24)
1 glass of red wine
2 fresh hot red chillies
2 celery stalks
2 Kaffir lime leaves
225 g / 8 oz onion
3 tbsp extra-virgin olive oil
2 garlic cloves
salt and pepper
handful of flat-leaf parsley, to
   garnish

FOR THE ALBONDIGAS:
450 g / 1 lb chicken thighs,
   skinned
2 tsp cumin seeds
1 slice of white bread, crusts
   removed
3-4 tbsp beer
1 tbsp chopped chives
1 tbsp chopped coriander
   [cilantro]
1 garlic clove
white of 1 egg
2-3 tbsp flour
3 tbsp sunflower oil

Soak the beans overnight in lots of cold water. Bring to the boil and boil hard for 10 minutes, then drain in a colander and rinse under cold running water.

Rinse out the pan, return the beans to it and add the chopped tomatoes and their liquid, then the chicken stock and wine, plus as much cold water as is needed to cover the beans completely. Add the chillies, celery, lime leaves and 1 teaspoon of ground black pepper.

Dice the onion and sweat in the olive oil until translucent. Smash and chop the garlic and stir that in. Increase the heat and fry, stirring continuously, until golden brown. Add to the beans.

Bring to the boil, lower the heat and simmer until done, about 1 hour. Season with salt after 45-50 minutes. Taste for seasoning when the beans are cooked and adjust if necessary.

You can finish the preparation immediately or leave to cool and reheat gently later, or keep covered in the fridge for up to 3 days.

Make the albondigas: bone out the chicken thighs, keeping the bones for stock. Cut off and discard most of the fat, retaining a little. Cube the flesh, put through the fine plate of a mincer [meat grinder] and transfer to a bowl. Alternatively, dice and then briefly pulse chop in a food processor.

Toast the cumin seeds in a dry pan over a low heat for 2-3 minutes, stirring. Grind in a coffee grinder and add to the bowl. Soak the bread in the beer, squeeze out any excess and add with the chopped herbs and crushed garlic. Add the egg white and mix with a fork to a coherent mass. Season with salt and pepper and mash thoroughly to distribute evenly.

Pull off a small piece, make it into a patty and fry it quickly in a hot pan. Taste to see if more salt and pepper is needed as you cannot adjust the seasoning later. Roll into balls about the size of walnuts on a floured surface, put on a lightly floured tray or plate and reserve.

Finish the soup: remove the chillies, celery and lime leaves from the beans and discard. Put half the beans in a food processor and purée. Add the cooking liquid through the feeder tube until you have a soup consistency. Return to the pan, stir with the whole beans and keep hot over the lowest possible heat.

Heat a large frying pan over a medium heat. Add the sunflower oil and fry the albondigas for 6-8 minutes, turning frequently until golden brown and cooked all the way through.

Ladle the soup into large warmed bowls, arrange the albondigas on top and scatter over whole parsley leaves.

San Francisco Clam Chowder

Clam chowder is usually associated with Boston and its East Coast environs, but chowder just as good can be had in San Francisco's Fisherman's Wharf restaurants. We rarely see clam chowder on British menus, which is a shame because it is an easy dish to make and invariably delicious. Palourde (carpet shell) clams are ideal for the job, but if you can't get hold of any, substitute clovisse, Venus, or other clams, or, for a different effect, cockles. Usually the clams are boiled in water as a preliminary, but I think they are better cooked in a closed pan with olive oil, garlic and a splash of white wine. As they open they give out a lot of delicious salty juices which make the base of the soup and give you a much better control of the final flavour. Canned clams and clam juice are excellent.

FOR 6

1 kg / 2¼ lb palourde or other
   hardshell clams
2 garlic cloves
5 tbsp extra-virgin olive oil
300 ml / ½ pt [1¼ cups] dry white
   wine
225 g / 8 oz canned clams and juice
225 g / 8 oz shallots
2 celery stalks, plus handful of leaves
30 g / 1 oz [3 tbsp] flour
1 small fresh hot red chilli
1 bay leaf
350 g / 12 oz [2 heaped cups] peeled
   potatoes, cut into 2 cm / ¾ in dice
12 threads of saffron
575 ml / 1 pt single cream [2⅓ cups
   light cream]
2 tbsp chopped flat-leaf parsley
salt and pepper

Wash the fresh clams, discarding any that don't close when tapped firmly. Smash and chop the garlic and put with 2 tablespoons of olive oil in a saucepan which has a tight-fitting lid. Put over a high heat and, as the garlic starts to sizzle, pour in the wine. Bring to the boil, add the clams, put on the lid and shake. Cook for 1-2 minutes, when the clams will be done and will have opened. Drain in a fine sieve set in a bowl, to keep the liquid. Remove the clams from their shells and reserve, discarding the shells. Put the canned clams with the fresh, and add the clam juice to the liquid in the bowl.

Slice the shallots thinly, then dice. All but the most tender inner celery stalks have stringy fibres running down the centre. You get rid of these by cutting almost all the way through at the top of a stalk and pulling away and downwards. Then slice the stalks across thinly. Sweat both shallots and celery in a large saucepan with the remaining olive oil until soft.

Stir in the flour and cook for 2 minutes, stirring. Turn up the heat and whisk in the wine and clam juice mixture, then add 1.1 litres / 2 pt [5 cups] water. Split the chilli, add with the bay leaf and bring to the boil. Add the potatoes. Return to the boil and immediately lower the heat. Add the saffron and then simmer for 12-15 minutes, or until the potatoes are just cooked. Fish out the chilli and bay leaf and discard.

Chop half the clams finely and stir in. Shred the celery leaves and add. Stir in the cream and, as the chowder returns to a simmer, stir in the chopped parsley and the remaining whole clams. Season with plenty of black pepper and taste. It should not need any salt, but you can only judge whether it does after the addition of the cream. If you do add salt, allow it to cook in for 2 minutes, otherwise it will sit on top of the taste rather than become an integral part of it.

Remove from the heat, allow to stand for a minute and then serve in large warmed soup bowls.

Cream of Sweetcorn Bisque with Tiger Prawns and Coriander Butter

Jeremiah Tower makes a sweetcorn soup with crayfish cream at Stars, his San Francisco restaurant, which gave me the idea for this bisque. It is a fine combination, made more special by the reduced shellfish essence from the tiger prawn heads and shells. If you have kept reduced shellfish fumet in the freezer (page 25), you can add a few cubes to intensify the flavour still further. Since tiger prawns are sold with heads on or off, it is difficult to be absolute about the unpeeled weight. When young corn is available use it, otherwise frozen kernels are fine. Fresh corn should ideally be used on the day of purchase. The longer you keep it the starchier and less sweet it becomes.

Peel the prawns and put the shells (and heads, if supplied) in a pan with the white wine, bay leaf and about 300 ml/ ^{1}/2 pt [1 ^{1}/4 cups] water. Bring to the boil, skim, lower the heat and simmer to reduce by half. If you have cubes of frozen shellfish reduction in the freezer, then add them at this stage.

FOR 6

*450 g / 1 lb peeled raw tiger
    prawns [large shrimp],
    about 1 kg / 2 1/4 lb in their
    shells*
*150 ml / 1/4 pt [2/3 cup] dry
    white wine*
1 bay leaf
*850 ml / 1 1/2 pt [3 1/2 cups]
    Shellfish Stock (optional, see
    page 00)*
*8 young ears of corn or 450 g /
    1 lb [2 3/4 cups] frozen corn
    kernels*
115 g / 4 oz shallots
30 g / 1 oz [2 tbsp] butter
1 garlic clove
*575 ml / 1 pt [2 1/3 cups]
    Chicken Stock (page 24)*
*300 ml / 1/2 pt single cream
    [1 1/4 cups light cream]*
*1 tsp fresh oregano leaves
    (optional)*
2 tbsp olive oil
salt and pepper
*55 g / 2 oz [4 tbsp] Coriander
    and Green Chilli Butter
    (page 41)*
small bunch of chives

While the stock is reducing, cut through the backs of the prawns and remove the intestinal threads. Wipe clean with a damp cloth or paper towels. Sweeten the prawns by putting them in a bowl of heavily salted water and swirling, rubbing gently between your fingers. Throw away the water, put the prawns in a colander and rinse under the cold tap. Leave to drain.

Shuck the corn, removing all the silky threads under the husks, and cut down the length between the kernels and the cob, taking the kernels off in slices. Others may open the packet of frozen corn with a theatrical flourish.

Slice and then dice the shallots. Melt the butter in a pan and sweat the shallot dice until soft and translucent. Smash and chop the garlic, stir into the pan and cook for 1 minute. Stir in the corn and continue to cook over a low heat, stirring, for 2-3 minutes. Add the chicken stock and the shellfish reduction, strained through a fine sieve. Bring to the boil, lower the heat and simmer for 3 minutes.

Put into a blender or food processor and blitz for a minute. Pour back into the pan through a fine sieve, pressing with the back of a spoon to push as much of the purée through as possible. Stir in the cream and return to a low heat on the hob. Taste and season with salt and pepper. Stir in the fresh oregano if you have it.

Put the prawns in a bowl with the olive oil. Season with plenty of pepper. Heat a heavy frying pan until smoking hot and sauté the prawns, stirring and tossing, until just done (when the blue-tinged flesh will have firmed to an opaque white, ribbed with red). This should take no more than 2 minutes. Turn the prawns out on a warmed plate (if you leave them in the hot pan they will overcook).

Ladle the bisque into warmed soup bowls. Distribute the prawns among the bowls, mounding them in the centre of each. Cut 1 cm / 1/2 in thick slices from the Coriander Butter and sit these at an angle on top of the prawns. Snip 4 cm / 1 1/2 in pieces of chives and criss-cross them around the edge.

Poached White Fish in an Intense Broth

Making fish soups at home is one of those things that few people do and for no good reason. One frequently hears from even very keen cooks that they buy jars of fish soup stock imported from France, which is just plain silly. A good fish soup is, more than anything else, a good fish stock, and since this is something that could not be easier or cheaper to make yourself and only takes half an hour, there is really no reason not to follow the procedure detailed in the stock section on pages 22-5. When you do, a whole range of opportunities opens up, of which the following soup is only the most obvious. Once you have the broth, you can make it specific with one type of fish, or come closer to a bouillabaisse by using several.

The broth is enriched with tomato and saffron, but its purpose, no matter how delicious, is to play a discreet supporting role to the chunks of boneless and skinless white fish which have been poached only to the point of just being cooked.

This recipe specifies cod, but there are many other eminently appropriate firm white-fleshed fish, like hake, haddock, turbot and brill. All are expensive, but you can substitute fillets of skate, plaice or flounder, coley or pollock or conger eel. Oily fish like salmon, mackerel, tuna, sardine and herring are not suitable candidates. The inclusion of a few tiger prawns is always a good thing. You can also use as many different kinds of fish as are available or fancy dictates, allowing about 200 g / 7 oz of filleted fish per person.

A very different result can be achieved by leaving out the saffron and tomato sauce, straining the stock through a muslin-lined sieve and adding a packet of Japanese dashi, the dried bonito and konbu seaweed broth.

We are treating this dish as a first course, but it can easily become a main item on the lunch or dinner agenda. Make it more substantial with chunks of potato and add more fish. If adding potato, always cook this in the broth until done before adding the fish, or cook it separately, stirring in just before service.

FOR 6

900 g / 2 lb cod fillets
575 ml / 1 pt [2¹/₃ cups] Quick
    Tomato Sauce (page 34)
¹/₂tsp saffron
about 1.75 litres / 3 pt [7¹/₂cups]
    Fish Stock (page 25)
16 raw tiger prawns [large
    shrimp], peeled and
    deveined as described opposite
    (optional)
1 tbsp Pastis or Pernod
parsley leaves, to garnish

Add the tomato sauce and saffron to the broth and return to a simmer.

Check that all pin bones have been removed from the fish by running your finger along the bone line against the direction of the bones. Pull out any you find using a strong pair of tweezers or a small pair of pliers. Skin the fillet or fillets by holding at the tail and cutting down to the skin before running the knife along, lifting the flesh away and removing the skin in one piece. Cut the fish into portion-size chunks or the largest chunks you think appropriate.

Add the fish to the broth with the prawns, if using, and poach for 2-3 minutes, judging when the fish is done by lifting a piece with a slotted spoon. When it is opaque with no trace of pink then it is cooked. Remember that it will go on cooking in the hot broth, so lift out the fish at once and transfer to warmed bowls.

Stir the Pastis or Pernod into the broth and ladle over the fish. Scatter whole leaves of parsley over before serving.

First courses can almost always be main courses too...

Some, like the artichoke dishes below or Rabbit Rillettes (page 125), conform more closely to our accepted idea of a first course, as do *salades tièdes*, but any of the tarts will do nicely as the main item on the menu.

In the Middle East and North Africa, *mezze* is really many first courses served at the same time. The implication of first course is sequential, and in the context of this book, has been considered as an aid to planning smooth progressions throughout a meal.

As recently as 20 years ago every meal in the USA was automatically prefaced with a salad, usually a quarter of an iceberg lettuce smothered with a heavy blue-cheese dressing. This effectively killed the appetite. None of the salads included here will do that kind of damage.

Artichokes with Norma Jean's Three Mayonnaise Sauces

All the artichokes grown in the USA come from California. Drive down Route 156 towards the Monterey Peninsula in the months from March through May and you are surrounded by fields of artichokes, for all the world like giant flowering thistles which, of course, is precisely what they are. This is where Italian immigrants started commercial artichoke cultivation in the 1920s, with production focused around Castroville in Monterey County, about 100

miles south of San Francisco, where the climate is ideal. Monterey County remains the heartland of artichoke growing, producing most of the USA's crop from fewer than 9,000 acres, an annual output valued at $40 million.

Restaurants tend to use only the artichokes' fonds, or bases, discarding the leaves, but this does not mean we have slavishly to follow their lead at home. Jane Grigson summed it up when she wrote, 'The artichoke above all is the vegetable expression of civilized living, of the long view, of increasing delight by anticipation and crescendo.' There is something very appealing about picking off a leaf, dipping the fleshy base in an appropriate sauce and nibbling it, before tossing the remains aside. How far you toss depends on how Caligula-like you feel that day. And, as you work your way slowly through the leaves, you have the pleasurable anticipation of the succulent base, the climax of the experience indeed.

In Italy much is made of baby artichokes, quaintly called castrati, which can be eaten whole before the choke grows and the leaves harden. The trade is now able to buy these during their brief season and it is worth talking to your greengrocer about whether he or she can get hold of some for you when they are to be had. You can buy them bottled in jars of olive oil all year round, carciofi alla romana, which are actually very good, if expensive.

When preparing artichokes, you may like to cut off the top third and trim the tops of the leaves. This is only a presentational nicety to assuage any guilt you might feel about producing a zero-effort first course. If you are trimming the artichokes, then have handy a bowl of water acidulated with a few tablespoons of vinegar in which to immerse them, as cut surfaces rapidly blacken if you don't take this precaution.

Why Norma Jean's three mayonnaise sauces? To honour the memory of Marilyn Monroe, who in 1947 was crowned California Artichoke Queen.

FOR 4

4 large artichokes
3 tbsp malt or white vinegar
150 ml / ¼ pt [²/3 cup]
   Mayonnaise (page 46)
150 ml / ¼ pt [²/3 cup] Green
   Chilli Mayonnaise (page
   46)
150 ml / ¼ pt [²/3 cup] Red
   Pepper Mayonnaise (page
   46)
salt

Put a big pan of salted water to boil, adding the vinegar. Put in the artichokes, put on a lid and simmer for 30 minutes. Turn off the heat and leave to cool in the liquid. Then remove and put to drain in a colander with the bases upwards. Remove the stems.

Adjust the thickness of the three mayonnaises to the consistency of double [heavy] cream by adding a little water. Put 1 tablespoon of each on the plate about 3 cm / 1¼ in apart and 3 cm / 1¼ in from the centre. Tilt the plate in different directions so they run and touch one another. Put an artichoke in the middle of each plate.

Artichokes and wine do not generally make a happy partnership, but a Chenin or Sauvignon Blanc seems to tolerate the strong and pervasive flavour acceptably, the former being the drier alternative. So does something powerful like a Barolo, but this is a serious sort of wine to serve with a first course, begging the question of what could possibly follow it.

Warm Artichokes with Bagna Cauda

FOR 4

4 large artichokes

FOR THE BAGNA CAUDA SAUCE:

6 garlic cloves

5 tbsp olive oil

*115 g / 4 oz canned anchovy
   fillets, drained*

*125 ml / 4 fl oz [¹/₂ cup] crème
   fraîche*

pepper

*Warm artichokes can be eaten with hollandaise sauce and are particularly nice
with a warm anchovy and garlic sauce, as in the bagna cauda of Northern Italy.
Ideally the sauce should be presented in a bagna cauda at the table. This is a
small earthenware bowl glazed on the inside only, which sits over a candle or
night-light.*

Cook, drain and cool the artichokes as described in the previous recipe.

   Make the dipping sauce by smashing and chopping the garlic as finely as you
can. Put it into a saucepan over a low heat with the olive oil and anchovies. Stir
from time to time until the anchovies break down and you have a thick paste.

   Off the heat, whisk in the crème fraîche and pepper to taste. Then transfer
to a bagna cauda or spoon on to individual plates next to the artichokes.

Artichoke Heart and Tomato Salad with Basil Vinaigrette

*Beneath the leaves and hidden by a fuzz of silky hair lies the fond, heart or
base of the artichoke and for this recipe you will need to cut everything away
to get at it. Start by snapping off the stems, then pull away the larger outer
leaves. Cut off the top cone of softer leaves. Once the choke hairs are revealed,
you have gone far enough. You can use the leaves to make a soup or to impart
an artichoke accent to a vegetable stock. As soon as you have the first one
done, immerse it in cold water acidulated with malt or white vinegar or lemon
juice to prevent discoloration from exposure to the air.*

FOR 4

*4 artichoke bottoms, leaves,
   choke and stems removed*

3 tbsp malt or white vinegar

20 basil leaves

juice of ¹/₂ lemon

*125 ml / 4 fl oz [¹/₂ cup]
   extra-virgin olive oil*

12 ripe plum tomatoes

2 shallots

salt and pepper

handful of flat-leaf parsley

Cook the artichoke bottoms in the acidulated water, simmering for 20-25
minutes or until they are easily pierced with a fork. Leave to cool in the cooking
liquid. Remove and scrape off the choke hairs.

   Chop the basil leaves and put them in a food processor with the lemon
juice, olive oil and a pinch each of salt and pepper, and blitz the mixture until
you have a uniform texture.

   Blanch the tomatoes briefly in boiling water and refresh in cold water. Slice
them and arrange overlapping in the centre of 4 large plates. Dice the shallots
very small and sprinkle over the tomatoes. Put an artichoke bottom in the
middle of each and spoon over the basil and lemon oil. Pick off whole parsley
leaves and scatter over.

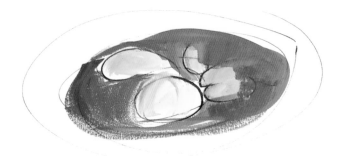

Chilli and Chive Gnocchi with Roasted Tomato Chilli Sauce

FOR 6

675 g / 1 1/2 lb potatoes
200 g / 7 oz self-raising flour
    [1 1/2 cups self-rising flour]
white of 1 egg
3 fresh hot green chillies
2 tbsp chopped chives
600 ml / 21 fl oz [2 1/2 cups]
    Roasted Tomato Chilli
    Sauce (page 33)
3 tbsp chopped flat-leaf
    parsley
salt and pepper
55 g / 2 oz [1/2 cup] Parmesan
    cheese, freshly grated, for
    sprinkling

Gnocchi are little dumplings made from flour and potatoes and also, less often, from semolina. They can be leaden, but here – spiked with hot chilli and chives – make a very Californian first course. Received wisdom decries the use of eggs in the mix, but the white of one egg offers the double benefit of lightening the dumplings while making them less likely to disintegrate in the cooking water.

The gnocchi can be prepared ahead of time, but they should be wrapped in plastic film and not held for more than two hours as they oxidize and blacken after extended exposure to the air.

This can also be served as a single supper dish, followed perhaps by a salad or some fruit.

Put a large pan of salted water on to boil.

Peel the potatoes, cut them into large chunks and boil in the salted water until just done. Drain, return to the pan and shake to dry excess moisture. Season with salt and pepper, then mash with a potato masher until lump-free. Add the self-raising flour and beat briefly to incorporate. Add the egg white and beat in.

Remove stem and seeds from the chillies; julienne the flesh, then cut across into tiny dice. Add to the potatoes with the chopped chives, mashing to distribute evenly throughout the dough. Turn out on a floured surface, knead briefly and divide into four. Roll each quarter into a tube about 2.5 cm / 1 in in diameter. Shake more flour over and cover with a cloth.

Preheat the oven to 180°C/350°F/gas4. Brush an ovenproof dish in which the gnocchi will fit in a single layer with olive oil. Put a large pan of salted water on to heat to a gentle bubble.

Cut the gnocchi cylinders into individual dumplings. You decide how big you want to make them, but on the small side is better because they puff up nicely. Poach in the simmering water. When you put them in they sink to the bottom; when they float to the surface they are done. Transfer to the ovenproof dish with a slotted spoon, taking care not to bring any water along with them.

Stir the chopped parsley into the sauce. Spoon the sauce over the gnocchi, bake for 10 minutes, when the sauce will be seething hot. Offer grated Parmesan at the table.

Dry-grilled Aubergine with Gremolata

Aubergines sop up oil like sponges. The more oil you put in the pan, the more they will happily absorb. So the best thing is to cook them dry, only dressing them with extra-virgin olive oil after they are cooked. This can be done on a non-stick pan or ridged grill pan. The alternative is to combine the two, as here, where the preliminary cooking is done dry in a non-stick pan. Then the cut surfaces are brushed with a little oil and the slices laid on the ridges of a very hot grill pan to finish. If they are cooked exclusively dry on a grill pan, the charring can be too pronounced and the slices may stick. This way, both the flavour and the presentation are improved. Small, plump aubergines are best for this treatment. Without the dressing, the cooked aubergines are ready for use in a moussaka or melanzane parmigiano.

Gremolata, a mixture of grated lemon zest, garlic and parsley, strikes just the right forceful note against the rather bland flavour of the aubergine. Because of the nasty chemicals and wax with which all but organic lemons are treated, scrub them in hot soapy water, rinse well and dry before grating.

Serve this dish as a first course with warm Wheat-flour Tortillas (page 57) or warm shop-bought pitta.

FOR 4

two 225 g / 8 oz purple
   aubergines [eggplants]
4 tbsp extra-virgin olive oil
salt and pepper

FOR THE GREMOLATA:
1 lemon
small handful of chopped
   parsley
1 garlic clove

First make the gremolata: grate the lemon zest into a bowl. Finely chop the parsley and add. Smash and chop the garlic finely. Add this, mix all together and reserve.

Preheat a non-stick frying pan over a low heat. Cut the aubergines lengthwise into 1 cm / ½ in slices and cook these for a few minutes on each side in the preheated dry pan over a medium heat. The slices will be browned on the surface and meltingly soft within.

While they are cooking, preheat a ridged grill pan over a medium heat until very hot. Brush both sides of the aubergine slices with olive oil and lay them on the ridges at an angle of 45 degrees. Turn after 15 seconds to stripe the other side at the same angle and then turn again in the opposite direction. This produces a neat cross hatch on one side and a slightly charred smoky flavour.

Transfer the cooked aubergine slices to a warmed serving dish, sprinkle over a little gremolata, season with salt and pepper and dress with extra-virgin olive oil. They make a lovely antipasto with no further embellishment.

Pommes à l'Huile

Reading Hemingway's A Moveable Feast *when I was 16 made me determined that one day I too would drink cold Alsace beer and eat* pommes à l'huile *in Paris's Brasserie Lipp. Hemingway obviously received a more friendly reception than I did. Unknowns — British and American — are usually banished to the dining room upstairs, but it is still a wonderful* fin de siècle *brasserie that was unchanged when Hemingway was there and remains unchanged to this day.*

This was the first piece of food writing that actually gave me a thrill of recognition that the simplest food could be exhilarating.

'I asked for a distingué, *the big glass mug that held a litre, and a potato salad… The beer was very cold and wonderful to drink. The pommes à l'huile were firm and, marinated with the olive oil, were delicious. When they were gone I ordered another serving and a cervelas. I mopped up all the oil and all the sauce with bread and drank the beer slowly until it began to lose its coldness and then I finished it and ordered a demi.'*

This entrancing salad is served warm and is a perfect treatment for the first Jersey Royals before they form a skin. If using potatoes with a fully formed skin, then peel them while still warm. They are great with any sausages or ham, hot or cold. For the bread, bake a ciabatta with a 25% rye content (page 54). Ask for a potato salad anywhere in the USA and you will be given diced potato in an oleaginous and tasteless mayonnaise. I often make the Lipp version in California and people are knocked out.

FOR 4

800 g / 1³/₄ lb new potatoes

4 shallots

125 ml / 4 fl oz [¹/₂ cup] extra-virgin olive oil

3¹/₂ tbsp sherry vinegar or balsamic vinegar

salt and pepper

2 tbsp chopped flat-leaf parsley

Chop the shallots finely and put them in a bowl with the oil to sit for 1 hour at room temperature.

Cook the potatoes in lots of boiling salted water until just tender, about 20 minutes. While they are cooking, mix the vinegar into the shallot oil and season with salt and pepper.

Drain the potatoes and, as soon as they are cool enough to handle, cut across into thin even slices. The hotter you can cut them, the better, so wear rubber gloves to avoid third-degree burns. Add the potato slices to the bowl of shallots as you cut them. Mix with the vinaigrette, dress with chopped parsley and serve at once.

Roasted Aubergine with Cipolline in Agrodolce

This is an interesting combination of textures and flavours, while the presentation is appealing – not always an easy thing to achieve with aubergines. They look so lovely raw, with their shiny purple-black skin, but are visually reduced by cooking, emerging dark, wrinkled and without lustre.

The sweet-and-sour (agrodolce) Italian onion relish, cipolline, is equally nice with cold meat or cheese, is very easy to prepare and can be served at room temperature or hot. Decide for yourself whether to make this a hot or cold first course, for the same is equally true of the aubergine.

When buying the aubergines, select four of equal size appropriate for serving one per person.

FOR 4

4 aubergines [eggplants]
2 red onions
4 tbsp olive oil
salt and pepper

FOR THE CIPOLLINE:

*450 g / 1 lb pickling onions
   [pearl onions]*
4 tbsp olive oil
2 tbsp red wine vinegar
*2 tbsp caster sugar [US
   granulated sugar]*
1 tsp salt
1/2 tsp black pepper

First prepare the cipolline: trim the onions and pour boiling water over them. Leave to stand for a minute, then refresh in cold water. This makes the tedious chore of peeling them a lot easier, but will never stop the tedium altogether, so try and get somebody else to do the job.

Fry the whole peeled onions gently in the olive oil, shaking from time to time, for 15-20 minutes, until you achieve an even golden colour. Add the vinegar, sugar and salt. Turn up the heat and caramelize, tossing and turning to coat the onions evenly. Transfer to a bowl, season with pepper and leave to cool. If keeping, pack into a sterilized jar and film the surface with olive oil before refrigerating.

Preheat the oven to 200°C/400°F/gas6. Working from just inside the stem so they remain attached, cut the aubergines lengthwise into 5 mm / ¼ in slices and fan them out. Cut the red onions across into 5 mm / ¼ in thick slices. Brush the cut surfaces of the aubergines and the onions with olive oil and season with salt and pepper. Slide an onion slice between every 2 slices of the aubergines and place on a baking sheet. Bake for about 30 minutes, when the aubergines will have crumpled.

Serve at once, with some cipolline on each plate, or leave to cool and eat at room temperature. This distinction is important. Never eat dishes like this straight from the fridge, but always allow them time to come back to room temperature first.

Roasted Pepper and Feta Soufflé Tart

Sweet and smoky roasted peppers are peeled and then baked in a crisp tart shell with cubes of feta in a souffléd savoury custard. This is fusion food as much as any exotic salad. It is great straight from the oven while still raised, but equally nice at room temperature. It is not as good after refrigeration, but the chances of there being any left to chill are pretty remote.

FOR 6

4 roasted red sweet peppers, peeled (see page 26)

12 saffron threads

1 pre-baked 23 cm / 9 in savoury tart pastry shell (page 59)

45 g / 1 ½ oz [3 tbsp] butter

45 g / 1 ½ oz [⅓ cup] flour

350 ml / 12 fl oz [1 ½ cups] full-fat milk

55 g / 2 oz [½ cup] Parmesan cheese, freshly grated

6 eggs

225 g / 8 oz feta cheese

salt and pepper

Preheat the oven to 180°C/350°F/gas4.

Put the peppers to drain on a rack for at least 1 hour to rid them of residual oil. Put the saffron in a small bowl with 1 tablespoon of boiling water to infuse. Place the pastry shell on a baking sheet. Cut the peppers into strips and arrange to cover the bottom of the shell.

Melt the butter in a saucepan, stir in the flour and cook this roux briefly until lightly coloured. Whisk in the milk. Add the saffron and soaking liquid. Cook over a low heat for 15 minutes, whisking frequently until you have a thick béchamel. Stir in the Parmesan and season with salt and pepper.

Separate the eggs and whisk the whites to soft peaks. Remove the béchamel from the heat and whisk in the egg yolks, one at a time. Transfer to a bowl and stir in a big spoonful of the whites, then fold in the rest, turning the bowl and folding with a big scooping action. Fold in the feta dice and pour and scrape into the tart shell.

Bake for 25 minutes, when the tart will be well risen and golden brown. Serve at once or leave to cool and serve at room temperature.

Bitter Greens with Sautéed Mushrooms and Crisp Shallots

The dark and slightly bitter greens that we associate in Britain with spring are, in reality, available all year round, many of them the leaf by-product of the primary vegetables – for example, turnips and sprouts. While they need no more than blanching before being served with a nut of butter (or a flavoured butter, see pages 41-4), this treatment turns them into a first course. You can add a poached egg and some garlic croutons, but they are not obligatory.

Use the large, flat-cap cultivated mushrooms or shiitake, both of which have a pronounced flavour, unless you are lucky enough to lay your hands on some true field mushrooms or Portobello mushrooms in the US, in which case lucky you. Button mushrooms taste of almost nothing at all and are best composted. If you are feeling lazy, crisp shallots can be bought ready-cooked from South-east Asian grocers.

FOR 6

675 g / 1 1/2 lb bitter greens
225 g / 8 oz mushrooms
350 g / 12 oz shallots
5 tbsp olive oil
2 garlic cloves
45 g / 1 1/2 oz [3 tbsp] Parsley, Garlic and Red Chilli Butter (page 42)
salt and pepper

Slice the shallots thinly. Put 2 tablespoons of the oil in a non-stick pan, add the shallots and fry over a medium heat, stirring, until crisp and golden brown. Transfer to paper towels to drain.

Discard the outer leaves of the greens, cutting out the thick end of the ribs running up into the leaves you will use. Wash and reserve. Put a large pan of lightly salted water on to boil.

Wipe the mushrooms, trim the bases of the stems and cut the heads into 1 cm / 1/2 in thick slices, cutting through the cap downwards so the central slices include the stem. Slice the garlic wafer-thin.

In a large dry frying pan, toss the mushrooms over a medium heat. Only when they start to soften and exude moisture, add the remaining olive oil and the sliced garlic. Sauté vigorously for 2 minutes. Remove from the heat but leave in the pan to keep warm. Season.

Plunge the greens into the rapidly boiling water and cook for 2-3 minutes. Drain in a colander, return to the pan and add the Parsley, Garlic and Red Chilli Butter. Toss to coat the leaves.

Distribute the leaves among 4 large bowls, mounding in the centre. Spoon the mushrooms around the sides. Sprinkle the crisp shallots on top of the leaves and serve at once.

Chilli Carrozza with Mozzarella and Feta

Mozzarella en carrozza (in carriages), or Italian fried cheese sandwiches, are usually shallow-fried in a lot of olive oil. The bread soaks this up like a sponge and they are seriously fattening and rich. Mozzarella on its own has a very subtle flavour, some might say bland. These sandwiches are cooked with very little oil in a non-stick frying pan and the mozzarella is mixed with feta, which lightens them while giving a better defined flavour. A little chilli and some spring onions complete the package.

Of course, you can use home-made bread here or baguette, but this is one of the few dishes where you can use sliced bread and nobody will complain or even notice. Maybe it's what it was invented for. This sweeping statement does not include American sliced bread which contains sugar or worse, and has the texture of rubber. Use a suitably sized pastry cutter to cut rounds out of the bread slices.

FOR 4

1 buffalo mozzarella cheese
8 slices of white sliced bread
85 g / 3 oz feta cheese
4 spring onions [scallions]
1 fresh hot green chilli
4 tbsp olive oil
salt and pepper

Cut the biggest rounds you can from the each of the bread slices.

Drain the mozzarella and cut into 1 cm / 1/2 in dice. Dice the feta in the same way. Trim the spring onions, then cut them into julienne strips. Cut the chilli in half, remove seeds, and shred. Mash all the cheese and flavourings together in a bowl with a fork and season with pepper.

Divide into four equal portions and press on to 4 of the bread rounds. Press another round on top of each and flatten with the heel of your hand so they hold together.

Put a non-stick pan over a low heat. Brush one side of each sandwich with olive oil and sprinkle on a little salt. Lay them in the pan, oiled side down, and fry for 4-5 minutes, or until the bottom piece of bread is crisp and golden brown and the cheese is beginning to melt. Brush the tops with oil and turn. Increase the heat slightly. As the cheese melts and starts to ooze from around the sides, they are ready.

Eat at once. Mozzarella is never nice after it has cooked and melted, then cooled and congealed. A tomato and basil salad sets the carriages off well.

Wild Mushroom Risotto Cakes with Chive Crème Fraîche

Ten years ago you had more chance of being mounted by a horse than finding a good risotto in an Italian restaurant outside Italy, never mind at a dinner party. These days there is a wider understanding of what a risotto should be in terms of the right rice and a seamless cooking process using boiling stock, but people still tend to follow the wrong restaurant lead and fall over with too much butter and, often, finish unnecessarily with double [heavy] cream. This delivers an overly rich dish to the table and one which is wholly inappropriate for a first course.

Here the risotto is made using a mixture of olive oil and butter, the rice being plumped with a wine-flavoured chicken-and-mushroom stock. The wild mushrooms are dried pleurottes, ceps or porcini and trompettes-de-la-mort – a standard mixture called forestière. If you just happened to have a pound of fresh ceps to hand, feel free to substitute. The finished risotto is left to cool, shaped into small cakes and given a double coating of egg and crumb before being shallow-fried until crisp. The resulting cakes are served with a dollop of crème fraîche spiked with chopped chives.

The portion size is deliberately small as it is really an appetizer to get the meal rolling on a high note. It can also be served in larger amounts as a main course or indeed as a supper dish on its own, to be followed by nothing more than a salad and perhaps a piece of cheese.

Pour hot water over the mushrooms to cover and leave them to rehydrate for 30 minutes. Drain in a sieve set in a jug, to keep the liquid. Rinse the mushrooms thoroughly under running water, chop to a uniform size and reserve. Pour the mushroom soaking liquid through a fine sieve again into the stock, add the wine and bring to the boil. Lower to a bare simmer.

Dice the onion. Smash and chop the garlic. In a heavy saucepan (ideally with rounded internal edges where the sides meet the base), melt the butter with the oil over a medium heat and fry the onion until translucent, stirring at regular intervals. Add the rice and garlic, then stir for 2 minutes to coat the rice before starting to add the stock a ladleful at a time, stirring until the liquid is absorbed before adding the next ladleful. Repeat this process until the rice is cooked and creamy, which will take about 20 minutes. If you use up all the stock before the rice is done, finish with ladlefuls of boiling water.

About 5 minutes before it due to be finished, add the mushrooms and continue stirring until you judge the rice to be done. The only way to do so is

55 g / 2 oz dried mushrooms
1.75 litres / 3 pt [7 1/2 cups]
    Vegetable Stock (page 24)
1 glass of dry white wine
1 onion
1 garlic clove
55 g / 2 oz [4 tbsp] butter
3 tbsp olive oil
350 g / 12 oz [1 1/2 cups]
    risotto rice, preferably
    Arborio
55 g / 2 oz [1/2 cup] Reggiano
    Parmesan cheese, freshly
    grated
2 eggs
about 85 g / 3 oz [2 cups] fine
    fresh white breadcrumbs
sunflower oil, for frying
salt and pepper
handful of flat-leaf parsley, to
    garnish

FOR THE CHIVE CREME FRAICHE:
300 ml / 1/2 pt [1 1/4 cups]
    crème fraîche
bunch of chives

by tasting. Stir in the Parmesan, taste and add salt and pepper as needed. Take off the heat and spoon into a tray to cool, then refrigerate for at least 2 hours or do this the day before and refrigerate overnight.

Whisk the eggs in one bowl and put the crumbs in another. Use a spoon to scoop out golf-ball-sized amounts of risotto, rolling them between your hands to give a uniform surface, and put them on a clean tray until all the mixture is used up. Wash and dry your hands before rolling one ball at a time in the egg, then transfer to the crumbs, shaking the bowl to coat evenly. Dip a second time in the egg and crumbs before flattening them into neat cakes. Refrigerate again for an hour or two before frying.

Make the Chive Crème Fraîche: finely chop the chives and add to the crème fraîche, seasoning lightly with salt and pepper.

Pour enough sunflower oil into a large frying pan to cover the bottom by 5 mm / $\frac{1}{4}$ in and place over a low heat. When hot, fry the cakes in it gently, turning once. They will take about 3 minutes a side.

Serve 2 or 3 cakes on individual warmed plates, with a heaped tablespoon of the crème fraîche. Scatter with some whole leaves of flat-leaf parsley.

Goats' Cheese Won-tons with Green Ratatouille

The idea of putting goats' cheese in won-ton comes from Brian Whitmer of Carmel's Pacific Edge Highland Inn.

The deliberate selection of green and white vegetables to make a ratatouille seems very calculated and Californian but is, in reality, more South London and came about because they were the only things I had to hand. The most frequent mistake made when cooking ratatouille is to fry everything together and to do so too aggressively. It takes time, but you should fry each vegetable separately and gently, transferring them when just done to a large pan and only stewing them together briefly at the end.

The quality of the olive oil really matters. The ratatouille benefits from being made the day before and refrigerated overnight. Always serve ratatouille at room temperature. If you should have some left over, try it in a frittata (page 132).

48 won-ton wrappers
handful of flat-leaf parsley
handful of coriander [cilantro]

FOR THE FILLING:
55 g / 2 oz shallots
1 garlic clove
1 red sweet pepper
1 yellow sweet pepper
115 g / 4 oz courgettes [zucchini]
2 tbsp olive oil
115 g / 4 oz soft young goats'
   cheese
12 black olives, pitted and
   chopped
2 tbsp chopped flat-leaf parsley
3 egg yolks
salt and pepper

FOR THE GREEN RATATOUILLE:
450 g / 1 lb green asparagus
225 g / 8 oz green beans
2 fennel bulbs
8 spring onions [scallions]
450 g / 1 lb courgettes
   [zucchini]
225 g / 8 oz onion
3 green sweet peppers
150-300 ml / 1/4 – 1/2 pt
   [2/3 – 1 1/4 cups] extra-virgin
   olive oil
2 celery stalks
2 garlic cloves
small bunch of chives

Make the won-ton filling. (This can be made the day before and refrigerated until needed, but must be wrapped in won-ton only just before poaching because the moisture will dissolve the dough.) Dice the shallots and garlic. Reserve. Remove seeds from the peppers, and trim the courgettes. Chop the peppers and courgettes in 5 mm / 1/4 in dice and sauté in the olive oil for 3 minutes. Add the shallots and garlic and cook for a further 1 minute, tossing and stirring. Transfer to a colander and leave to drain.

Put into a bowl with the cheese, crumbled, the chopped olives and the parsley. Mix all together with a fork. Season.

Make the ratatouille: blanch the asparagus in rapidly boiling salted water for 3 minutes and reserve. Blanch the green beans for 3 minutes and reserve. Cut the fennel into 2 cm / 3/4 in dice. Trim the courgettes and cut into 2 cm / 3/4 in dice. Cut the onion in half and then into 2 cm / 3/4 in dice. Cut the green peppers in half, remove stem and seeds, and cut into similarly sized dice. Cook the spring onions whole.

The order in which you fry the unblanched vegetables does not matter, but do each separately over a low heat, stirring frequently until wilted, taking care not to brown. Put a couple of tablespoons of oil in with each batch. Transfer each to a large pan when they are done. These should all still retain some bite. Finish by frying the celery and garlic, sliced into wafer-thin shavings.

When all are done, chop the chives in 5 mm / 1/4 in lengths and stir in. Add the blanched beans and asparagus, season with salt and pepper and cook all together gently, stirring for 4-5 minutes. Transfer to a bowl, cover with plastic film and refrigerate overnight. Remove an hour before you want to serve.

Make the won-ton: lay 24 of the wrappers on a table. Whisk the egg yolks and brush the edges. Put a heaped teaspoon of the filling on each. Lay the remaining wrappers on top of them and press the edges to seal. Trim the edges with a sharp knife, since the bulge of the filling will mean the top wrapper will not go all the way to the edge of the bottom wrapper.

Poach in simmering salted water for 1 minute. Remove the won-ton with a slotted spoon, putting four on each plate. Just before serving, pick off the parsley and coriander leaves. Stir half of them into the ratatouille. Spoon ratatouille on each plate and sprinkle the rest of the leaves over each portion.

Goats' Cheese and Potato Tart with Flaky Pastry Crust

In the Loire valley they serve tourte de Châteaumaillant, a tart of goats' cheese and potato which is cooked in a shell made from puff pastry. This puffs up around the edges but, of course, the base comes out just like any other pastry.

Making the base of spinach solves this defect and the crisp pastry top contrasts nicely with the creamy filling. Those who can't be bothered to make the pastry may use shop-bought frozen puff without disgrace. The lightness which the spinach crust imparts is the sort of thing which makes this dish fit for an evening meal in Sonoma County – or any other Californian county come to that.

I first cooked it for a dinner party at a friend's house high in the Hollywood Hills. We ate outside as night fell, the shapes of cyprus and palm trees outlined against the lights of the city below. Max and Prima – golden retrievers with spotted bandannas around their necks – waited hopefully, but there was none left.

FOR 6

285 g / 10 oz mild goats' cheese
550 g / 1 1/4 lb potatoes
225 g / 8 oz spinach
6 spring onions [scallions]
85 g / 3 oz [6 tbsp] butter
4 eggs
150 ml / 1/4 pt [2/3 cup] crème fraîche
1/4 nutmeg
1 tbsp olive oil
450 g / 1 lb Flaky Pastry (page 60)
salt and pepper

Remove stems from the spinach and blanch in fast boiling salted water for 30 seconds. Refresh in cold water and put to drain in a colander.

Peel and thinly slice the potatoes and plunge into the same boiling salted water for 4 minutes. Refresh in cold water, drain, pat dry and reserve.

Trim the spring onions and cut across into thin rings. Sauté briefly in 15 g / 1/2 oz [1 tbsp] of the butter to wilt and extract moisture. Reserve.

Butter a 23 cm / 9 in tart pan, then lay the spinach leaves in it, overlapping to form a base. Preheat the oven to 190°C/375°F/gas 5.

Put the goats' cheese in a food processor with 3 of the eggs, the crème fraîche, grated nutmeg, salt and pepper. Blitz to a paste.

Put half the potatoes on the bottom of the tart and scatter on the remaining butter, cut into small dice. Put the spring onions on top of that, then spoon the cheese custard on top and spread to cover the potatoes evenly. Lay the remaining potatoes on top, brush them with the olive oil and season with plenty of pepper.

Roll out the pastry and cut to make a round to fit on top of the potatoes. Brush the pastry with the remaining egg, lightly beaten.

Bake for 30 minutes, when the pastry will be risen and golden brown. Serve as soon as it comes from the oven.

Lobster Salad with Yogurt and Lime Dressing

Lobsters are not as expensive as they used to be, but they will never be cheap. A lobster salad is a good way of making the most of not very much. You will need two 550g/1¼lb lobsters to serve 4 people. Mayonnaise is usually served with cold lobster, but this is a much lighter dressing.

When boiling shellfish – which really means to simmer with an occasional bubble bursting to the surface, and not at a rolling boil – the cooking water should be as salty as the sea, a salinity equivalent achieved by adding about 140g/5oz [1 cup] coarse sea salt to every 5 litres/8pt [5 qt] of water. The size of the lobster will determine the size of the pot and the amount of water you need. Give the lobster a short swim to check this out.

There is a theory that if you bring the water to the boil from cold with the lobster in it that it won't suffer. This is probably just wishful thinking. Ask a lobster its preference and it will always plead the Fifth.

Bring the salted water to the boil and drop the lobster in. A 550g/1¼lb specimen will take 13 minutes, a 675g/1½lb one 15 minutes, and one up to 1.125kg/2½lb 20 minutes. Over that weight, allow an extra 5 minutes per 450g/1lb. If it is that big it is quite a venerable character and you will be terminating the crustacean equivalent of a senior citizen.

Cutting a lobster in half is easiest with a heavy, pointed and sharp-bladed knife. If you are right-handed, position the lobster on its belly and with the head pointing to the right. Insert the point where the carapace joins the tail section then drive down and cut towards the head, slamming down with the flat of your hand on the knife to cut cleanly through the shell. Turn the lobster, reinsert the knife in the same line and cut through to the tail. Only the gravel sac and intestinal track towards the mouth are inedible. The green tomalley in the carapace is delicious and the tail meat lifts out in one piece. Use the shell to make stock, which can be reduced and frozen.

FOR 4

two 550g/1¼lb lobsters
1 garlic clove
1 tsp Dijon mustard
juice of 1 lime
300ml/½pt [1¼ cups] Greek-
    style or other thick plain
    yogurt
small bunch of chives
1 tbsp extra-virgin olive oil
4 Little Gem lettuces [Romaine
    hearts]
2 bunches of watercress
salt and pepper

Prepare and cook the lobsters as described. Leave to cool completely before cutting in half. Extract the meat, and crack the claws open to remove that meat too. Cut the meat into fine strips.

Smash and chop the garlic finely and put into a bowl with the mustard, lime juice, yogurt, half the chives cut into 5mm/¼in lengths, the oil and salt and pepper. Stir to mix.

Cut the lettuces in quarters lengthwise; add them to the bowl with the watercress and toss to coat. Put 4 pieces of lettuce on each plate and mound the watercress in the middle. Arrange the lobster on top and snip over the remaining chives.

Too-good-for-the-band Crab Cakes

In 1982 I had my one experience of being a chef when I cooked for six months at The Studio in Swallow Street off Piccadilly, a one-time jazz club under Bentley's Oyster Bar and an ill-starred venture. The food was well received, but a financial success we were not. Music was reintroduced to boost trade and feeding the band became an irksome daily chore.

I made an effort to cook them decent food, but it was always received and consumed in sullen silence. I asked Charles Campbell, the manager, what he thought the problem was. 'Don't give the buggers anything edible,' he advised. 'Just trick the dish up so it looks complicated.' He demonstrated what he meant, arranging various bits and pieces and leftovers on a large metal flat, flashing it briefly under the grill and garnishing it with every conceivable tomato slice and vegetable vulgarity, the whole ghastly arrangement much bedecked with chopped curly parsley. I sent the plate out shaking my head. Half an hour later the usually taciturn drummer shoved his head around the kitchen door, grinning and giving me the thumbs up. 'Bloody brilliant, chef. That's more like it.'

These crab-and-monkfish cakes would have been too good for the band, but received a standing ovation in California, whose influence can be felt in the revised spicing and the inclusion of coriander. You can use canned or frozen crab-meat, but for true sensation boil one specially for this dish. The inclusion of monkfish means you won't have to spend all day picking crab-meat to make the required weight. It also combines in a particularly delicious way with the crab. The bigger the crab, the easier to pick.

These crab cakes are based on a very thick béchamel and when you make the mixture you will think it too runny to work, but after a couple of hours in the fridge it becomes manageable.

MAKES 16

225 g / 8 oz white crab-meat

225 g / 8 oz monkfish fillet

4 spring onions [scallions]

1 celery stalk

1 garlic clove

1 fresh hot green chilli

1 roasted red sweet pepper, peeled (see page 26)

55 g / 2 oz [4 tbsp] butter

55 g / 2 oz [1/3 cup] flour

200 ml / 7 fl oz [7/8 cup] full-fat milk

2 tbsp chopped coriander [cilantro]

225 g / 8 oz [1 cup] dry freshly mashed potato

2 tbsp Worcestershire sauce

1 tsp Salsa Picante (page 39) or Tabasco sauce

2 eggs

115 g / 4 oz [about 2 cups] olive-oil-toasted bread-crumbs (sliced white bread brushed with oil, toasted and pulverized)

salt and pepper

sunflower oil for deep-frying

575 ml / 1 pt [2 1/3 cups] Green Chilli Mayonnaise (page 46), to serve

Trim the spring onions, trim the celery, peel the garlic, and remove seeds from the chilli. Cut all of these and the red sweet pepper to a uniform brunoise dice (5 mm / 1/4 in) and sweat in the butter until limp but not brown.

Add the flour and cook, stirring, for 2 minutes, then add the milk and chopped coriander, beating and cooking until you have a thick shiny paste.

Off the heat, add the mashed potato, Worcestershire sauce and 6 drops of salsa or Tabasco and season with a little salt and pepper.

Cut the monkfish fillet across into 5 mm / 1/4 in slices, then cut these across into dice. Stir in with the crab-meat and spread the mixture on a Swiss-roll [shallow baking] pan or tray and allow to cool. Then refrigerate until very cold. (This could be overnight.)

Heat the sunflower oil for deep-frying to 190°C/375°F. Beat the eggs in a bowl and put the breadcrumbs in another. Using a heaped dessertspoonful at a time, roll the crab mix into small balls, coat in egg and then roll in the crumbs. Deep-fry for 3-4 minutes. You can also flatten them and shallow-fry on either side until brown and crisp.

Serve with the mayonnaise.

Scallop Couscous with Squid Ink Sauce

Scallops are best when heavily seared outside but only barely cooked within. Couscous is now available in an easily reconstituted, pre-cooked form, and squid ink comes from Spain in neat sachets or you can use the ink sacs from squid cleaned for another dish (see page 106). Put them together and you have pretty near instant delight. Fast food can be great food, and this particular combination of seared scallops on a bed of yellow couscous flecked with gremolata and chilli has it all – freshness, vitality, contrasting textures and vivid visual impact. The recipe was given to me by London chef Redmond Hayward.

FOR 4

8 large scallops [sea scallops]
about 2 tbsp olive oil

FOR THE COUSCOUS:
225 g/8 oz [1 1/3 cups] instant couscous
2 shallots
2 tbsp olive oil
1 fresh hot red chilli
30 g/1 oz [2 tbsp] unsalted butter

FOR THE SQUID INK SAUCE:
300 ml/1/2 pt [1 1/4 cups] Fish Stock or Shellfish Fumet (page 25)
4 sachets (about 1 tsp each) squid ink
150 ml/1/4 pt [2/3 cup] crème fraîche
salt and pepper

FOR THE GREMOLATA:
2 garlic cloves
1 lemon
large handful flat-leaf parsley

Ask the fishmonger to open and clean the scallops for you.

Make the gremolata: smash and finely chop the garlic. Wash the lemon, dry and then grate the zest and add to the garlic. Chop 3 tablespoons of parsley leaves, and mix with the lemon and garlic. Reserve.

Start the sauce: put the stock or fumet to heat in a pan with the squid ink.

Prepare the couscous: dice the shallots and fry them gently in the olive oil. Remove stem and seeds from the chilli, chop it and add to the shallots. Stir together for a minute, then remove from the heat and reserve.

Reconstitute the couscous in a saucepan with boiling water in the ratio recommended on the packet. Season with salt and pepper, and add the shallots and chilli. Add the butter and stir in. Cover with a lid and put in a warm place.

Finish the sauce: add the crème fraîche to the inky fumet, taste and season as needed. Keep hot.

Detach the corals and slice each scallop across into 2 discs. Brush corals and white flesh with olive oil, season with salt and pepper and lay carefully in a very hot dry frying pan. Cook for 1 minute each side and transfer immediately to a warm plate. Overcook and you will end up with expensive erasers.

Stir the gremolata into the couscous. Mound some couscous in the middle of each warmed plate, arrange 4 scallop slices on top and carefully spoon the black sauce around the outside. Put 2 corals on opposite sides of the plate on the sauce. Scatter with a few whole leaves of parsley.

Seared Squid with Thai Shallots and Deep-fried Tentacles

Cleaning squid is not a thrilling job but at least it is easy. Pull firmly but gently by the head and the insides will slither out. Cut through just behind the eyes. Discard the guts, remove the hard knob from behind the tentacles and remove the quill from within the body sac. Try to leave the ink sacs intact and freeze them for use in Scallop Couscous with Squid Ink Sauce (page 105). Slit the body open down one side along the seam and trim to a rough rectangle. Incise a shallow 1 cm / ½ in diamond pattern on both sides, taking care not to cut all the way through. Rinse and refrigerate until needed.

One of the nice things about this dish is the contrast in texture between the meaty bodies and the crisp fried tentacles.

FOR 4

1 kg / 2¼ lb small squid
450 g / 1 lb shallots
3 tbsp sunflower oil, plus more oil for deep-frying
1 garlic clove, smashed and chopped
3 fresh hot red chillies
flour for dusting
salt and pepper
bunch of chives, to garnish

Heat the oil in a deep-fryer to 190°C/375°F.

Slice the shallots thinly, then sweat them in a frying pan in the 3 tablespoons of oil. When soft, turn up the heat and fry, stirring, until browned and starting to crisp. Stir in the garlic and one of the chillies, seeded and cut into julienne strips. Cook for 30 seconds. Stir and leave in the pan off the heat.

Heat a heavy frying pan until smoking hot. Season the squid with salt and pepper and lay the squid in a single layer in the pan. They will bubble and tremble within seconds. Turn after 30 seconds. The squid will almost immediately roll up. As soon as this happens, remove and transfer to a warmed plate. Cook any longer and the flesh will toughen. Repeat with the remaining rectangles.

Fill the squid tubes with the shallot mixture. Cut the tentacles into four and toss in seasoned flour. Deep-fry in the hot oil for 60 seconds.

Distribute among the plates (depending on their size, put 1 or 2 squid on each plate) and finish with some shredded chilli and chives snipped into 3 cm / 1¼ in lengths.

Seared Sesame Scallops with Angel-hair Bean Salad

Follow Sunset Boulevard west and you move from Hollywood through Beverly Hills, with its bizarre jumbo houses with their Doric columns, turrets and manicured lawns, WesTech Armed Response signs on every electric gate. You don't see people on foot, except joggers. Walkers without sportswear are promptly arrested.

The roads off to left and right are lined with palm trees, the traffic pretty much non-existent by European city standards, so it is an easy 30-minute ride out to the ocean. You hang a right and strike north on Pacific Coast Highway, leaving Santa Monica behind, and pretty soon you are in Malibu.

If your initial reaction is 'so what?', then it is the same as everybody else's. Houses all squidged up together present their prosaic backs to the traffic streaming by. They have nothing in common architecturally, their only shared attribute being giant satellite dishes. Many of them look like garages. Even the meanest runs around $2 million and upwards.

As you continue north, things get smarter and you no longer have properties immediately on the highway. Now more exclusive houses hide down the hillside. And then you reach The Colony, where the real heavy-hitters have their private beach and partial seclusion from the Star Map seekers who, with the dangerously obsessed and crazy people, make celebrity in America a questionable benefit.

In a shopping mall beside a car park and close by The Colony is Granita, one of Wolfgang Puck's restaurants. It is big and light, its walls studded with seashells and ocean bric-à-brac in a style reminiscent of a Miro fantasy.

This dish is close in spirit to much of Puck's food, which frequently combines hot and cool elements. The finest French beans are called angel-hair. Here we toss them in a soy-based dressing and serve them still crunchy but piping hot, with the scallops on top. The sesame and pepper form a gently tongue-tingling crust. This is not too spicy and therefore does not mask the delicate flavour of the scallops' sweet flesh.

Have the fishmonger open the scallops and clean them for you. Keep them refrigerated and cook as soon as possible.

8 large king scallops [sea
    scallops]

450 g / 1 lb fine French beans
    [green beans]

1 tbsp sesame seeds

1 tsp black peppercorns

2 tsp flour

1 tsp salt

2 tbsp extra-virgin olive oil,
    plus more for serving

small handful of flat-leaf
    parsley

FOR THE SOY DRESSING:

2 tbsp Kikkoman soy sauce

2 tbsp olive oil

1/2 garlic clove, chopped finely

2 tsp lime juice

2 tsp Dijon mustard

Bring a pan of lightly salted water to the boil. Trim the stems from the beans, but don't cut off the hair-tip ends. Reserve.

Toast the sesame seeds and peppercorns in a small dry non-stick frying pan over the lowest heat for 2-3 minutes, stirring. Grind briefly in a coffee grinder (you don't want a powder) and mix with the flour and salt in a bowl; reserve.

Mix the dressing ingredients in a large bowl.

Cut each scallop laterally through the middle and detach the corals. Brush the scallops and corals with olive oil and press the flat surfaces into the bowl of spice mix.

Preheat a dry heavy frying pan until smoking hot.

Blanch the beans in the boiling water for 4 minutes. Remove and drain. Put in the bowl with the dressing and toss to coat.

While the beans are cooking, lay the scallops and corals in the hot frying pan. Sear one side for 60 seconds. Turn and sear the others for 30 seconds. Immediately transfer to a warm plate. Don't leave them in the pan or they will overcook even off the heat.

Mound the dressed beans on large warmed plates. Lay the scallops and corals on top. Spoon a tiny bit of extra-virgin olive oil over the scallops. Scatter with whole flat-leaf parsley and serve at once.

Tiger Prawn Risotto

You can buy tiger prawns fresh or frozen. The price should take account of this and also whether or not they have their heads on. If you do get them with their heads on then these, with the shells, will make a very good stock. Avoid buying prawns which have been defrosted in the shop. Ask the fishmonger to get you some from his freezer and defrost them gently yourself. If you buy them defrosted you don't know whether that was done the day before or worse. If you cannot get any celeriac, the knobbly root vegetable, then substitute celery. While the inclusion of crème fraîche is definitely not something they would do in southern Italy it is entirely acceptable in San Bernardino or even Berwick-upon-Tweed. It gives a finish to the dish which is sumptuous without being overly rich.

900 g / 2 lb raw tiger prawns
   [large shrimp]

1 litre / 1 $^3/_4$ pt [1 qt] Shellfish
   Stock (page 25)

16 threads of saffron

1 fennel bulb

1 large leek

8 shallots

2 garlic cloves

170 g / 6 oz celeriac [celery root],
   peeled weight

5 tbsp extra-virgin olive oil

300 g / 10 $^1/_2$ oz [1 $^1/_4$ cups] risotto
   rice, preferably arborio or
   vialone

3 tbsp crème fraîche

2 tbsp chopped flat-leaf parsley

salt and pepper

If frozen, defrost the prawns at room temperature. Never speed the process with hot water as this will toughen the flesh. Peel and remove the intestinal thread. Reserve the shells and augment the shellfish stock with them as described in the stock section on page 25. Pour a few tablespoons of the simmering stock over the saffron threads and leave to infuse.

Chop all the vegetables into 5 mm / ¼ in dice, then sweat in olive oil in a large heavy-based pan until soft. Add the rice and stir, turning to coat each grain with oil.

Start adding the simmering stock, a ladleful at a time, stirring between additions until all the liquid has been absorbed by the rice, which will take 16-20 minutes depending on the rice. Towards the end of cooking, add the saffron and its soaking liquid. Always add saffron towards the end of cooking and never at the beginning. If cooked for too long the flavour reduces. Less saffron added towards the end of the cooking delivers more thumps a thread (cf. bangs per buck). You want a creamy finish but the rice grains should still be distinct and will only just resist a bite. This is not as firm as al dente, but must not be a mush.

Stir in the raw prawns and cook for about 2 minutes. Add the crème fraîche and stir in, then taste and season with salt and pepper.

To serve, mound the risotto in the centre of large warmed soup plates. Scatter over whole parsley leaves just before bringing to the table.

Skewered Tiger Prawns with Coriander and Parsley Pesto

Americans call all prawns 'shrimp' and do not differentiate between the tiny shrimp (French écrevisse) and the Dublin-Bay-sized varieties. Those of us old enough to have shivered on British summer beaches in seaside towns in the 'Fifties will have done so with a shrimping net in one hand and a tin bucket and spade in the other. Today, young Californians probably think of shrimping as a sophisticated option on an Internet pornographic bulletin board. I dare say theirs is a more entertaining holiday choice, bucket and spade notwithstanding.

When planning to use bamboo skewers, first soak them overnight then bag and freeze them. This slows down the rate at which they char and burn, though it will not make them impervious to flame. The best thing to cook these prawns on is a heavy grill pan without sides, but they can also be cooked on the barbecue or under a very hot grill [broiler].

FOR 4

1 kg / 2 1/4 lb (to give 20) large raw
   tiger prawns [large shrimp],
   peeled, deveined and
   sweetened in salted water
   (see page 84)

FOR THE MARINADE:
1 garlic clove, finely chopped
5 tbsp sunflower oil
2 tsp lemon juice
1/2 tbsp Salsa Picante (page 39)
1 tsp salt
1/2 tsp pepper
1/2 tsp ground cumin

FOR THE CORIANDER AND PARSLEY
PESTO:
2 handfuls of coriander [cilantro]
2 handfuls of flat-leaf parsley
1 garlic clove
1 small fresh hot green chilli
juice of 1 lemon
small bunch of chives
2 tbsp cashew nuts
1 tsp salt
1 tsp black pepper, coarsely
   ground
175 ml / 6 fl oz [3/4 cup] extra-
   virgin olive oil

Pesto with basil must be one of the most delicious of cold sauces but this variation on the theme is pretty amazing too, unless, of course, you hate coriander in which case you had best leave California alone and give this book to a deserving friend.

The day before: put 20 bamboo skewers to soak in cold water, then freeze as above. Put the prawns into a zip-lock bag with all the marinade ingredients. Refrigerate overnight.

Make the pesto: wash the coriander and parsley and spin dry. Pick over, discarding the largest stems. Chop coarsely and put in a food processor. Smash and chop the garlic, and cut the chilli into tiny dice. Add to the food processor with half the lemon juice and all the other dry pesto ingredients. Blitz to a crumb, then scrape down the sides. With the machine running at full speed, pour in the oil through the feeder tube. Taste, adding more salt, pepper and lemon juice as you like.

Preheat the grill pan, charcoal grill or overhead grill [broiler]. If using an overhead grill, put a metal tray under it to heat through in order to give a broiling effect.

Straighten the prawns and push a skewer through the middle of each, reserving the marinade.

Just before you grill the prawns, brush them with the marinade. Grill for about 90 seconds each side, taking care not to let the wood come in direct contact with flames. Serve 5 skewers to a plate, arranged around a ramekin in the centre of each filled with the pesto to dip into.

Sashimi

Sashimi (raw fish) and sushi (vinegared rice and seaweed) were popular in California long before the rest of the world woke up to how delicious these very Japanese dishes are. Perfect sashimi is, I believe, one of the highest forms of food. The quality of the experience depends on the freshness and quality of fish but also in the knowledge and skill which goes into its preparation. Japanese chefs spend years learning to become qualified sashimi chefs, and in Japan there are masters of the art, living National Treasures even. However, there is no reason not to try raw fish at home if you are confident in its selection. There is no mystique to worry about, just the freshest fish, the sharpest knife and a scrupulously clean cutting surface.

One of my proudest possessions is a hand-made sashimi knife. It comes from the last traditional forge in Tokyo near the old Central Fish Market and is so precious it has its own wooden scabbard to protect the scalpel-like edge. It is kept sharp on a succession of water-stones used in conjunction with a paste made from soft nagura stone. It is 'true-forged' which means that the knife is beaten by hand using the same technique developed 1,000 years ago for Samurai swords. The steel is folded over and hammered repeatedly so the end blade is made up of literally thousands of layers.

The more skilled the sashimi chef, the longer the blade employed. The length of my blade far exceeds my skill, and don't go reading anything Freudian into that remark. There are some excellent Japanese knives on the market now which have incorporated the best qualities of the old knives into a high-tech product in which the handle and blade are bonded in one continuous piece of lightweight steel.

Make a small selection of sashimi from sea bass, tuna, salmon and squid. You do not need very much because raw fish is very rich. Always serve the fish with a dipping sauce of Kikkoman soy sauce, mirin – Japanese rice wine – and wasabi – Japanese green horseradish. Some shredded daikon – mild white radish – is usually served too.

one 900 g / 2 lb sea bass (or two
   170-175 g / 6-6¹/2 oz fillets)
350 g / 12 oz tuna fillet
350 g / 12 oz salmon fillet, cut
   from the middle
450 g / 1 lb squid
about 15 cm / 6 in length of
   daikon (optional)
about 2 tbsp wasabi
about 6 tbsp Kikkoman soy sauce
about 3 tbsp mirin (optional)

Have the fishmonger fillet the sea bass for you and remove the pin bones. Check there are none left by running a finger along the bone line against the grain. Remove any that have been missed with a strong pair of tweezers. Lay a fillet, skin side down, on the board and skin it by sliding a knife down to the skin at the tail end, gripping the end and running the knife along its length while pulling gently. Cut into 1 cm / $\frac{1}{2}$ in thick slices at a 45 degree angle. Each slice will have a trace of the skin which will give a pink sheen at the edge.

Arrange 3 pieces overlapping on chilled plates. Rectangular plates are ideal for the presentation, which should always be slightly asymmetrical. Next time you eat Japanese food in a restaurant look at how they do it and copy as best you can.

Trim the tuna fillet into a neat brick, removing any black bits or blood spots. Cut this into 1 cm / $\frac{1}{2}$ in thick slices and again arrange 3 pieces overlapping. Skin the salmon and do the same with it.

Clean the squid (see page 106), reserving the tentacles for another dish. Cut a diamond pattern into the flesh and slice into neat bite-sized pieces.

Shred the daikon, if using, and put a little pile on each plate. Mix the wasabi to a thick paste with water and mould into six little balls each about the size of a small marble. Put one on each plate. Put a tablespoon of soy sauce and a little mirin, if using, in one small dish per person.

Each of you adds wasabi to the soy according to individual taste, mixing to a thin paste into which you dip the fish. Eat with chopsticks and drink warm sake. Look out across the Pacific, eyes narrowed against the sun. *Hai, Anjin san.*

Tempura Skate with Saffron Hollandaise

Skate is a terribly undervalued fish. It is characterized by having an edible cartilaginous and flexible skeleton instead of true bones. There is an enduring piece of received kitchen wisdom about skate that when very fresh the fish smells of ammonia. The truth is a strong whiff of ammonia means that whatever you do in the way of cooking and saucing will not eliminate this. If it smells, throw it away.

The skate is very similar to a ray and propels itself underwater by flapping its wings; these are the only part of the fish that are eaten. A typical portion may weigh as much as 675g/1¹/₂lb and is cut into a triangular shape. The amount of fish specified sounds a lot, but the bone-to-flesh ratio is higher than with most fish. Classically it is pan-fried and served with black butter, which is actually not black at all but just brown.

When deep-fried, skate is usually cooked on the bone, but this is not really the ideal treatment unless you actually like eating the bones because by the time the middle is done the tender flesh is likely to be overcooked at the surface.

The batter used here is a Japanese tempura-style coating and as light as air, while the hollandaise is given both colour and flavour with saffron and mustard. The moist skate contrasts nicely with the crisp white batter and the rich sauce sets the whole thing off brilliantly.

If you prefer, serve the skate fillets with one of the other flavoured mayonnaises. Tartare and gribiche sauce are also good with any type of deep-fried fish.

FOR 4

4 skate wings, weighing about
   450g/1 lb each
salt and pepper
sunflower oil, for deep-frying
flour, for dusting
4 bunches of watercress, to serve

FOR THE SAFFRON HOLLANDAISE:
1 tsp saffron threads
140g/5oz [10 tbsp] butter
3 egg yolks
1 tbsp lemon juice
salt and pepper

The skate wings fan from a solid pinkish main bone down to a thin edge. Using a small sharp knife, follow the edge of this bone along its length, sliding and cutting with the knife angled downwards to the secondary bones. Lift the flesh away and work to the tip, sliding and cutting to lift the flesh away in a neat fillet. One side will be larger than the other and 2 fillets from one wing make a single portion.

Make the hollandaise: pour 1 tablespoon of boiling water over the saffron and leave to infuse for 20 minutes. Melt the butter over a low heat. Put the egg yolks, lemon juice, saffron and soaking liquid, and salt and pepper into a food processor. Blitz, pouring the melted butter in a thin stream through the feeder tube. Taste and adjust the seasoning. Transfer this sauce to a bowl over hot water and keep warm, stirring occasionally.

Preheat the oil in a deep-fryer to 190°C/375°F.

2 eggs

250 ml / 8 fl oz [1 cup] ice-cold lager

pinch of bicarbonate of soda [baking soda]

pinch of salt

115 g / 4 oz fine plain flour [^{3}/$_4$ cup all-purpose flour], sifted

Make the batter: beat the eggs in a bowl. Continue to beat, adding the lager in a thin stream. Add the bicarbonate of soda and salt to the sifted flour then dump this in one go into the liquid and stir a few times barely to mix. (There should be lumps in this batter! Stir until smooth and you will end up with a heavy coating when it is fried.) Leave to stand for 10 minutes.

Dip the skate fillets in seasoned flour, knocking off any excess, then dip in the batter and deep-fry for about 4 minutes, turning once. Drain briefly on kitchen paper and serve on warmed plates with a generous spoonful of saffron hollandaise on one side and a bunch of watercress on the other.

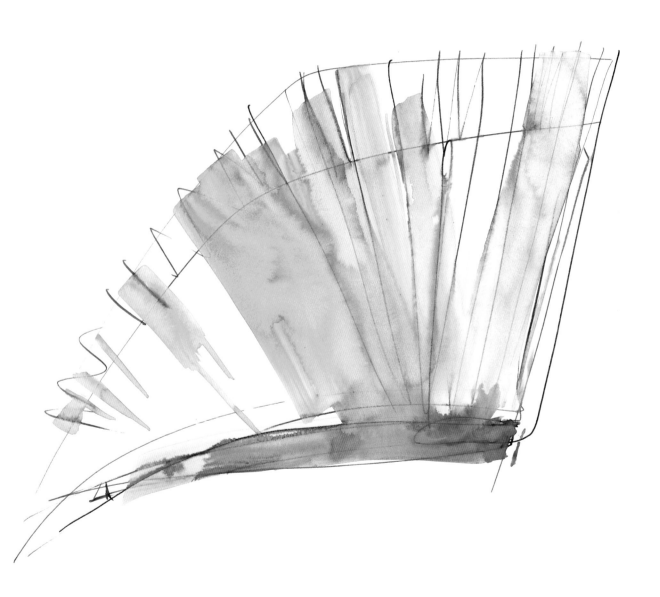

Thai-style Fish Cakes with Tomato Salsa and Coriander Pesto

Thai flavours – notably the Holy Trinity of Thai cooking, lemon grass, coriander and fish sauce – can today be enjoyed by a much wider eating public, for the ingredients are now available in most supermarkets. Thai fish sauce is made from salted and fermented small fish and squid. It smells a bit alarming when you open the bottle, but delivers an intriguing flavour to the finished dish. Although in South-east Asia the fish sauce is used more as we would use soy sauce at the table, it adds a further dimension to any cooked dish in which it is included and plays an important part in making these fish cakes taste quite different.

Any white fish will do, but as you are using very strong flavouring ingredients you can take this opportunity to use something cheap and cheerful like coley or pollock. The inclusion of swordfish in this version upgrades the cakes, but they are fine with just the white fish. Alternatively, you could include fresh tuna or salmon in the same proportion.

MAKES 12 (4 SERVINGS)

550 g/1 1/4 lb white fish fillets,
   cut into pieces
225 g/8 oz swordfish
1 stalk of lemon grass
handful of coriander leaves
   [cilantro]
2 fresh hot green chillies
1 tbsp Thai fish sauce
1 egg, plus white of 1 extra egg
3 tbsp mashed potato
   (optional)
285 g/10 oz leeks
olive oil, for frying
sunflower oil, for frying
flour, for dusting
Coriander and Parsley Pesto
   (page 111), to serve
Basic Salsa Cruda (page 37), to
   serve
2-3 tbsp extra-virgin olive oil
salt and pepper

Skin the fish, cut the flesh into chunks and put in a food processor. Peel off the thick outer leaf of the lemon grass and discard, then cut across into the thinnest rings you can manage. Finely chop the coriander and green chillies. Add these to the fish along with the fish sauce and egg and egg white. Blitz to a smooth purée, add the mashed potato, if using, and whizz again briefly. Scrape into a bowl, cover the top with plastic film and refrigerate for at least 2 hours or overnight.

Trim the leeks, slice down their length to the middle and stand upright in cold water for 10 minutes to ensure they are clean. Cut into julienne strips and fry over a low heat in the olive and sunflower oils. When softened, increase the heat to medium and stir-fry until crisp. Drain on paper towels and reserve.

Using a tablespoon to give the right amount, form the fish mixture into 12 balls and then flatten these into cakes. Dredge with flour and shallow-fry in sunflower oil until golden brown on both sides. This will take only about 3 minutes on each side.

Adjust the consistency of the sauces with a little extra-virgin olive so they are thin enough to swirl on a plate. Put a tablespoon of each on either side of the plate, tilting and turning so the two come together in the centre. Arrange 3 cakes on top and serve with a garnish of crisp-fried leeks.

Deep-fried Chicken Won-tons with Roasted Pepper Coulis

MAKES 24 (4 SERVINGS)

24 rectangular won-ton
  wrappers (freeze the rest
  of the pack for another
  dish)
small bunch of chives, to
  garnish

FOR THE FILLING:

4 cm / 1 1/2 in piece of root
  ginger
1 garlic clove
small handful of coriander
  [cilantro]
2 spring onions [scallions]
115 g / 4 oz sliced Parma ham
  [prosciutto]
450 g / 1 lb skinned and boned
  chicken breasts
white of 1 egg
salt and pepper

FOR THE ROASTED PEPPER COULIS:

4 red sweet peppers
about 4 tbsp extra-virgin olive
  oil
4 garlic cloves
4 shallots
1 tbsp paprika
1 fresh hot red chilli
2 tsp balsamic vinegar
salt and pepper

Won-ton wrappers are a universal boon to cooks, providing us with an instant and light form of ravioli which we can fill as taste and imagination dictates. There is nothing intrinsically wrong in using bought-in components when constructing a dish, and when – as in the case of won-ton wrappers and filo pastry – it is highly unlikely that you could make something as well as the large-scale producer, then to insist on doing it yourself is a perverse waste of time which could be better spent on other more rewarding and creative kitchen projects. Like staring out of the window planning tomorrow's menu.

Won-ton can be pretty grim. They disappoint with the quality of filling – invariably low-grade tasteless pork. Sampling them in the China Towns of Los Angeles and San Francisco was no more alluring. Discovering that one could buy ready-made won-ton wrappers cheaply in Chinese markets prompted experimentation at home and I soon discovered that by creating fillings which were delicious in their own right, by filling the wrappers more generously and by folding and sealing them with care, one could create memorable won-tons using lobster, tiger prawns, Dover sole, turbot, fillet steak – the opportunities are only limited by the imagination or what is to hand.

In this case, the won-tons are filled with minced chicken breasts and Parma ham and are deep-fried rather than poached, before being served on a spicy roasted pepper coulis.

First make the coulis (this can be done the day before and the coulis stored in a jar in the fridge until needed): preheat the oven to 190°C/375°F/gas5. Halve the peppers and remove seeds and stems. Arrange them cut side up in a roasting pan and brush generously with olive oil inside and out. Smash and chop the garlic and divide equally among the peppers. Roast until the peppers start to collapse, about 30 minutes. If the top edges blacken this is fine.

Transfer the peppers to a bowl and cover the top. Leave for 15 minutes, then peel. The skin comes off easily. Transfer the peeled pepper halves to a food processor with the garlic and all the juices.

Dice the shallots and sweat them with 1 tablespoon of olive oil until soft. Stir in the paprika and cook for 1-2 minutes, then transfer to the processor.

Split the chilli and remove seeds. Cut it across into thin strips, then cut these across again into tiny dice. Add to the peppers with the vinegar and 2 tablespoons of olive oil. Process to a purée and push through a sieve.

Make the won-ton filling: peel the ginger and grate it on to a plate so as not to lose any of the juice. Grate the garlic on top of it. Chop the coriander and spring onions. Add to the ginger and garlic. Dice the Parma ham. Cut the chicken breasts into small dice. Season with a little salt and pepper (the ham is very salty so be very sparing with the salt at this stage).

Put a small saucepan of water on to boil.

Put the mixed ingredients and the egg white into the processor and pulse-chop just until it holds together. You do not want a formless mush, but a mixture that has discernible elements of the constituent parts.

Take a teaspoon of the mixture, slide it into the simmering water and poach for 2 or 3 minutes. Remove and eat it to check the seasoning. If the filling needs more salt then add some to the mixture in the processor now and pulse for a couple of seconds to distribute it evenly.

Put some water in a cup or ramekin. Flour a baking tray and have it beside you. Brush the edges of a won-ton wrapper with a little water from the cup or

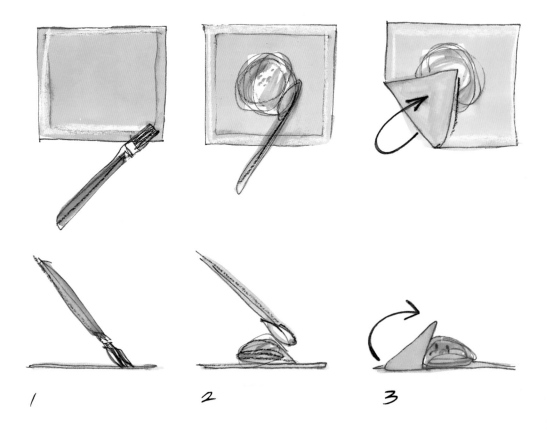

1   2   3

ramekin. Put a heaped teaspoon of the filling mixture in the middle. Fold opposite sides together and pinch the edges firmly to seal. Bring up the remaining corners and pinch together, then pinch along the open edges to seal. Repeat until you have finished all the mixture and wrappers, transferring the finished won-tons to the floured tray. They can be wrapped in plastic film and kept in the fridge for up to 6 hours before the wrappers deteriorate.

Preheat sunflower oil for deep-frying to 185°C/365°F in a wok or electric deep-fryer.

Put the coulis to warm over a low heat. If it is too thick, add a little water. It should have a spoonable consistency to coat the plate.

Fry the won-tons in batches of 6-8 for 3-4 minutes each batch, when they will be puffed up and golden brown. Remove with a wire strainer and drain on paper towels. Keep warm while you cook the remaining batches.

Spoon the coulis on to warmed soup plates, tilting to cover the central base. Arrange 6 won-tons on each and decorate with 4 cm/ 1 1/2 in strips of chives.

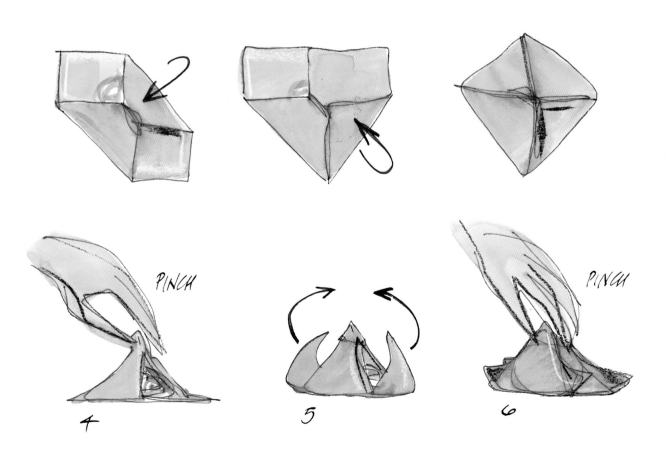

Caramelized Chicken Livers on Garlic Croûtes

Caramelizing implies sugar, and since chicken livers have a tendency to bitterness, the addition of a few teaspoons of sugar to the pan along with shallots produces a nice crunchy effect while ameliorating the strong flavour. The Chinese use sugar quite a lot in stir-frying, while in South-east Asia palm sugar is a frequent addition to many savoury dishes.

When cooking chicken livers in a pan always do so over a very high heat and quickly. You can usually find chicken livers frozen in tubs in any supermarket, but they are generally not of good quality and almost certainly came from battery chickens. Ask your butcher to check out the wholesale market for imported French chicken livers, which come fresh and vacuum-packed in kilo bags.

FOR 4

550 g / 1 1/4 lb chicken livers
2 garlic cloves
100 ml / 3 1/2 fl oz [7 tbsp] extra-
    virgin olive oil
4 slices of white bread
225 g / 8 oz shallots
1 fresh Anaheim-type
    (medium-hot) chilli
1 tbsp flour
1 tbsp caster sugar [US
    granulate sugar]
1 tbsp sherry vinegar
salt and pepper
small bunch of chives, to
    garnish
handful of flat-leaf parsley, to
    garnish

The day before: smash and chop the garlic. Put it into a screw-top jar and pour the olive oil over it. Leave at room temperature until just before you start cooking, then strain it through a fine sieve into a bowl.

Preheat the oven to 200°C/400°F/gas6. Cut the crusts off the bread, brush both sides with the oil and put on a baking sheet. Bake for about 10 minutes, or until crisp and golden brown. Keep an eye on it because it burns the instant you do something else. Remove and keep warm.

While the croûtes are baking, pick over the livers, cutting off any tubes or bits of fat and removing any green-tinged parts. These have been in contact with bile and will be unpleasantly bitter. Pat dry with paper towels and reserve.

Put a large heavy frying pan over a medium heat. Cut the shallots and chilli into 1 cm / 1/2 in strips. Put into the pan with the remaining olive oil, turn down the heat and sweat until the shallots are translucent.

Toss the livers with the flour, salt, sugar and coarsely milled black pepper. Turn up the heat to high, throw the livers into the pan and sauté for 2-3 minutes. Add the sherry vinegar and toss.

Put the olive oil croûtes on warmed plates and mound the livers on top. Give a couple more turns of the pepper mill, snip chives over generously and scatter over some whole parsley leaves. Serve at once. Sing *Viva Tijuana* as you rattle your castanets and flamenco-dance the plates to the table.

Warm Salad of Sugar-snaps with Peppered Chicken Livers

A warm salad makes a perfect light first course for a summer lunch. Sugar-snap peas – the young pods eaten whole – tossed in a balsamic vinaigrette are excellent with chicken livers, their natural sweet taste balancing the richness of the livers nicely. The chicken livers are seared and peppery outside but moist and pink inside, while the garlic croutons add a satisfying crunch to this unusual salade tiède.

FOR 4

450 g / 1 lb sugar-snap peas
225 g / 8 oz chicken livers
2 garlic cloves
about 100 ml / 3 1/2 fl oz [7 tbsp]
  olive oil
2 slices of white bread, crusts
  removed and cut into
  5 mm / 1/4 in cubes
30 g / 1 oz [2 tbsp] unsalted
  butter or 1 tbsp clarified
  butter
5 tbsp Chilli Balsamic
  Vinaigrette (page 36)
salt and pepper
handful of flat-leaf parsley, to
  garnish

Two hours before cooking: smash and finely chop the garlic and stir with 2 tablespoons of the olive oil in a bowl. Leave for the garlic flavour to infuse. Just before cooking begins, strain this through a fine sieve into another bowl, discarding the garlic residue. If you leave it in, it may burn on the croutons as they fry, giving them a bitter taste.

Add the bread cubes to the oil, season lightly with salt and pepper and toss to coat. Then fry gently in a dry heavy pan over a low heat to prevent burning. Turn and toss to cook to an even crunch.

Trim the pea pods and blanch for 2 minutes in lots of rapidly boiling lightly salted water. They should barely be cooked. Refresh in cold water and drain.

While the pods are cooking, season the chicken livers with plenty of coarse pepper and a little salt and sauté quickly in the remaining olive oil and butter. This will only take a couple of minutes, leaving the livers pink in the middle.

To serve, plunge the sugar-snaps back into the boiling water for 15 seconds, drain and put into a bowl with the vinaigrette and toss to coat. Then mound them on individual plates. Share out the livers, arranging them on top, and scatter with the warm croutons and flat-leaf parsley.

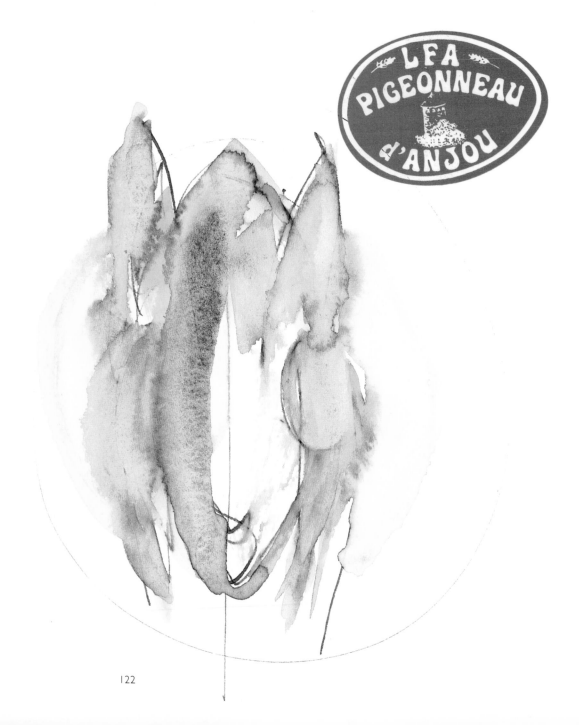

Spiced Squab with Tagliatelle in Broth

This is an excellent way of making the most of these small, succulent but very expensive birds (see page 174). In this dish one 500 g/1 lb 2 oz squab serves two people. The birds are cooked ahead and left to rest for 20 minutes before carving. Twelve to fifteen minutes at 250°C/475°F/gas9 will produce a very rare result which, since the flavour is both rich and delicate, is sufficient for my taste, particularly as the meat will be bathed in very hot broth. You may, however, prefer to take them a little further, say 15 minutes. If serving immediately, a squab should still rest for 10 minutes.

The carcasses from the birds make the most sensational stock. Even one carcass added to chicken bones will deliver a good result (see page 24).

Tagliatelle replaces the more obvious and ubiquitous instant soup noodles. You can make your own if you are keen on cranking the pasta machine, but supermarkets now sell very good fresh tagliatelle.

FOR 4

2 dressed squab, each weighing about 500 g/ 1 lb 2 oz
about 2 tbsp Chilli Oil (page 40)
450 g/1 lb fresh tagliatelle
1.1 litres/2 pt [5 cups] well-flavoured Chicken or Squab Stock (page 24)
4 tbsp Kikkoman soy sauce
3 cm/1¼ in piece of root ginger
1 fresh hot green chilli
8 spring onions [scallions]
salt and pepper
handful of coriander leaves [cilantro], to garnish

Remove the squab from the fridge 1 hour before cooking to allow to come to room temperature. Brush all over with chilli oil and reserve.

Preheat the oven to 250°C/450°F/gas9.

Put the squab, breast side down, in a roasting pan. Strew on salt and coarsely cracked pepper and put to roast for 7 minutes. Turn breast side up, spoon on a little more oil and season with a little salt and lots of pepper. Roast for a further 5 minutes for a very rare finish, 8 minutes for medium. (Cook it until well done and you have committed a crime against squabdom). Take out of the oven and leave for 10 minutes before carving.

While the squab are waiting for the knife, put on a pan of salted water to boil for the tagliatelle, and in another pan heat the stock with the soy sauce to a gentle simmer. Cut the ginger and chilli into julienne strips and shred the spring onions. Reserve.

Carve the birds by cutting down on one side of the breastbone with a small very sharp knife, following around the contour of the bird and cutting through the joints of the thigh and wing. Repeat on the other side. Detach the legs and thighs from the breasts. Slice each breast at an angle into 4 pieces.

Cook the tagliatelle for 4 minutes or until al dente. Drain and divide between 4 warmed bowls. Arrange the meat equally on top and pour over the steaming hot stock. Scatter on the ginger, spring onions and chilli. Finally, grind over some pepper and garnish with lots of whole coriander leaves.

Drink a chilled Manzanilla or Fino if serving for a first course, or something red and beefy with it as a main course.

Seared Foie Gras with Sweetcorn and Black Bean Pancakes

FOR 4

4 slices of raw duck foie gras,
    about 5 mm / 1/4 in thick
salt and pepper

FOR THE PANCAKES:
115 g / 4 oz [3/4 cup] corn
    kernels
85 g / 3 oz [1/2 cup] cooked
    black beans
1 tbsp cornflour [cornstarch]
300 ml / 1/2 pt [1 1/4 cups] plain
    yogurt
450 g / 1 lb [2 heaped cups]
    dry mashed potatoes
60 g / 2 oz [7 tbsp] flour
4 eggs, separated, plus whites
    of 2 more eggs
2 tbsp chopped coriander
    leaves [cilantro]
salt and pepper
sunflower oil, for brushing

Increasing numbers of people take exception to foie gras as the unnatural product of a cruel and unusually intensive regime, the implication being that this is something new. They may not realize that cramming geese to enlarge livers was originally based on the geese's own greedy behaviour and has been going on since the Fifth Egyptian dynasty. It was common practice in ancient Greece from the third millennium BC and was very much a part of the grand Roman table. Throughout history, foie gras has always been the voluptuary's ultimate treat and a potent symbol of culinary decadence.

The lunatic homosexual Emperor Heliogabalus fed his dogs exclusively on foie gras. He was murdered in an army barracks latrine by having a sponge stick rammed down his throat, presumably by a military gourmet who found such waste intolerable.

Foie gras terrines were exported to America from France as long ago as 1791. Two hundred years later, Americans can at last cook fresh livers for themselves.

Californians, for years denied foie gras by import restrictions, are now allowed to bring in as much as they like and it features proudly on the menus of many of the state's finest restaurants. Frying raw foie gras – the enlarged livers of corn-fed geese and ducks – is not difficult, just expensive. However, since it is very rich, you need only 55 g-85 g / 2-3 oz for a first-course portion. The liver's high fat content means quite a lot of it runs out when it hits the hot pan, and acrid smoke billows forth.

These pancakes make a perfect foil for the rich foie gras. If foie gras is not to hand or ethical considerations exclude it from your diet, try the pancakes with bacon and a fried egg on top with a spoonful of Basic Salsa Cruda (page 37) on the side.

Any large floury potatoes will do for the pancake base. Indeed, if you have some mashed potatoes left over these will form the basis of an excellent batter, and by all means use frozen corn. If using fresh corn you will need to blanch it first. The cooking of black beans is described on pages 30-31.

First make the pancake batter: mix the cornflour to a paste with a little water, stir into the yogurt and bring to the boil. Lower the heat and simmer the mixture for 10 minutes.

While still very hot, beat the yogurt into the potatoes. Whisk in the flour and leave to cool. Whisk in the egg yolks, the corn and the black beans.

Season with salt and pepper. Fold in the coriander, then the lightly beaten egg whites. You should have achieved the consistency of a very thick pancake batter. Leave to stand for an hour before using.

Heat a non-stick frying pan over a low heat. When hot, raise the heat a little. Wipe the surface with an oiled piece of paper towel. Stir the batter and ladle enough in to make a pancake the size of a saucer. Cook until bubbles start to come to the surface. Turn with a spatula and cook the other side. Transfer to a plate and keep warm in a low oven while you cook the rest.

Put a dry heavy frying pan over a medium heat. When the pan is smoking hot, season the foie gras with salt and pepper and sear. Turn after 20 seconds and cook the other side for 20 seconds. Transfer immediately using a spatula and sit each slice on top of a pancake. Finish with a little black pepper and serve immediately.

Rabbit Rillettes

FOR 6

550 g / 1 1/4 lb rabbit pieces

1 onion

1 carrot

3 garlic cloves

4 celery stalks

12-15 rosemary leaves

200 g / 7 oz pork belly [fresh pork side]

55 g / 2 oz unsmoked streaky bacon [unsmoked thick-sliced bacon]

55 g / 2 oz [1/4 cup] goose or duck fat or lard

350 ml / 12 fl oz [1 1/2 cups] dry white wine

1 bay leaf

3 tbsp Jack Daniels, Jim Beam or sour mash whiskey

salt and pepper

Americans have a surprisingly ambivalent attitude to rabbit, considering they never had the taint of myxomatosis to put them off. I put my children off rabbit when they were little with an ill-judged joke about Flopsy, Mopsy and Cottontail Pie, creating an aversion which has lasted into adulthood. Since rabbit meat has a good flavour and is virtually fat-free, people are coming round to it and even those who are fairly anti-coney can be won over when it is served as rillettes.

In this recipe a uniquely American slant is given by the inclusion of bourbon. Shelly Berger, whose eponymous salad is described later on page 162, was a convert to rabbit in his 50th year, when I persuaded him to try it grilled at Bibendum in London. He then startled everybody by ordering it his first day back at Le Dôme, with mustard sauce and a bottle of claret, a marked change from his daily routine of chopped salad and iced tea. His usual waiter had to be helped back to the kitchen in shock.

The meat is slowly poached in white wine and fat with aromatic flavourings until it is so tender you can shred it with a fork. Rillettes by definition, therefore, are not for cholesterol cowards but are an excellent alternative to a terrine and particularly good with slices of sourdough bread that have been toasted on a ridged grill pan.

The rillettes benefit from being kept for a week before eating, which allows their flavour to develop. If you have packed the rillettes down firmly enough and filmed the surface with fat to make an airtight seal, they will keep in the fridge for a month.

Rillettes can be served traditionally as a first course or as a single lunch dish with something red but light, like a good Beaujolais, to drink with them.

California lunchers often drink iced tea throughout lunch. The very thought of iced tea on the side while eating good food makes me shudder. I have actually seen people drink tea while eating soup, and if that isn't intolerable behaviour I don't know what is. Conclude the meal with a palate-cleansing dandelion or frisée salad.

Cut the onion in half and the carrot into 4 lengthwise. Slice the garlic into transparently thin slices. Trim the celery and cut it into 4 cm / 1 ½ in lengths. Pick off the rosemary leaves and chop.

Cut the pork belly and bacon into lardon strips and put them into a saucepan with the fat or lard, wine and 250 ml / 8 fl oz [1 cup] water. Bring to the boil and skim. Add the onion, celery, carrot, garlic, bay leaf and rosemary. Season with 1 teaspoon of salt and ½ teaspoon of pepper. Lower the heat so that only the occasional bubble breaks the surface and simmer gently, uncovered, until the liquid is reduced by half.

Remove the onion, carrot and bay leaf. Add the rabbit pieces and the whiskey, put on the lid and continue to cook for a further 1 hour or so, when the meat will have pulled away from the bones and you can push a fork into the rabbit without resistance.

Drain in a sieve set in a bowl, reserving the fat in the bowl. Transfer the rabbit to a board, pull the meat off the bone and tear into shreds with 2 forks. Put into another bowl with the belly pork and bacon, add 2 tablespoons of the reserved fat and mix lightly. Taste and add more salt and pepper if needed, then pack into a Kilner or other preserving jar. Pour on some more fat to seal and refrigerate. Any remaining fat is great for frying potatoes.

Warm Puy Lentil Salad with Poached Egg and Pancetta

Lentilles de Puy, the nutty-flavoured dark-green royalty of the world of pulses, cook quickly while retaining separate, slightly al dente lentils. Once exclusively the product of the Puy area of France, they are now also grown in Canada and are more widely available.

California has many French chefs, very many very French restaurants and a large expatriate French community. Some of its most interesting food fusions have come with the mixing of French and Eastern cuisines. This salad is not an example of such fusion cooking, but the sort of dish you might be served at The French Laundry in Napa Valley or at one of the great wineries, a perfect foil for any wine, either white or red.

With all pulses you can calculate that 450 g/1 lb [about 2 1/2 cups] dried will give you 6-8 portions for a first course and about 4-6 for a main course when rehydrated and cooked. There is never a problem having some left over. They reheat well and are as nice-cold as hot and, of course, all pulses can be puréed to good effect.

Pancetta, the very best Italian bacon with a lovely strong flavour, is a global success story. You can buy it in various grades from Italian food shops, the finest being sliced thin like Parma ham [prosciutto] and eaten raw as an antipasto. For cooking you want to buy pancetta in a piece and cut into lardon strips yourself. It is also delicious boiled as you would a piece of gammon or ham, though it tends to be very salty and needs lengthy soaking first. On reflection it is so expensive this treatment may be sacrilegious. If you cannot find any pancetta, then substitute a good quality streaky bacon [thick-sliced bacon].

The salad can be made without any pancetta or bacon, but the combination with the poached egg is one of the main points of the dish. Poaching eggs is not difficult, so long as the eggs are very fresh. Every day that passes makes poaching more tricky, since the egg will not cohere in the water once it is stale. Stale for poaching purposes is a fresh egg by most standards. To see how fresh your eggs are, break one on to a plate. The white should stand up closely around the yolk. If it spreads, the egg is unsuitable for poaching.

FOR 4

285 g/10 oz [1 1/3 cups]
    lentilles de Puy
115 g/4 oz pancetta or
    streaky bacon
3 tbsp olive oil
175 g/6 1/2 oz onions
2 garlic cloves
115 g/4 oz carrot
2 celery stalks, plus their
    leaves
150 ml/1/4 pt [2/3 cup] dry
    white wine
1 bay leaf
1 fresh red serrano-type (hot)
    chilli
4 very fresh large eggs [US
    extra large eggs]
1 tbsp vinegar
handful of flat-leaf parsley
salt and pepper

FOR THE VINAIGRETTE:
5 tbsp extra-virgin olive oil
1 tbsp balsamic vinegar
1 tbsp Dijon mustard
salt and pepper

Put the lentils in a sieve and rinse well under cold running water. Reserve.

Cut the pancetta into fat lardon strips and fry gently in the olive oil until much of its fat has run into the pan and the bacon is beginning to brown.

Cut the onion, garlic and carrot into 5 mm/1/4 in dice and stir into the pan. Slice the celery across as thinly as you can, add to the pan and sweat the vegetables until soft and translucent, stirring from time to time. Add the lentils and stir for 2 minutes. Turn up the heat and add the white wine, bay leaf and chilli. Bring the wine to the boil, then pour over cold water just to cover the lentils and bring back to the boil. Turn down the heat and simmer gently for 15-20 minutes. Remove from the heat and remove the bay leaf and chilli. Put a lid on the pan to keep the lentils warm.

About 10 minutes before the lentils are done, put on a wide shallow saucepan of lightly salted water to boil. Add the vinegar. You want the water bubbling but not at a ferocious rolling boil. There is no need to stir the water as received wisdom suggests. Break the eggs on to saucers and slide them into the water, one at a time. The white will start to set at once and the eggs will be done in 1 1/2–2 minutes. Remove carefully with a slotted spoon and put on a warm plate. Trim ragged edges with scissors. Alternatively eggs can be poached ahead and held in cold water until needed. They are then returned briefly to simmering water to heat through.

While the water is heating, make the vinaigrette by mixing all the ingredients in a large bowl and reserve.

Chop half the parsley and all the celery leaves and stir into the lentils. Drain in a sieve, put into the bowl with the vinaigrette and toss.

Mound the lentils in the centre of 4 large plates. Carefully put an egg on top of each and scatter on a few whole leaves of parsley to finish.

Onion and Pancetta Tart

A real quiche Lorraine is a delightful creation. This variation on the theme, generously filled with onions and cooked lardons of pancetta, is a fine lunch dish which needs no more than a crisp Chardonnay to drink with it and a simple green salad to follow. The tart is best eaten hot, but is still delicious at room temperature.

FOR 4-6

170 g / 6 oz pancetta

3 tbsp olive oil

675 g / 1 1/2 lb onions

30 g / 1 oz [2 tbsp] butter

one 23 cm / 9 in savoury tart pastry shell, baked blind (page 59)

575 ml / 1 pt [2 1/3 cups] whipping cream

4 eggs

85 g / 3 oz [3/4 cup] Gruyère cheese, shredded

1/4 nutmeg

salt and pepper

Cut the pancetta into lardon strips and fry gently in the olive oil until the bacon darkens in colour and its fat runs into the pan. Transfer to paper towels to drain.

Slice the onions thinly and add to the pan with the butter. Sweat over a low heat, stirring from time to time, until soft and translucent. It is very important not to allow the onions to brown as this would ruin the tart.

Preheat the oven to 180°C/350°F/gas4. Put the savoury tart pastry shell on a baking sheet.

Whisk the cream with the eggs and season with salt and pepper. Remove the pan from the heat. Stir the cheese into the onions.

Distribute the pancetta evenly over the bottom of the tart shell. Stir the onion mixture into the custard, then pour and spoon into the tart. Grate the nutmeg on top and bake for 30 minutes.

Brunch and Eggs

Brunch is a strange institution for those of us who think of lunch on Sunday as being later rather than earlier. It is a meal which mixes breakfast classics – eggs are invariably included – with sugary items like Danish pastries. The drink is Bloody Mary (page 66), the total effect bloody odd and intolerable if you are in a state like Georgia where brunch starts promptly at 10 am but the bar does not open until noon. Worse still is Tallahassee, the state capital of Florida, which the last time I was there (to interview the Governor on the subject of electrocution) was dry all day on Sunday, even so far as hotel residents were concerned. I have not been back to see whether the regime has improved.

Classic Omelette and Hash Browns

Why a recipe for an omelette? Because nobody ever gives you one and because people endlessly ask for advice. There are no substitutes for watching somebody who knows how to cook one, but determination and a willingness to practise – and throw away the first dozen attempts – will get you there.

La Mère Poulard, who had a restaurant in Mont-Saint-Michel in Normandy, was known throughout France for her omelettes and roast chickens. When asked what was the secret of her omelettes she famously – and I think irritatingly – replied that she beat the eggs well, used a well-seasoned pan and a good-sized lump of the best unsalted Normandy butter. Merci, Madame. Thank you for sharing that with us.

The important thing is not to overcook the eggs. The centre of the omelette should be baveuse, dribbling moist.

An omelette does not need to be served with anything, but all egg dishes go well with hash browns. A lot of American recipes use diced potatoes, but grated are better. The kind of potato does not really matter. An American diner would almost certainly cook hash browns in bacon fat, which gives them their distinctive flavour; but if this does not appeal, butter or a mixture of oil and butter works well.

12 very fresh eggs
85 g / 3 oz [6 tbsp] unsalted
    butter

FOR THE HASH BROWNS:
675 g / 1 1/2 lb potatoes
55g / 2 oz [4 tbsp] butter
4 tbsp sunflower oil
salt and pepper

First make the hash browns: peel and coarsely grate the potatoes into a bowl of cold water to remove excess starch, then spin dry in a salad spinner or press in a colander to squeeze out as much liquid as you can. Spread out on a cloth. The drier you can get them, the better.

Melt the butter with the sunflower oil in a heavy frying pan. Distribute the grated potato in an even layer and press down hard with a metal spatula to compress into a cake. Season with salt and pepper and cover. Lower the heat and cook gently for 15 minutes. Remove the lid, raise the heat to medium and fry for a further 5 minutes.

Slide the spatula under the potato mass, making sure it has not stuck. If you feel bullish about the whole thing, flip the cake over and cook the top for 5 minutes to crisp and brown. If a more wimpish mood holds sway, put a warmed plate upside down on the top and turn out the cake on to it, browned base upwards. Cut into wedges to serve. Crisp bacon crumbled over is traditional though not essential.

To make the omelettes: put a 23 cm / 9 in omelette pan dry over a medium heat. Whisk 3 of the eggs in a bowl with salt and pepper for 3 minutes or until light and frothy.

Throw a nut of the butter into the pan, tilt and swirl about and immediately add the beaten eggs before the butter burns. With the flat of a fork, stir the centre vigorously for 5 seconds, tilting the pan to move uncooked egg to the edges. Work around the omelette, pulling the eggs gently towards the centre. The eggs are going to continue cooking after they come out of the pan so remove from the heat while the middle is still moist and creamy.

To serve the omelette, tilt the pan and then give the handle a firm tap to turn the furthest edge over, tipping on to a plate with a rolling movement to give a cylindrical shape. This is as hard to do as it is to describe, but practice will make perfect. Omelettes are like crêpes: they get better as you go along. Repeat with the remaining eggs 3 at a time to make the 3 other omelettes, serving them as they are done.

Parmesan Soufflé Omelette with Spinach Sauce

The soufflé omelette is easy and quick to prepare and more forgiving than a classic omelette. The combination of spinach and cheese is invariably delightful, described in the French kitchen as florentine. The very first thing I ever cooked at the age of 14 was a cheese soufflé omelette, which confirms how easy they are.

Although you can make individual soufflé omelettes, they really work better when cooked on a larger scale. This omelette is for four.

FOR 4

85 g / 3 oz [6 tbsp] butter
30 g / 1 oz [3 tbsp] flour
575 ml / 1 pt [2¹/₃ cups] milk
5 tbsp dry sherry
1 bay leaf
¹/₄ nutmeg
450 g / 1 lb spinach
30 g / 2 oz [¹/₂ cup] Parmesan
*   cheese*
10 eggs
salt and pepper

Put on a pan of salted water to boil. Melt 30 g / 1 oz [2 tbsp] of the butter in a saucepan, stir in the flour and cook this roux briefly until lightly coloured. Whisk in the milk and sherry. Cook over a medium heat, whisking, until it starts to thicken.

Lower the heat to the lowest setting. Add the bay leaf and grate in the nutmeg. Season with a little salt and plenty of pepper. Cook, stirring from time to time, for 20 minutes, when the sauce will be reduced by almost half. Remove the bay leaf.

Pick over the spinach, cutting out the stems. Blanch in the boiling water for 30 seconds. Drain in a colander, then refresh in cold water. Gently squeeze out excess moisture. Chop the leaves and add to the finished sauce. Grate half the Parmesan and stir in. Keep warm.

Put a heavy 25 cm / 10 in frying pan to heat over a low flame. Separate 5 of the eggs and whisk the whites until they form soft peaks. Don't take them too far; they should not be stiff. Whisk the 5 whole eggs and 5 yolks with 2 tablespoons water and season with a little salt and pepper. Stir in a spoonful of whites and then gently fold in the rest.

Turn on the overhead grill [broiler] to medium. Turn up the heat under the frying pan and when it is smoking hot, throw in the remaining butter. Swirl and immediately pour and scrape in the eggs. Turn down the heat to medium and cook until the base is set, about 2 minutes.

Transfer the pan under the grill [broiler] and cook until the surface is risen and golden brown. Move the pan three times, sliding it around to get as even an exposure to the heat as possible. It will take about 4-5 minutes. You don't want the omelette wet in the middle, but just set. All grills vary, while the thickness of the frying pan and how hot you have made it will also affect the cooking time.

Slide the omelette out flat on to a cutting board. Pour the sauce down the middle and fold it over. Cut into 4 and serve on warmed plates with the remaining Parmesan shaved over, spooning any remaining sauce alongside.

Roasted Pepper and Parmesan Frittata

This differs from a classic Italian frittata, which tends to be a skinny, overcooked affair, by being more moist and substantial and in the two-stage cooking method. Cooking the eggs in two layers, the second layer finished under a medium overhead grill [broiler], has the effect of holding the filling in the middle while the protective egg base prevents it sticking or breaking up.

FOR 4-6

4 roasted red pepper halves, peeled (see page 26)
55 g / 2 oz [1/2 cup] Parmesan cheese, freshly grated
10 eggs
8 spring onions [scallions]
8 basil leaves
2 tbsp olive oil
salt and pepper

Trim the spring onions and slice thinly. Cut the peppers into 1 cm / 1/2 in dice.

Beat 4 eggs in one bowl and 6 in another. Season both with salt and pepper, and stir the grated Parmesan and the basil leaves torn into strips into the bowl with more eggs.

Preheat an overhead grill [broiler] to medium. Put a 20 cm / 8 in non-stick frying pan over a low heat. When hot, turn up the heat to medium and add the olive oil. Pour in the 4-egg mix and swirl to cover the bottom of the pan.

When just set, cover with the pepper dice and onions, then pour over the remaining eggs. Lower the heat and cook for 4 minutes, then transfer the pan to under the grill [broiler] and continue to cook until done. This can only be judged with practice, but you can pull the surface away at the centre to check. The frittata should be cooked all the way through, but only just.

Slide on to a board and leave to cool. Do not refrigerate, and serve at room temperature.

Variations on this theme will become obvious. Diced new potatoes, oven-roasted tomatoes, dry-grilled aubergine [eggplant] and fried courgettes [zucchini] offer a few alternative fillings, either alone or in combination.

Eggs and Leeks in a Mustard Saffron Cheese Sauce

This is a sophisticated version of the classic supper dish of childhood, reminiscent of the nursery and as comforting to advancing years as it is resolutely delicious. It is a magical combination and one that never fails to please at any age. While nostalgically a supper dish, it is also ideal on a brunch or lunch menu. A tablespoon of mustard powder sounds a lot but is very gentle once cooked. Hard-boiled does not mean that the eggs are cooked to the consistency of squash balls. The yolks should only just be set.

FOR 4

8 hard-boiled eggs

16 baby leeks

850 ml / 1 1/2 pt [3 1/2 cups] milk

about 15 threads of saffron

30 g / 1 oz [2 tbsp] butter

30 g / 1 oz [3 tbsp] flour

1 tbsp mustard powder

1/4 nutmeg

5 tbsp dry sherry

1 bay leaf

85 g / 3 oz [3/4 cup] Parmesan
    cheese, freshly grated

30 g / 1 oz [1/4 cup] farmhouse
    Cheddar cheese, grated

1 tbsp breadcrumbs

salt and pepper

Heat a few tablespoons of the milk, add the saffron and leave to infuse.

Melt the butter in a saucepan, stir in the flour and cook this roux briefly until lightly coloured. Stir in the mustard powder and grated nutmeg, then whisk in the milk and sherry. Add the bay leaf and bring to the boil, stirring. Turn down the heat and cook for 20 minutes, stirring from time to time.

Remove the bay leaf and add the saffron milk and grated cheese. Continue to cook until amalgamated and the sauce is silky textured. Season with pepper, adding salt only after you have tasted, since both cheeses already contain quite a lot of salt.

Preheat the oven to 180°C/350°F/gas4.

Trim the leeks and wash carefully. Cook in lightly salted boiling water until barely cooked, about 4 minutes. Refresh in cold water and drain in a colander. Shell the eggs and cut in half lengthwise. Reserve.

Arrange the eggs, cut side upwards, and the leeks in an appropriate ovenproof dish. Pour over the sauce, scatter the breadcrumbs on top and bake for 25 minutes, when the crumbs will have gratinéed and the sauce will be volcanic, bubbling hot.

Serve with proper sourdough bread if you can get hold of some.

Chilli, Corn and Coriander Soufflé

The 'Big Three' of Mexican cooking – corn, chilli and coriander – like being treated in this Gallic way. A novel brunch dish, it is equally good as a single lunch or supper dish. Serve overlooking the Ocean. Hola! French and nautical.

FOR 4

115 g / 4 oz [²/3 cup] corn kernels
1 tbsp olive oil
1 tbsp white breadcrumbs
55 g / 2 oz [4 tbsp] butter
45 g / 1 ¹/2 oz [¹/3 cup] flour
450 ml / ³/4 pt [2 cups] milk
5 tbsp dry sherry
1 bay leaf
2 spring onions [scallions]
1 fresh red serrano-type (hot) chilli
30 g / 1 oz [¹/4 cup] Parmesan cheese, freshly grated
6 eggs
salt and pepper

If using fresh corn, cut the kernels from the ears and blanch them for 3-4 minutes in rapidly boiling, lightly salted water. Refresh in cold water and drain. If frozen, defrost in a colander, allowing water to drain off.

Preheat the oven to 180°C/350°F/gas4. Brush a 20 cm / 8 in soufflé dish with olive oil. Add the breadcrumbs and turn the dish to impart a thin coating all over.

Melt the butter in a saucepan, stir in the flour and cook this roux briefly until lightly coloured. Then whisk in the milk and sherry. Add the bay leaf and season with salt and pepper. Cook over a low heat for 20 minutes, stirring from time to time.

Trim the spring onions, and remove seeds from the chilli. Shred both as finely as you can. Stir the shreds into the sauce after 15 minutes. Stir in the corn and Parmesan. Remove from the heat.

Separate the eggs and beat 4 of the yolks into the sauce, one at a time. Whisk the whites to soft peaks. Stir in 1 heaped tablespoon to lighten the sauce, then add the sauce to the whites and fold in gently.

Pile the mixture into the soufflé dish. Put on a baking sheet and bake for about 12-15 minutes. When cut open, the centre should still be quite liquid.

Huevos en Rabo de Mestiza

Eggs poached in a tomato-and-chilli sauce sounds good, but not as glamorous as huevos en rabo de mestiza. Serve the dish at the table from the pan in which it is cooked, with some warm ciabatta (page 54) on the side to mop up the sauce.

Good-quality tomato ketchup, being made exclusively from tomatoes, vinegar, salt and sugar, is beneficial to many dishes. If you don't add ketchup to the sauce, then put in a little sugar to accentuate the natural sweetness of the tomatoes.

A heavy non-stick frying pan is ideal for cooking and serving the eggs. Whatever the pan, choose one which has a lid. At the risk of stating the obvious, you will almost certainly have a saucepan lid which will fit. I hesitate to point this out, but somebody did write to me once complaining that frying pans don't have lids. Hmm.

FOR 6

6 eggs
225 g / 8 oz onions
4 tbsp olive oil
2 garlic cloves
900 g / 2 lb canned plum tomatoes
4 tbsp tomato ketchup or
   2 tsp sugar
1 bay leaf
handful of flat-leaf parsley
4 fresh green Anaheim-type
   (medium-hot) chillies
55 g / 2 oz [¹/₂ cup] Parmesan
   cheese, freshly grated
salt and pepper

Slice the onions thinly. Fry them gently in the olive oil until they are soft and translucent.

Chop the garlic and add that, together with the tomatoes (with their liquid), the ketchup or sugar and the bay leaf. Increase the heat and bubble, stirring, until most of the liquid has evaporated.

Remove the bay leaf and put the sauce into a food processor with half the parsley, chopped. Blitz to a purée and return to the pan. Remove seeds from the chillies, cut into strips and add. Season with salt and pepper and return to a simmer for 5 minutes.

Break the eggs one at a time into a saucer, then slide them into the sauce. Put a lid on the pan and cook gently until the whites have set but the yolks are still liquid.

Scatter the Parmesan and remaining whole parsley leaves over, and take to the table bubbling hot.

Smoked Salmon with
Scrambled Eggs and Latkes

Stay up Saturday night, clubbing, ending up in a casino so you can lose all your money at roulette or blackjack. Do not go to bed before 6am. Doze fitfully until 9am. Shower, take two Alka-Seltzers with an espresso and try to pick up the papers. Discover they are too heavy to lift. Drive in a fragile fashion to brunch where Bloody Marys are drunk from 11 am. You will need them as your fellow brunchers are ghastly and, yes, they do help the hangover. When the food arrives, switch to champagne. Your appetite has returned just as they take away your untouched plate. Eat a croissant with strawberry jam and some melon with ginger. Drink Marc de Champagne throughout the afternoon. Around 4, decide that brunch is GREAT. Funny how you can jump to the wrong conclusions: your fellow brunchers are really special human beings. Let's do this again next Sunday, people! Bribe the valet to keep your car parked and go home by cab. Retire to bed wounded for a little pre-dinner nap at 6 pm. Wake at 1.30 am. Drink a litre of cold San Pelegrino. Eat aspirins and Temazepam. Consider a contemplative and reclusive life. Stare at the ceiling and await Monday morning feeling pretty grim about everything.

LA's Tinsel Town has a very big Jewish community. Latkes are Jewish potato cakes that can be heavy enough to break the plate, particularly when fried in chicken fat, and in Fit World they are now a rarity produced exclusively by people's mothers for duty get-togethers like Chanukah. These are lighter and, being fried in only a little sunflower oil in a non-stick pan, not quite as engrossant. So eat.

Preheat the oven to 180°C/350°F/gas4.

First make the latkes: whisk the eggs and milk in a mixing bowl. Whisk in the matzo meal. Cut the onion into tiny dice and stir this in. Season with salt and pepper.

Wash the potatoes and pat dry, but don't peel. Grate them in a food processor using the finer of the 2 grating discs. Put into a drying-up cloth and squeeze dry. Stir into the bowl.

8 eggs
30 g / 1 oz [2 tbsp] butter
2 tbsp crème fraîche
350 g / 12 oz smoked salmon
salt and pepper
small bunch of chives, to garnish

FOR THE LATKES:

2 eggs
125 ml / 4 fl oz [½ cup] milk
4 tbsp matzo meal (from the
    kosher section of any
    supermarket)
115 g / 4 oz onion
450 g / 1 lb baking potatoes
    (peeled weight)
4 tbsp sunflower oil
salt and pepper

Heat a large non-stick pan over a low heat. When the pan is hot, turn up the heat and add a tablespoon of oil. Spoon the mixture into the pan to make 4 individual cakes with a diameter of about 5 cm / 2 in. Turn down the heat and cook slowly for 6-8 minutes, when the underside will be crisp and golden brown. Turn and give them 3-4 minutes on the other side. Transfer to a metal tray and put into the oven while you cook the next batch.

While the last batch of latkes are cooking, scramble the eggs. Whisk them lightly and season with a little salt and pepper. Melt the butter in a pan and pour in the eggs. Cook gently, stirring with a wooden spoon. At the outset you only need to stir once a minute, pushing the spoon firmly into the base rim because that is where the curds form first. As the curds start to form properly you must stir continuously and remove the pan from the heat before they are completely done as their internal heat and the residual heat of the pan will continue the cooking process. Stop the cooking process and enrich the eggs at the same time by beating in the crème fraîche.

Put the smoked salmon on cold plates and spoon the scrambled eggs next to them (never on top). Add 2 latkes and garnish with 3 cm / 1¼ in lengths of chives. Serve at once, while the eggs and latkes are still hot.

Appropriately in a book which takes its inspiration from a place where all rules are made to be broken...

… the choice of main courses draws on many cultural starting points and influences. These are the kinds of dishes which you can eat over and over again without ever getting bored, which ultimately is the true test of what is good food and what is not.

Gado-gado

Gado-gado is an Indonesian salad which could have been created to hit the California fusion salads spot. It is made from a mixture of cooked and raw vegetables, which may include beansprouts, green beans, cucumber, carrots, cauliflower, cabbage and spinach, but which is always bathed in a sweet peanut sauce. New Jersey Royal potatoes are best for this dish but when they are not available use a small waxy potato like Pink Fir Apple or Charlotte.

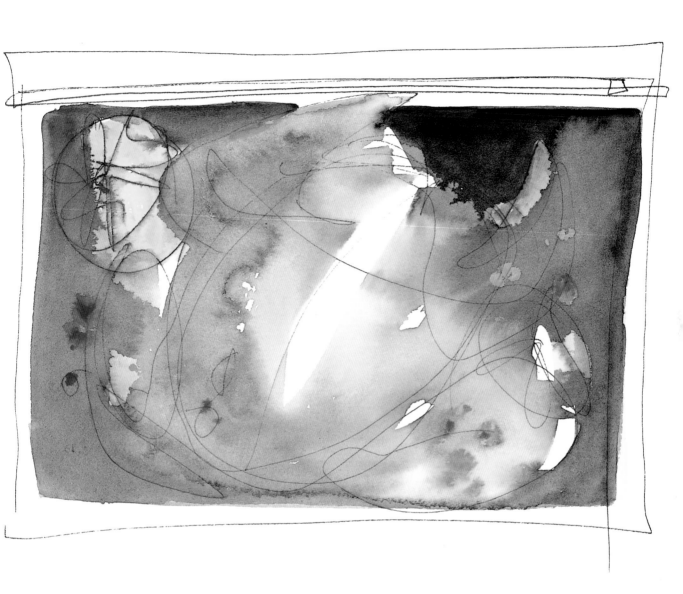

I large carrot

170 g / 6 oz green beans

I small cauliflower

225 g / 8 oz spinach

225 g / 8 oz white cabbage

350 g / 12 oz potatoes

115 g / 4 oz beansprouts

½ cucumber [English hothouse
    cucumber]

FOR THE PEANUT SAUCE:

170 g / 6 oz [1⅓ cups] raw
    peanuts (in the shell)

115 g / 4 oz onion

3 tbsp sunflower oil

2 garlic cloves, chopped

2 fresh hot red chillies,
    deseeded and shredded

2 tsp caster sugar [US
    granulated sugar]

2.5 cm / 1 in piece of root
    ginger, peeled and grated

juice of 1 lemon

salt and pepper

Cook the vegetables in a large pan of salted boiling water using a blanching or chip basket so you can do them individually, giving each the minimum time in the water to deliver a barely cooked result.

Peanuts tend to be sold roasted, salted and shelled. You can buy raw peanuts in Asian grocers or pet shops – they sell them for parrots, apparently…

First make the sauce: shell the peanuts into a food processor and blitz to a fine grainy mush. Dice the onion and fry in the sunflower oil until lightly caramelized, then add the garlic and the chillies. Fry for another minute, then add the peanuts with the sugar and the ginger. Turn up the heat and add 375-450 ml / 12-15 fl oz [1½–2 cups] water. Bring to the boil, reduce to a simmer and cook gently for 20 minutes, stirring from time to time. Remove the sauce from the heat and stir in the lemon juice. Season with salt and pepper to taste.

While the sauce is finishing, peel the carrot and cut into neat batons. Trim the beans and cut in half. Cut out the base of the cauliflower and separate the florets. Pick over the spinach and pull off any large stems. Shred the cabbage. Boil the peeled potatoes until just tender in lots of lightly salted water. Drain in a colander set in another pan and return the water to the boil. Refresh the potatoes in cold water, peel and cut across into thick slices.

Now cook the beans and carrots for 2-3 minutes, the cauliflower florets and cabbage for 1 minute, and the spinach and beansprouts for 30 seconds, refreshing each batch of vegetables in cold water before draining. Arrange on a large serving plate.

Cut the cucumber into matchstick strips and scatter these over the top. Pour over the sauce while it is still warm and serve the dish at room temperature.

Spanish Rice

Older Californians – a species not always immediately identifiable other than by tortoise-neck, now octogenarians watch morning TV from the Stairmaster – will tell you that before the war, Spanish rice was pretty close to being the Californian national supper dish. The recipes I was given were pretty basic stuff, but this rather more contemporary version is made special by the inclusion of both oven-roasted tomatoes and red sweet peppers. The rice is also cooked first rather than measuring the liquid and doing the whole thing in one go. Traditionally Spanish rice is topped with Monterey Jack cheese, America's inferior version of Cheddar. Here we replace it with mozzarella, making it even less Spanish but much nicer.

Oven-roasted tomatoes and sweet peppers crop up so often you should cook them once a week and keep them in oil in the fridge until needed. They are great things for impromptu meals when people turn up unexpectedly. You can make an instant tomato or pepper tart by arranging them on a sheet of frozen puff pastry, do a brilliant frittata or make a pipérade with a difference, all in minutes. And roasted peppers on their own make a lovely salad, dressed with lemon juice and oil.

FOR 4

285 g / 10 oz [1²/₃ cups] long-
    grain rice
1 red onion
125 ml / 4 fl oz [¹/₂ cup] olive
    oil
2 fresh hot green chillies
4 tsp fresh oregano leaves or
    1 tsp dried oregano
6 roasted red pepper halves,
    peeled (see page 26)
about 16 roasted tomato
    halves (see page 26)
115 g / 4 oz fresh buffalo
    mozzarella cheese
salt and pepper
45 g / 1¹/₂ oz [3 tbsp] butter
slices of toasted baguette and
    unsalted (preferably
    Normandy) butter,
    to serve

Preheat the oven to 180°C/350°F/gas4 and grease a gratin dish with a little of the butter.

Slice the onion and put in a heavy-based saucepan with a little oil over a low heat. Cook until it wilts. Cut the chillies in half lengthwise, strip out the seeds and discard. Cut the chillies into julienne strips, add to the pan and cook for 2-3 minutes. Add the oregano.

At the same time, bring a large pan of salted water to a fast boil. Pour in the rice and cook for 8 minutes. Test a grain. It should be just al dente. If not, continue to cook, testing every 30 seconds until you are happy. Drain the rice through a sieve and reserve. This basic technique will give you perfect fluffy rice every time.

Add the cooked rice to the onion mixture and stir to coat. Cut the roasted peppers into strips and stir these in, then season with salt and pepper to taste.

Arrange the tomato halves on the bottom of the prepared gratin dish, then spoon the rice mixture over, pressing down gently with the back of a spoon. Dot the top with the remaining butter and bake in the preheated oven for about 15 minutes.

Drain the mozzarella, slice thinly and then dice small. Remove the dish from the oven and sprinkle the cheese evenly on top. Return to the oven to bake for a further 10 minutes, or until the cheese is melted and bubbling hot.

Mill lots of black pepper over the top before bringing to the table in the dish. Serve immediately with slices of toasted baguette and unsalted Normandy butter.

Variation:

If you are so inclined, you can add 115 g / 4 oz pancetta, smoked streaky bacon [smoked thick-sliced bacon] or ham. Cut into lardon strips and fry gently with 4 tablespoons of olive oil until they start to crisp, then stir them into the rice mixture.

Tiger Prawns in Sesame Yeast Batter with Spiced Potatoes

FOR 4

20 raw tiger prawns [large
    shrimp], peeled and
    deveined
sunflower oil, for deep-frying
bunch of chives, to garnish
2 bunches of watercress, to
    serve
2 limes, to serve

FOR THE SESAME YEAST BATTER:
350 ml / 12 fl oz [1 1/2 cups]
    hand-warm water
6 g / 1/4 oz sachet of easy-blend
    instant yeast
I tsp salt
1/2 tsp caster sugar [US
    granulated sugar]
225 g / 8 oz plain flour [1 2/3 cups
    all-purpose flour], plus more
    for dusting
2 tsp turmeric
2 tsp sesame seeds
I tsp salt
I tsp pepper

FOR THE SPICED POTATOES:
550 g / 1 1/4 lb small waxy potatoes
2 tsp mustard seeds
2 tsp cumin seeds
I tsp coriander seeds
I tsp black peppercorns
2 tbsp sunflower oil

This has entertaining parallels with fish and chips. The batter delivers a very crisp finish and the spiced potatoes are baked in the oven rather than deep-fried. Use a small waxy potato, like Desirée, Charlotte or Belle de Fontenay.

Tiger prawns are widely available frozen and you can sometimes get them fresh. Along with squid, they freeze exceptionally well, though the quality varies from brand to brand as does the amount of frozen water you pay for. They are usually sold headless. This obviously affects the price and the value by weight.

Never force defrosting by putting them in hot water as this will make them go fibrous and soggy when cooked. To sweeten them, put into quite heavily salted water and swirl for a minute or two, rubbing gently with your fingers. Throw away the salt water, rinse the prawns under cold running water and leave to drain in a colander.

First make the batter: put the water in a bowl and whisk in the yeast, salt and sugar. Then whisk in the flour, turmeric, sesame seeds, salt and pepper. Cover the top with plastic film and leave for 2 hours at room temperature.

Preheat the oven to 220°C/450°F/gas7.

Prepare the spiced potatoes: toast the mustard, cumin and coriander seeds with the peppercorns in a small dry frying pan over a low heat for 3 minutes. Grind coarsely in a coffee grinder. Cut the potatoes lengthwise into quarters. Put the oil in a large bowl and stir in the spices. Add the potatoes and toss and turn to coat. Transfer to a baking sheet or Swiss-roll pan [shallow baking pan] and bake for 35-40 minutes, occasionally shaking the pan. About 10 minutes before the potatoes are ready, preheat the oil for deep-frying to 190°C/375°F.

Stir the batter. Turn the prawns in flour, shake off any excess and dip into the batter, tapping them on the side of the bowl to get rid of any excess. Deep-fry for 4 minutes and drain on paper towels.

Serve with the potatoes, a handful of watercress and half a lime on each plate. Scatter snipped chives over the potatoes and sprinkle with salt.

Tiger Prawn Sauté with Fresh Chilli Salsa

Tiger prawns are the best kind of fast food, taking no more than 2-3 minutes when stir-fried in a heavy pan that you have preheated to smoking hot.

People have been encouraged to think that stir-frying is something exclusively carried out in a wok. This is not true, and the wok for most people is an inefficient piece of kit because they use it on ordinary hobs. The round base of the wok was originally used buried in red-hot charcoal, and today Chinese restaurants have special gas ranges with holes into which the base comes in contact with a ferocious flame. The woks now available with flat bases are obviously better in the usual domestic kitchen and the only kind which can be used with an electric hob.

A large and heavy iron pan is what you want for stir-frying the prawns for this dish and it is also the best thing for searing fish. Non-stick pans, like the Le Creuset range, are great to work with, but non-stick surfaces do not like being exposed dry to very high heat. Indeed, Le Creuset states specifically that you should not do so because it damages the surface quickly and their pans are too expensive to treat as disposable.

To get the maximum life out of any non-stick pan, each time you use it first warm it through over the lowest heat, gradually increasing it. Never put a non-stick pan straight on to a high heat or indeed, into an oven hotter than 200°C/400°F/gas6. Inevitably you break these rules, but the less often you do so, the longer your pans will stay in good shape.

FOR 4

*900 g / 2 lb raw tiger prawns
   [large shrimp]*
3 tbsp Chilli Oil (page 40)
1 tsp ground cumin
1/2 tsp salt
1/2 tsp black pepper
4 fresh hot green chillies
5 cm / 2 in piece of root ginger
12 spring onions [scallions]
*4-6 tbsp Basic Salsa Cruda
   (page 37)*
handful of coriander [cilantro]

If the prawns are frozen, take them out of the freezer and spread on a tray to defrost at room temperature. This usually takes about 3-4 hours, but will take less if the kitchen is hot or if you are preparing them in Death Valley, where the hottest temperature ever recorded was 57°C/134°F. Sweeten them as described on page 142.

Peel them and cut down through the back to remove the intestinal thread. Wipe clean with a paper towel. When cutting down through the prawn, go about halfway through. This exposes a larger surface area to speed cooking and also means the prawn will fan open attractively. Rinse the shells (and heads, if any) and use to make a fish stock (freeze them only if fresh).

Put the prawns into a bowl with the chilli oil, cumin, salt and pepper. Toss to coat and reserve. The prawns can now be refrigerated for several hours before cooking but, if so, remove them at least 30 minutes beforehand to bring them to room temperature. Note that the raw prawns have a bluish tint and are ringed with darker blue stripes.

Remove stem and seeds from the chillies. Cut into julienne strips. Peel the ginger and cut into similar very thin sticks. Put on small plates and reserve.

Put the pan to heat through. When smoking hot, throw in the prawns, the whole spring onions and half the ginger strips. Sauté, tossing, stirring and turning, until you judge them to be done. The flesh will be white and opaque and the blue rings will now be red. Immediately add the salsa and toss all the contents of the pan together.

Remove from the heat and serve at once on warmed plates. If you leave them in the hot pan they will continue cooking and toughen. Scatter with whole coriander leaves and offer the julienned green chillies and the remaining ginger on the little plates for people to help themselves.

Seared Scallops with Fennel and Olives

The simplest cooking treatment is best for scallops and they must only be cooked very briefly or their expensive and delicate flesh will be turned into rubber. Here they are briefly seared and served with a clean-tasting salad of fennel, tomatoes, olives and flat-leaf parsley.

Ask your fishmonger to open and clean the scallops for you, quite a tricky task. You could use fillets of cod, bream or red mullet if decent-sized scallops are not obtainable.

FOR 4

12 king scallops [sea scallops] with coral

1 fennel bulb

5 tbsp extra-virgin olive oil, plus more for brushing

juice of 1 lime

4 spring onions [scallions]

12 pitted black olives

4 oven-dried (8 halves) plum tomatoes (see page 26)

good handful of flat-leaf parsley leaves

salt and pepper

extra-virgin olive oil, to dress

Wash and trim the fennel, saving the feathery leaves if present. Shave the fennel into wafer-thin slices on a Benriner mandolin (see page 200) and put into a bowl with the olive oil and lime juice. Top and tail the spring onions, shred and add to the bowl. Cut the tomato halves in half and add with the olives and a good handful of whole parsley leaves, reserving some for garnish. Season with salt and pepper and toss again, then mound on 4 plates.

Heat a non-stick pan over a low heat and, when hot, turn up the heat to hot. Detach the corals from the scallops and slice each scallop across into 2 discs. Brush corals and white flesh with olive oil and season lightly. Lay them in the pan, flat surface downwards, for 30-45 seconds. Turn and give the other surface 30-45 seconds.

Place around the salads. Dribble over a little extra-virgin olive oil. Sprinkle salt and grind pepper over the scallops.

Sea Bream with Basil Beurre Blanc

FOR 4

4 sea bream [porgy] fillets,
*   each weighing about 170g/*
*   6oz*
450g/ 1 lb spinach
2 tbsp extra-virgin olive oil, plus
*   more for dressing*
bowl of ice-cold water
salt and pepper

FOR THE BASIL BEURRE BLANC:
55g/2oz shallots
1 garlic clove
170g/6oz [³/4 cup] chilled
*   unsalted butter*
100ml/3¹/2fl oz [7tbsp] dry
*   white wine*
100ml/3¹/2fl oz [7tbsp] white
*   wine vinegar*
3tbsp crème fraîche
12 basil leaves

Sea bream is a firm, lean fish and perfect for pan-broiling – the technique by which it is placed in a very hot dry pan and then, after a brief exposure to heat from below, is finished under the grill [broiler]. The dish is served on a bed of spinach, which also benefits from the sauce. The beurre blanc sauce could as easily be scented with tarragon, chervil or rosemary.

Beurre blanc must be the restaurant sauce of the 'Eighties and 'Nineties, which is particularly ironic in California where butter is generally viewed with the same warmth a rat feels for Warfarin. Restaurants frequently mount as much as 450g/1 lb of butter into a sauce for four, but this recipe calls for only 170g/6oz.

Have the fishmonger cut the bream off the bone for you to produce four 170g/6oz fillets and ask him to remove the pin bones. It is still advisable to check there are none left by running your finger along the bone line of each fillet against the grain. Pull out any that have been missed with a heavy-duty pair of tweezers or small pliers.

Put on a large pan (ideally with a blanching basket) of lightly salted water to boil. Pick over the spinach, detaching any large stems. When the water is boiling fast, blanch the spinach for 20-30 seconds and immediately transfer to a bowl of ice-cold water to refresh and stop the cooking. Reserve, keeping the water in the pan hot.

Brush the fish fillets with olive oil, season with salt and pepper and reserve.

Start the basil beurre blanc: finely chop the shallots and garlic. Put the shallots and garlic in a pan with 30g/1 oz [2 tbsp] of the butter and sweat gently until soft, but do not allow them to colour. Add the white wine and wine vinegar, increase the temperature and bring to the boil. Reduce quickly until you are left with only 1 tablespoon of syrupy residue.

Add the crème fraîche and lower the heat. Cut the remaining butter into 2 cm / ¾ in dice and whisk into the residue, one piece at a time. The sauce will emulsify and become smooth and homogenous. Taste, adding salt and pepper as liked. Pass through a fine sieve into a bowl set over the hot water. Shred the basil and stir in.

While finishing the sauce, preheat a hot grill [broiler] and heat a dry pan until very hot. Lay the fillets in the hot pan, skin side down, for 60 seconds to brown them. Then put the pan under the grill for 2-3 minutes.

During this time, plunge the spinach back into fast boiling water for 15 seconds. Drain well and distribute between 4 warmed plates, mounding into a neat pile in the centre and spooning 3 tablespoons of basil beurre blanc around the spinach. Lay the bream on the spinach, skin side up. Brush the skin with a little olive oil to gloss the surface and serve at once.

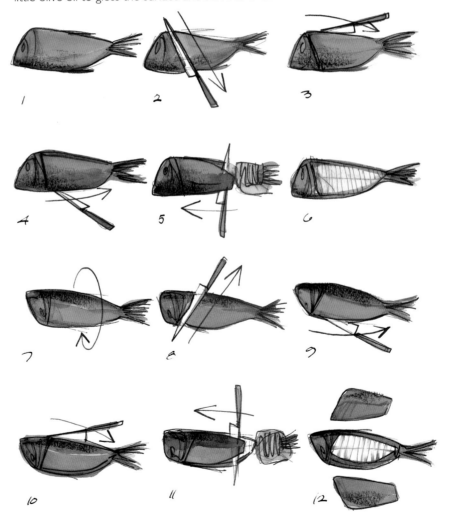

Pan-fried Lemon Sole in Polenta Crumbs with Cajun Rémoulade

FOR 4

*4 whole white-skinned slip
   sole [or flounder]*

30 g/ 1 oz [3 tbsp] flour

2 eggs, lightly beaten

*115 g/4 oz polenta flour [1 cup
   polenta or cornmeal]*

4 tbsp olive oil

55 g/ 2 oz [4 tbsp] butter

little sunflower oil

salt and pepper

2 bunches of watercress, to serve

*1 lemon, cut into quarters
   lengthwise, to serve*

FOR THE CAJUN RÉMOULADE:

*575 ml/ 1 pt [2^1/3 cups] Basic
   Mayonnaise (page 46)*

6 spring onions [scallions]

2 tbsp chopped flat-leaf parsley

2 anchovy fillets

*2 fresh hot red chillies,
   deseeded*

2 tbsp chopped chives

1 tbsp capers

1 tbsp Dijon mustard

3 tbsp tomato ketchup

juice of 1 lemon

1 tbsp Worcestershire sauce

Sand dabs are a great Californian treat, small flat fish that are usually simply fried in butter. You eat several at a serving. I used to spear fish for dabs while snorkelling as a child, but you rarely see them on the fishmonger's slab. However, slip or small lemon sole are as good treated the same way and are here served with a spicy Cajun rémoulade. Cajun cooking may be a long way east, but this is too good a sauce to be geographically picky about it. Serve with boiled new potatoes, mashed potatoes or fries. Alternatively, serve with the spinach in a nutmeg béchamel (see opposite).

First make the Cajun rémoulade: chop the spring onions, parsley, anchovies, chillies, chives and capers and beat these into the mayonnaise, together with the other ingredients.

Lightly dust the fish with flour. Brush with beaten egg, then coat with polenta flour.

Put 2 frying pans (each large enough to hold 2 fish) on to heat. Put the olive oil in and heat over a medium heat. When hot, add the butter, swirl and immediately lay in the fish. Fry for 3 minutes and turn. Add a little sunflower oil to either pan if all the fat has been absorbed frying the first side. Cook for a further 2 minutes, when the soles will be golden brown and nicely crisped but moist and succulent within.

Serve on warmed plates with a bunch of watercress and a quarter of lemon on each. Offer the rémoulade in a sauce-boat for people to help themselves at the table.

Broiled Halibut and Hallucinatory Spinach

Spinach cooked this way is delicious as a dish in its own right or it can set off any grilled or poached fish or chicken admirably. Cheese, spinach and nutmeg go together so well you know their partnership must have been ordained by a higher power.

The nutmeg gives the title to the dish. Did you know it contains a volatile oil called myristicin which will, in large quantities, makes you see things? I got quite excited when I first heard this from an old hippie whom I met in Santa Barbara zoo as we both ducked the excrement being thrown at the visitors by a cross elephant. The conversation inevitably turned to grass and other substances, as you would expect, talking to somebody whose thin and fragrant cigarette was clearly not a product of any known tobacco giant. 'There's a lot of things the good Lord put on this earth to get you high and nutmeg's one of them,' he said. I grated on a lot to see if hallucinations would attend the next meal, but it turns out you would have to eat about three whole nutmegs before your vision even flickered and even then you would get a vile headache. Don't worry: myristicin is also present in carrots, and when did you ever get high on them?

Nutmeg is the seed of the fruit of Myristica fragrans, the tropical nutmeg tree which originated in the Moluccas (the so-called Spice Islands), but is today cultivated in many tropical countries, with Grenada the single largest producer. The seed is covered with a red fibrous membrane which separates it from the flesh of the fruit. When dried and flattened this becomes mace. Mace and nutmeg do smell and taste similar and are interchangeable, though mace is stronger in flavour. In the seventeenth and eighteenth centuries, nutmeg was so popular that people had their own silver nutmeg-holders and - graters that they would take with them when they went out to dinner.

Mace and nutmeg should be kept whole in small quantities in airtight jars, since the oil is given off in time and the flavour lost. Their unique flavour enhances both sweet and savoury custards and is particularly good in cheese

*sauces. It can be used instead of cloves in a bread sauce and as an
alternative to vanilla in ice-cream. It is invariably added, as here, to a
béchamel sauce.*

*For some reason you find halibut steaks on every fish counter in California.
This dish is equally good with cod or haddock cooked in the same way or with
poached brill or turbot.*

FOR 4

*4 halibut steaks, each weighing
    about 200g / 7 oz*
450 g / 1 lb spinach
30 g / 1 oz [2 tbsp] butter
30 g / 1 oz [3 tbsp] flour
575 ml / 1 pt [2¹/₃ cups] milk
5 tbsp dry sherry
¹/₄ nutmeg
85 g / 3 oz Parmesan cheese
1-2 tbsp olive oil
*55 g / 2 oz [4 tbsp] Roasted Red
    Pepper, Chive and Parmesan
    Butter (page 44), chilled*
salt and pepper

Pick over the spinach and blanch briefly in rapidly boiling salted water, refresh
in cold water, then drain. Melt the butter in a saucepan, stir in the flour and
cook this roux for 2 minutes, until lightly coloured. Whisk in the milk and
sherry. Season with salt and pepper and grate in the nutmeg. Simmer, stirring
from time to time, for 20 minutes. Then grate in two-thirds of the Parmesan.
Whisk again, fold in the spinach, heat through gently and keep warm while you
cook the fish.

Heat a dry heavy frying pan (large enough to hold the halibut steaks in one
layer) over a medium heat, and preheat an overhead grill [broiler]. Brush the
fish with olive oil on both sides and season with salt and pepper.

Lay the halibut steaks in the smoking-hot pan and transfer it to under the
grill after 30 seconds. Cook until the flesh of the fish is white and just firm to
the touch, say 2-3 minutes.

Put a halibut steak on each warmed plate, top with a disc of chilled
flavoured butter and mound the sauced spinach beside it. Shave the remaining
Parmesan over the spinach.

Roasted Monkfish in Fig Leaves

The idea of wrapping delicate flesh in leaves to keep it moist while imbuing them with their flavour during cooking no longer seems a radical treatment, but the use of fig leaves had never occurred to me until, at Alice Water's suggestion, I tried roasting halibut in them and discovered that they impart a delicate taste of coconut to the fish. You can try this with any firm-fleshed white fish fillet, but it is particularly effective with monkfish, which is more moist than halibut and has a greater resilience to the oven. It is served with a mound of Thai fragrant rice flavoured with cardamom seeds. A rice steamer is a desirable piece of special kit and not expensive.

FOR 4

2 tail sections of monkfish, each weighing 400-450 g/ 14-16 oz

225 g/8 oz [1 1/3 cups] Thai fragrant rice

5 cardamom pods

4 large fig leaves

bowl of iced water

4 tbsp extra-virgin olive oil

salt and pepper

1 lime, to serve

About 45 minutes before you want to eat, wash the rice in a sieve under cold running water until all the starch has gone and the water runs clear. Leave to stand and dry for 15 minutes. Put into the steamer with the rinsed cardamom pods and the requisite amount of water as the manufacturer instructs and switch on. When the rice is cooked, the steamer automatically switches to the 'keeping warm' mode and will hold the rice in perfect condition for several hours. (For how to cook measured amounts of rice and water in an ordinary saucepan, see page 196.)

Cut off the slippery outer membrane from the monkfish tails, then cut the fillets away from the flexible central bone. Alternatively, cut down either side of the bone and slide the knife outwards at an angle to the membrane, pushing outwards. This detaches it.

Preheat the oven to 200°C/400°F/gas6.

Holding them with tongs, dip the fig leaves into boiling water for 2 seconds, then refresh in a bowl of iced water.

Lay a leaf on the work surface, shiny side up. Brush a fillet on both sides with olive oil and season lightly with salt and pepper. Place on a leaf and fold the leaf up and around the fish, tucking it in to make a package. Place folded side down on a Swiss roll [shallow baking] pan or tray. Repeat with the other 3, then pour 100 ml/3 1/2 fl oz [7 tbsp] of water around them.

Roast for 10-15 minutes, checking after 10 minutes to see if they are done. Do this with the tip of a knife – the flesh should be firm and opaque.

Serve the fish beside a pile of fragrant rice, together with a wedge of lime cut lengthwise.

Salmon Teriyaki with Roasted Carrots and Fragrant Steamed Rice

Teriyaki is a Japanese grilling sauce made from soy sauce, sake and sweet rice wine. It is perfect with oily fish like mackerel and salmon. Seared salmon and tataki are my favourite ways of eating the great fish, which is actually not a big treat for me because I had far too much of it as a child growing up by the River Tweed, one of our finest salmon rivers. Salmon would appear in different guises but tasting, unfortunately, all too strongly of salmon: salmon fish pie, salmon fish cakes, pan-fried salmon and so on ad infinitum. The trouble is that when you have to face salmon on a regular basis the flavour becomes too intense, almost cloying. Perhaps if I had been given salmon teriyaki the way Californians like to eat it I might have felt differently.

FOR 4

4 wild salmon tail fillets, each about 2 cm / ^{3}/$_4$ in thick

2.5 cm / 1 in piece of peeled root ginger

2 lemons

5 tbsp Kikkoman soy sauce

4 tbsp mirin (Japanese rice wine)

3 tbsp sake

450 g / 1 lb carrots

2 tsp caster sugar [US granulated sugar]

3 tbsp olive oil

350 g / 12 oz [2 cups] Thai fragrant rice

salt and pepper

Grate the peeled ginger on to a piece of muslin or cheesecloth. Squeeze this into a bowl to extract the juice. Add the juice of 1 lemon and reserve. Bring the soy, mirin and sake to a boil in a small saucepan, remove from the heat and allow to cool. Then add to the citrus and ginger juices. This glaze can be made well in advance and kept covered in the fridge.

Preheat the oven to 230°C/450°F/gas8.

Peel the carrots and cut off the stems. Cut lengthwise into 1 cm / ^{1}/$_2$ in slices. Put these in an ovenproof dish, sprinkle on the sugar, spoon the olive oil over and season with salt and pepper. Roast for 40 minutes, turning halfway through. The exterior should caramelize.

Cook the rice in an electric steamer or in an ordinary saucepan as described on page 196.

Preheat an overhead grill [broiler] to medium. Brush the fillets all over with the glaze and put under the grill, skin side up. Cook for 3 minutes, brushing more glaze on while it grills. Turn and cook the other side for 2 minutes, again brushing on more glaze. When done the salmon will be glazed dark brown.

Serve on warmed plates with a mound of carrots and some steamed fragrant rice. Quarter the remaining lemon lengthwise and put a piece of it on each plate.

Grilled Tuna with Borlotti Beans and Wasabi Soy Dressing

If there is one fish that shouts California at you then it is tuna. Perhaps it is so popular because this is the fish closest to meat, and a lot of Californians now don't eat meat. Tuna, however, gives them a meat experience while they feel good thinking fish. It is also caught in the Pacific.

Of course, it is never called just plain 'tuna' there, but by specific type – ahi, yellow-tail, blue-fin, all sounding sexier on the menus. It is a very fashionable fish, whatever you call it, and one which is now more widely available though its quality is often unacceptable. I have seen tuna on supermarket wet fish counters that should not have been on sale, but then it deteriorates very fast once butchered and whatever they say to the contrary, supermarkets are not good with fish.

If you were to take a Japanese to look at the tuna sometimes on offer in my local market he would commit seppuku rather than eat it. Incidentally, if you are lucky enough to have a Japanese fishmonger near you, then this is the best place to buy tuna. Wherever you do manage to find it, the flesh should be a shiny moist red and not have an iridescent oily sheen on the surface or be dull-coloured. Both indicate oxidization from exposure to the air.

It may sound excessive, but when buying fish it is a good idea to take a cold bag with you, particularly in the summer. If you put your lovely fresh tuna in the boot of a car on a hot day and leave it there for a couple of hours, give it to the cat immediately when you get home because it won't be fit for human consumption. You will be spending a lot of money on it, so it pays to keep it cold.

As soon as you get it home, take it out of the bag, trim off any bloody bits and skin, then brush with olive oil. Wrap in plastic film and refrigerate until ready to use, which must be the same day. It is not going to become technically inedible, but the sooner you eat it the better.

We are cooking it here Japanese-style, seared crusty on the outside and raw in the middle. The dressing is very Japanese too.

4 tuna steaks cut from the
    belly, each weighing about
    140-200g/5-7oz
350g/12oz [2 cups] dried
    borlotti beans
2 garlic cloves, peeled and
    sliced
1 fresh hot red chilli
1 bay leaf
3 tbsp extra-virgin olive oil,
    plus more for brushing and
    dressing
4 tbsp Kikkoman soy sauce
2 tsp wasabi powder
1 tbsp Dijon mustard
handful of flat-leaf parsley
salt and pepper
1 lemon, to serve

The day before: rinse the beans, cover with cold water by 5 cm/2 in and leave to rehydrate overnight.

Next day, bring to the boil and boil hard for 5 minutes. Drain, rinse, return to the pan, cover with fresh water and return to the boil. Add the garlic, chilli and bay leaf. Lower the heat and simmer for 1–1½ hours or until just tender. Season with salt and pepper. Stir, remove from the heat and reserve in the cooking liquid.

Heat a dry ridged grill pan until very hot. Brush the tuna steaks with oil and season with salt and pepper on both sides. Lay the steaks on the pan at an angle of 45 degrees to the ridges. Sear for 30 seconds and turn to sear the other side, laying it in the same direction. Turn after 30 seconds and this time lay at 45 degrees in the opposite direction. Turn finally after 30 seconds, laying it in precisely the same direction. This will produce on both sides a neat cross-hatch called quadrillage (see pages 202-3). Transfer to a cold plate.

Mix to a paste 3 tablespoons of soy sauce with 3 tablespoons of olive oil and the wasabi powder. Drain the beans and toss with this dressing while still hot. Mound on 4 plates.

Mix the remaining soy sauce with the Dijon mustard and brush the outside of the steaks with this. Cut the steaks on the bias into 5 slices. Serve the tuna on top of the beans. Dress with a little extra-virgin oil, scatter around with whole parsley leaves and serve at once, still warm. Quarter the lemon lengthwise and put a piece on each plate.

Cheese and Anchovy Peppers with Fry-and-steam Courgettes

Once you have roasted and peeled your peppers, you have ammunition for many meaningful skirmishes. Here they form the basis for a quick lunch. Total preparation and cooking time is 15 minutes.

Preheat the oven to 250°C/475°F/gas9. Lay the roasted pepper halves in a roasting pan.

Drain the mozzarella and cut it into 8 pieces. Shave the Cheddar into wafer-thin slices with a cheese slicer. Shave 2 of the garlic cloves into paper-thin slices.

8 roasted pepper halves,
    peeled (see page 26)
1 buffalo mozzarella cheese
55 g / 2 oz Cheddar cheese
4 garlic cloves
16 anchovy fillets (1¹/₂ x 60 g /
    2 oz cans)
450 g / 1 lb courgettes
    [zucchini]
2 tbsp olive oil
6 pitta breads
small bunch of chives
salt and pepper

Put 2 anchovy fillets in each pepper half. Distribute the Cheddar evenly among them on top of the anchovies. Lay the garlic slices on top, then cover them with the mozzarella. Dribble over the oil from the anchovy can(s) and grind on some pepper. Reserve.

Put a frying pan or shallow saucepan with a lid over a low heat.

Trim the courgettes, cut in half lengthwise and then slice into 5 cm / 2 in pieces at an acute angle. Slice the remaining garlic as before.

Put the peppers in the oven, and preheat the grill [broiler]. Put the olive oil in the pan and turn the heat up to high. Throw in the courgettes and sauté vigorously for 1 minute. Add the garlic and shake. Put on the lid, turn down the heat and cook for 3 minutes. Remove the lid and shake again. Some of the cut faces will have browned. Remove from the heat and leave in the pan, uncovered.

Toast the pitta breads briefly under the grill, say 1 minute one side and 30 seconds the other. Cut them in half.

Divide the courgettes among 4 warmed plates. Snip 3 cm / 1¹/₄ in lengths of chives over them and put 3 pitta halves next to them.

The peppers are done when the cheese is melted and bubbling. They should be ready just as you finish putting the pitta on the plates. Put 2 halves of peppers on the remaining third of each plate and serve immediately

Red Snapper en Papillote with Fennel and Potato Purée

An ideal fish for roasting or baking, red snapper has long been popular along the West Coast of the United States and is now widely available in Britain. Try cooking it en papillote in foil parcels and serving it with a creamy fennel and potato purée.

Preheat the oven to 210°C/425°F/gas7. Trim the fennel bulb and wrap it in foil with 1 tablespoon of the olive oil and the garlic clove. Bake for 40 minutes.

Meanwhile, cut out 4 foil circles large enough to fold in half and crimp sealed with the fish inside.

Wash and trim the leeks, slice into fine strips and sweat in the butter for a few minutes until soft. This procedure eliminates some of the excess water from the vegetable.

Pile equal quantities of leek on each of the 4 foil circles, positioning it to one side of the centre. Lay the fish on top, spoon over the butter, season with salt and pepper and place a lime leaf on top of each. Then fold the foil over and crimp the edges to make a moisture-resistant seal.

While the fennel is cooking, bring a pot of salted water to the boil and cook the potatoes. Drain and return to the pan, then mash dry with a potato masher. Keep warm.

Place the four papillotes in an ovenproof dish in which they will just fit in a single layer and put in the oven towards the end of the fennel cooking time. Open one papillote after 15 minutes and test to see if the fish is cooked by pushing the tip of a sharp knife in at the backbone and lifting gently. If the flesh comes away easily it is done; if not, reseal and cook for a further 5 minutes.

When the baked fennel and garlic are done, put them in a food processor with the parsley, reserving a few whole leaves for garnish. Add the remaining olive oil and purée. Add to the potato and mash together. Taste and season. Put in a warmed serving bowl. Put a disc of the chilled flavoured butter on top and scatter over the remaining whole leaves of parsley.

Put the papillotes on plates and let your guests open them themselves, with the purée in the centre of the table.

Pan-broiled Cod with Spiced Lentils and Coriander

This technique, where the fish is started skin side down in a smoking hot dry pan and then finished under a grill [broiler], is very effective with a lot of fish and delivers a beautifully crisp and golden brown skin. Lentilles de Puy are the finest lentils in the world, dark green and with a marvellous flavour. They take less cooking than other lentils so should be cooked only until just done, never to a porridge like an Indian dal. While agonizing over the potential demise of the cod, I hypocritically continue to cook it.

FOR 4

900 g / 2 lb cod fillet(s)
350 g / 12 oz [1 $\frac{3}{4}$ cups] Puy
   lentils
4 plum tomatoes
4 garlic cloves
6 shallots
2 fresh hot red chillies
5 tbsp sunflower oil
2 Kaffir lime leaves
2 whole cardamom pods
2 tsp turmeric
1 litre / 1 $\frac{3}{4}$ pt [1 qt] fish stock
   (page 25)
juice of 1 lime
150 ml / $\frac{1}{4}$ pt [$\frac{2}{3}$ cup] crème
   fraîche
2 tbsp Thai fish sauce
3 red onions
4 tbsp olive oil
handful of coriander [cilantro]
$\frac{1}{2}$ tsp dried hot chilli flakes
salt and pepper

Remove the pin bones from the fillet(s) with small pliers, pulling in the same direction as the grain of the fish. You can feel them running along the side of the fillet where the thick part meats the thinner edge. They are quite tough to extract and, if you find it impossible, cut down on the thick side of the bones, detaching the thick part from the thinner flap. This can be used in a different dish, for example the Too-good-for-the-band Crab Cakes (page 104) or frozen and kept for a fish soup. Trim the fillet(s) into 4 neat rectangular portions.

Blanch the tomatoes in boiling water for 30 seconds, refresh and peel. Scoop out the pulp and seeds, cut the flesh into 1 cm / $\frac{1}{2}$ in dice and reserve. Smash and chop the garlic. Dice the shallots and shred the chillies.

Put 3 tablespoons of sunflower oil in a pan over a low heat, add the chopped vegetables, the lime leaves, whole cardamom pods and turmeric and fry over a low heat, stirring, for 5 minutes. Add the lentils, stir and pour in the fish stock and lime juice. Bring to the boil, lower the heat and simmer for 15 minutes, when the lentils should be just cooked.

Remove the lime leaves and cardamom pods and discard. Stir in the crème fraîche and fish sauce. Taste and season with salt and pepper. Keep warm over the lowest heat.

Cut the onions in half, then across into the thinnest slices you can manage. Sweat in the olive oil for about 5 minutes, or until translucent. Pick the leaves from the coriander and reserve.

Put a dry frying pan over a medium heat to get it smoking-hot and preheat the grill [broiler]. Brush the fish steaks with sunflower oil, then season with chilli flakes, salt and pepper and lay them in the pan. After 60 seconds, transfer the pan to under the grill for about 3 minutes. The cod should just be cooked through but not falling apart. Remove.

Stir half the coriander into the onions and half into the lentils. Put a ladleful of lentils and sauce on each warmed plate. Lay a cod steak on top, crisp skin up, and finish with a spoonful of wilted onions and coriander around the fish.

Broiled Cod with Angel-hair Beans

FOR 4

4 portions of white fish, skin on but pin bones removed, each weighing about 200g/ 7oz
450g/ 1 lb angel-hair (fine) green beans
bowl of ice-cold water
5 tbsp olive oil
1 garlic clove
salt and pepper
1 lime, to serve
extra-virgin olive oil, to dress

Trim the beans and blanch for 3 minutes in rapidly boiling salted water. Refresh in ice-cold water, drain and reserve.

Brush the fish steaks with oil on both sides and season generously with sea salt and black pepper.

Smash and chop the garlic finely. Put with 3 tablespoons of the oil in a pan with a lid and reserve.

Preheat a dry heavy frying pan to smoking-hot. Preheat an overhead grill [broiler]. Lay the fish skin side down in the pan and sear for 60 seconds. Transfer the pan to under the grill and continue cooking for about 2 minutes. The flesh should now be opaque and firm to the touch, just cooked but still moist. Transfer to warmed plates or soup plates.

Heat the oil and garlic over a high heat. As the garlic bubbles, add the beans, toss and put on the lid. Cook for 30 seconds and serve immediately, mounding the beans next to the cod and putting a quarter of lime, sliced lengthwise, on each plate. Fashion dictates that the cod is served skin side up, an irritation you can safely ignore. Dribble a little extra-virgin olive oil on the fish and serve at once.

Cod Fillet al Mojo de Ajo

Walk to the end of Santa Monica pier and you will find a group of rather sad-looking men casting their lines into the ocean. Their melancholy may be caused by the signs warning that the state government wants you to know that the sea is so polluted you eat what you catch at your own risk, a depressing state of affairs. By the boardwalk at the shore end of the pier you can sit at a muscle-man bar, eating nachos and sipping ice-cold beer, watching the in-line skaters loop by, one beautiful girl after another in figure-hugging haute couture sportswear. The bar also has two warning signs, the first threatening what amounts to system meltdown if you drink alcohol, the second saying that you are in a designated smoking area and that it has been determined that passive smoking can cause lung damage, birth defects and premature death. Since the bar is open-fronted you feel that the risks may be somewhat exaggerated.

A brilliant way of cooking any fish from clean sea water is al mojo de ajo – with garlic sauce – a dish I first ate in Mexico, far from the ocean but as fresh as if the fish had just been landed. The technique of slow-cooking thinly sliced cloves of garlic until golden brown is very Mexican and opposes received wisdom that browned garlic is bitter garlic. To avoid bitterness, the garlic is slowly cooked until golden in a mixture of olive oil and butter, but must not be allowed to take on too dark a colour. The result is sweet, aromatic and nutty.

FOR 4

*4 cod fillet steaks, skin on, each
    weighing about 200 g / 7 oz
55 g / 2 oz [4 tbsp] unsalted butter
5 tbsp olive oil
12 large garlic cloves
juice of 2 limes
handful of coriander leaves [cilantro]
flour, for dusting
salt and pepper*

Over a low heat, put the butter and olive oil in a frying pan large enough to hold the fish in a single layer and not touching. Peel the garlic and cut into wafer-thin slices. Fry gently, stirring, for 3-4 minutes or until just taking colour. Pour into a sieve set in a bowl and leave to drain.

Dredge the fish in seasoned flour. Turn up the heat, pour the oil and butter back into the pan and fry the fish, skin side down, for 2 minutes. Turn carefully, lower the heat a little and cook for a further 2-3 minutes. Transfer to warmed plates, skin side up.

Return the garlic to the pan, add the lime juice and 1 tablespoon of chopped coriander. Stir, bubble through and spoon over and around the fish. Garnish with whole coriander leaves.

Roast Herbed Chicken

Wherever you travel in California you will find a chicken turning on a spit in front of an upright grill, the flames glowing and flickering. This is quintessential California cuisine, simple and pure. The technique is what was originally called roasting and there is no better way of cooking a bird to this day. Twenty years ago, many domestic ovens came with rôtisserie attachments. These days you hardly ever see them. The best we can do is learn how to emulate the process by using our ovens to maximum effect.

The first prerequisite is a genuine free-range chicken. Our supermarkets are understandably secretive about what precisely they mean by the labels they stick on chickens claiming a free-range provenance, since most of them are raised in hangar-like sheds. Forget any rosy images of Rhode Island Reds strutting around farmyards. All we can assume is that they are not the product of a battery. The point is that if you want a genuine free-range chicken you can buy a poulet de Bresse imported from France. The only snag is the price, around £6 per 450 g / 1 lb at retail. Other controlled denominations – poulet jaune, poulet noir and label rouge – are also fine free-ranging chickens, and are not quite so expensive.

Given you have a decent bird, the next requirement is fresh herbs and sea salt, and the last fruity olive oil. Those who have tradition driven deep will insist on using lots of butter when oven-roasting chickens. There is a distressing tendency in restaurants the world over to use butter excessively and automatically, swirling it into sauces by the handful, ladling it over fish and swamping it over vegetables. If people knew how much butter and cream some chefs use their heart attacks would be precipitated earlier than God had planned from sheer disbelief. This chicken manages very nicely without butter, as do most roast birds in California.

Over the years my roasting technique for chicken has changed. I started out slavishly rotating the bird to sit on its back, breast, each side and back to breast but have found that the effort involved delivers no discernible benefit. For a couple of years I stuffed something under the breast skin – herbs, pancetta, you name it, it got stuffed. I have experimented with higher temperatures and lower temperatures, with convection and without it and with a grill-and-fan combination which delivers the best result of all. Working with chefs who rarely time anything and always work with hot ovens has moved me to cook at a hotter temperature, but has not persuaded me that basting is essential. If you cook the bird on a rack, breast side down for the longest period, only moving it breast side up for the last 10-15 minutes, it will always be succulent, the skin crisp, the presentation pleasing. If the bird has been stored in the refrigerator, remember to take it out well ahead of time to let it come to room temperature.

When carving, remove the legs and thighs first before cutting off the breasts whole. These are then cut on the bias into thick slices. The legs are cut through the joint and separated from the thighs and all are presented on a serving dish with the cooking juices from the roasting pan poured over. People then help themselves.

With the chicken, serve unpeeled baby potatoes roasted in chilli oil with whole garlic cloves or mashed potatoes and a simple gravy reduction. The small potatoes roast in 40-45 minutes, the garlic in 20.

FOR 4

1 free-range chicken, weighing
about 1.35 kg/3lb
2 garlic cloves
handful of flat-leaf parsley
1/2 tbsp chopped tarragon
1 tbsp fresh oregano
4 tbsp extra-virgin olive oil
juice of 1 lemon
salt and pepper

Preheat the oven to 250°C/475°F/gas 9.

Smash and mince the garlic. Pull herb leaves from the stems and chop. Rub the body cavity with the garlic, then fill loosely with the herbs. Brush the chicken all over with olive oil and season generously all over with salt and black pepper.

Put to roast on a rack, breast side down. After 35 minutes, turn breast side up. Squeeze the lemon juice over, spoon over the remaining olive oil and sprinkle with a little more salt, then return to the oven for a final 15-20 minutes roasting, turning the temperature down to 220°C/425°F/gas7.

Remove from the oven and allow to rest in a warm place for 15 minutes before cutting up and carving.

Chicken Teriyaki with Oyster Sauce Beansprouts

Teriyaki is a lovely grilling glaze, but it is sticky because of the sake and mirin – dry and sweet rice wines – and burns easily. It is therefore important to start grilling the meat with nothing on it but salt and pepper, before brushing with the glaze as it starts to cook. Both sake and mirin can be bought from Oriental markets. Chicken is one of the nicest things to grill teriyaki-style and you should use a mixture of thigh and breast meat.

Make 12 skewers, which should not be overloaded but look pleasingly minimalist. Soak and chill the bamboo skewers before grilling, as on page 110.

675 g / 1 1/2 lb mixed chicken
   breasts and thighs
juice of 1 lemon
5 tbsp Kikkoman soy sauce
4 tbsp sake
4 tbsp mirin
3 cm / 1 1/4 in piece of root ginger,
   peeled
8 spring onions [scallions]
sunflower oil, for brushing
salt and pepper

FOR THE OYSTER SAUCE BEANSPROUTS:
450 g / 1 lb [4 cups] beansprouts
2 garlic cloves
4 spring onions [scallions]
5 cm / 2 in piece of root ginger,
   peeled
1 tbsp toasted sesame oil
2 tbsp sunflower oil
2 tbsp oyster sauce

The day before, start by boning out the thighs. Then cut the thigh meat and breast meat into rectangles about 3 x 2 cm / 1 1/4 x 3/4 in. Put into a zip-lock bag with the lemon juice, soy sauce, sake and mirin and leave to marinate in the refrigerator overnight.

Pour the marinade into a pan. Peel and chop the ginger and cut it into tiny dice. Add to the marinade, bring to the boil and immediately remove from the heat. Allow to cool, then strain through a sieve to remove the ginger.

Preheat an overhead grill [broiler] or charcoal grill. Wipe the chicken with a damp cloth and thread on to 12 skewers, putting a quarter of a spring onion crosswise between each piece. Brush the chicken with a little sunflower oil and season with salt and pepper.

Grill, starting 13 cm / 5 in away from the heat. Brush on the marinade after 2 minutes and turn. Brush the other side and turn back after a further 2 minutes. Repeat, giving them a total of 5 minutes each side. They should be a burnished mahogany colour outside and cooked all the way through, but still moist and tender within.

While the chicken is grilling, cook the beansprouts: put a wok or large frying pan over a medium heat. Smash and chop the garlic and trim the spring onions. Slice the onions at an angle into thirds. Cut the ginger into matchstick strips. Put the sesame and sunflower oil into the pan and, as they start to smoke, throw in the garlic, spring onions and ginger. Stir-fry for 30 seconds, then add the beansprouts and stir-fry vigorously for 2 minutes. Stir in the oyster sauce and toss to coat evenly.

Mound to one side of each plate, with 3 teriyaki skewers on the other.

Salad S. Berger Style

Le Dôme on Sunset Boulevard is a legendary Hollywood restaurant where top agents deal over lunch, sipping endless glasses of iced tea. It sits discreetly on the south side of Sunset and has a vaguely classical frontage of honeyed stone and glass, with tiny lights strung in the trees outside that shine at night like diamonds. The chef is French, the waiters are professional waiters.

It is necessary to spell this out since the majority of LA's smart dining rooms are staffed by resting actors who make a point of not writing down your order but memorizing it and showing you a lot of porcelain-capped teeth when they insist on taking you through the menu and the day's specials. If you are very unlucky this will be done in a crouch next to the table so you get sympathy twinges at the back of your knees. By the time they conclude their recitation you have forgotten everything except that the last dish was not anything you would ever want to eat.

Le Dôme isn't like that. It is a proper restaurant, it serves terrific food and it is presided over by Eddie. It is his place and he runs it as a restaurant should be run – without familiarity and with complete professionalism. Restaurants come and go, but it remains my favourite place to eat in LA unless I want to eat Chinese and then it is Joss, just down the road.

In the main dining room of Le Dôme at a table which commands the best view of the room and immediate eye-contact with his assigned waiter sits Shelly Berger, a manager and agent who came to LA many years ago from his native Brooklyn. Shelly started out as an actor, sensibly moved to the controlling side of Tinsel Town and has, over the years, run some of the biggest names in show business, among them Diana Ross and Michael Jackson. For several years he was part of Berry Gordy's team, helping make Motown great, and his current acts still include The Temptations and The O.J.'s. He is a very funny man, who will keep you breathless with laughter throughout lunch. He loves good food and good wine. He liked it when I told him that you never grow old at the table. And he is the only person in the long and distinguished history of Le Dôme to have a dish named after him. There it is on the menu, 'Salad S. Berger Style'.

Like all the best deal-making salads this one is chopped. This means you don't have to take your eyes off the person opposite to do anything distracting like manipulate a knife on the plate, which might make you miss some tell-tale duplicitous blink or facial tick.

FOR 4

1 free-range corn-fed chicken,
    weighing about 1.35 kg / 3 lb
1 onion, halved
1 carrot, cut into 4
2 bay leaves
2 celery stalks
12 black peppercorns
140 g / 5 oz inner leaves from
    a Savoy cabbage
140 g / 5 oz red cabbage
4 ripe plum tomatoes
20 pitted black olives
115 g / 4 oz [^{2}/$_3$ cup] cooked
    chickpeas [garbanzo beans]
    salt

FOR THE DRESSING:

300 ml / ^{1}/$_2$ pt single cream
    [1 ^{1}/$_4$ cups light cream]
300 ml / ^{1}/$_2$ pt [1 ^{1}/$_4$ cups] Basic
    Mayonnaise (page 46)
1 ^{1}/$_2$ tbsp red wine vinegar
1 ^{1}/$_2$ tbsp Dijon mustard
1 tbsp Worcestershire sauce
salt and pepper

Put the chicken in a pot and cover with cold water. Bring to the boil, skim and reduce the heat to a simmer. Add the onion, carrot, bay leaves, celery, ^{1}/$_2$ tablespoon of salt and the whole black peppercorns and cook for 50 minutes. Remove and leave to cool. Keep the cooking liquid in the pan.

Cut off the base of the Savoy cabbage and strip off the outer leaves. (Keep these to use for a stuffed cabbage dish like Chicken and Cabbage Dolmades on page 169) Weigh 140 g / 5 oz of leaves, cut into bite-size pieces [about 2 cups] and put into a mixing bowl.

Cut off the base of the red cabbage, strip off the outer leaves and discard. Cut in half. Weigh one half and then cut off 140 g / 5 oz. Cut into bite-size pieces [about 2 cups] and add to the bowl.

Blanch the tomatoes for 30 seconds. Refresh in cold water and peel. Cut into quarters, strip out the seeds and pulp and discard. Cut each of the quarters into three and add to the bowl. Chop the olives and add. Stir in the chickpeas.

Pull the skin off the chicken and remove the breasts and thighs. Cut the thigh meat off the bone and cut into bite-size pieces. Slice the breast meat on the bias into bite-size pieces. Add to the salad.

Put the bones back into the cooking broth, return it to the boil, lower the heat and simmer for 3-4 hours. Strain and keep this stock for another dish.

Whisk all the dressing ingredients together. Taste and season with salt and pepper. Pour over the salad and toss before mounding on individual plates.

Eat while looking intently at the person opposite. Drink a decent Merlot. Make them laugh. Salad S. Berger style.

Pan-roast Chicken with Chilli Balsamic Vinaigrette and New Potatoes

California leads the world in dietary awareness. People there are now so worried about animal fat they think you are a button man if you put any on their plates. Chicken breasts cooked in a dry pan without any lubricant save the fat from the skin are hardly fried, so perhaps pan-roast is a more accurate description.

Chicken breasts benefit from slow and gentle cooking, emerging succulent and tender. Cooked aggressively over a high heat, they are in danger of being dry and tough. This recipe specifies chicken suprêmes, that is the breast attached to the first joint of the wing, but this is really a matter of aesthetics rather than flavour.

They will take about 15 minutes to cook, but precisely how long will depend on how low the heat is under the pan. With experience you can gauge when they are done by pressing gently with a finger. This is good practice since in a busy kitchen it is all too easy to forget exactly when you put the chicken on the hob.

The first Jersey Royal new potatoes in early May are delightful. They will not have formed a full skin and need only to be scrubbed before being boiled. Steaming new potatoes makes no sense at all. Plenty of just boiling water is the best method. Serve them with a knob of the Lime, Orange and Mint Butter (page 42). If using Jersey Royals towards the end of the season, it is probably best to peel them.

FOR 4

4 chicken suprêmes, skin on
500 g / 1 1/4 lb Jersey Royal or
  other new potatoes
I tbsp olive oil
55 g / 2 oz [4 tbsp] Lime,
  Orange and Mint Butter
  (page 42)
4-5 tbsp Chilli Balsamic
  Vinaigrette (page 36)
handful of flat-leaf parsley
salt and pepper

Make the vinaigrette as directed and reserve.

Put a large pan of lightly salted water on to heat. As it boils, add the potatoes to it, then put a dry non-stick pan over a low heat.

Brush the flesh side of the suprêmes with oil and season both sides with salt and pepper. Lay them in the pan, skin side down. Turn the suprêmes after 5 minutes and again after a further 5 minutes. Continue cooking until you judge them to be done, when they feel resilient to the push of a finger, which will take about 15 minutes.

Drain the potatoes when they are just tender. Transfer the chicken to a cutting board and leave to stand for 5 minutes, then slice on the bias into 4 pieces. Put on warmed plates, overlapping.

Stir the vinaigrette and spoon over and around the chicken. Put a few potatoes on each plate, with a piece of the Lime Butter on top. Scatter a few whole parsley leaves over all and serve at once.

Pan-roast Chicken Sandwiches with Bread and Butter Pickles and Superior Slaw

FOR 4

4 chicken suprêmes, skin on
I tbsp olive oil
8 thick slices of good bread
plain crisps [potato chips], to
    serve
salt and pepper

FOR THE BREAD AND BUTTER
PICKLES:
1.5 kg / 3½ lb pickling
    cucumbers
450 g / I lb onions
iced water
I litre / 1¾ pt [I qt] cider
    vinegar
I kg / 2¼ lb caster sugar [5
    cups granulated sugar]
3 tbsp salt
3 tbsp yellow mustard seeds
2 tbsp celery seeds
I tbsp dill seeds
I tbsp coriander seeds
I tbsp white peppercorns
2 bay leaves

America is sandwich land and the diner sandwich – which includes hamburgers in buns and huge split rolls called heroes – will always be close to the nation's soul. Pickles, coleslaw and potato chips are constant companions. This sandwich can be made with any kind of bread, but is especially nice served on a ficelle or baguette. Alternatively, give it a very different feel and use warm focaccia (page 53). This coleslaw is a very superior version, not remotely bland like the commercially produced stuff, and you won't have to pay silly prices for it.

Cindy Pawlcyn's Fog City Diner is situated on the Embarcadero by the edge of San Francisco Bay and is a joyous reinvention of the American classic roadside diner, where you stop for hamburgers and fries. She has moved the quality of the diner experience several hundred miles down the road, but it remains a place to celebrate American food at its best. Cindy's bread and butter pickles are famous, as delicious as they are easy to prepare. You need to find the small pickling cucumbers, otherwise the ingredients are straightforward. When eating pickles, always remember that old Jewish saying, 'a pickle on your lips, a pound on your hips'.

This pickle recipe is essentially hers, and only some of the amounts have been changed to protect the innocent.

FOR THE SUPERIOR SLAW:

1.35 kg / 3 lb hard white cabbage

2 garlic cloves

575 ml / 1 pt [2¹/₃ cups] Basic
    Mayonnaise (page 46)

2 tbsp Dijon mustard

2 tsp sugar

2 tbsp white wine vinegar

1 tsp salt

1 tsp black pepper

3 carrots

1 red sweet pepper

1 green sweet pepper

1 fresh jalapeño-type (very
    hot) chilli

1 red onion

6 spring onions [scallions]

3 celery stalks, with their
    leaves

3 tbsp chopped flat-leaf parsley

At least a day ahead, make the pickles: slice the cucumbers 1 cm / ¹/₂ in thick. You could do this lengthwise or across. Peel and cut the onions into wedges and put with the cucumbers in a large bowl. Cover with iced water and leave to soak for 2 hours.

Put the cider vinegar into a pan with 500 ml / 16 fl oz [2 cups] water, the sugar, salt, mustard seeds, celery seeds, dill seeds, coriander seeds, white peppercorns and bay leaves. Bring to the boil.

Drain the cucumbers and onions and return to the bowl, then, just off the boil, pour the pickling liquid over them. Stir, weight with a plate to keep them all submerged and, when cool, refrigerate for at least 24 hours before serving.

If you keep them in sterilized screw-top jars and only ever remove the pickles using a scrupulously clean slotted spoon or tongs, they will keep in the fridge for 3 or 4 months, maybe more.

To make the coleslaw: smash and chop the garlic and put into a bowl with the mayonnaise. Beat in the mustard, sugar, wine vinegar, salt and pepper. Shred the cabbage and peeled carrots. Slice the red and green peppers. Cut the chilli into strips, then cut them across into 5 mm / ¹/₄ in dice. Peel and dice the red onion. Trim the spring onions and slice them thinly. Trim and dice the celery. Chop the celery leaves and stir in with the parsley. Mix all the ingredients together so that every element is coated with mayonnaise. If not, add a few more spoonfuls of it and toss to cover evenly.

Make the chicken sandwiches: brush the suprêmes with the oil and season with salt and pepper. Cook in a dry non-stick pan over a low heat, starting skin side down and turning at intervals until just done, which will take about 15 minutes depending on size and how low you have the heat. Allow to rest for 10 minutes, then carve at an angle into thick slices. Make the sandwiches without butter.

Put the sandwiches on plates with bread and butter pickles, coleslaw and plain crisps next to them.

Lemon Grass Chicken with Fragrant Rice

For this dish use chicken thighs, which you can buy in packets in supermarkets. Cut through the bones using a cleaver for authenticity. Alternatively, bone them and cut across into bite-size pieces.

Lemon grass is a stiff elongated bulb-like grass made up of tightly rolled, rather tough leaves of which only the bottom 15-17.5 cm/6-7 in are used. It has a sweet, aromatic and powerful lemony flavour and features widely throughout South-east Asia. It is one of the fundamental flavourings of Thai cooking, where it is called takrai. Trim off the hard base, then cut across into the thinnest slices you can achieve. Never use dried lemon grass, which tastes like cheap soap.

The following recipe is from Vietnam, though variations on the theme can be found in Thailand, Malaysia, Indonesia and California – which has embraced South-east Asian themes with a vengeance.

If you can't find palm sugar, substitute muscovado.

The day before: chop the chicken into bite-size pieces or bone and cut each into 3.

Make the marinade: trim the lemon grass and slice across as thinly as you can into rounds. Put into a bowl, pour over the boiling water and leave to soak for an hour.

Now smash and chop the garlic clove and add with the ginger, tomatoes, palm sugar, turmeric, chillies and seasonings. Mix together, then put in the chicken pieces and turn to coat evenly. Cover the bowl with plastic film and refrigerate overnight.

Next day: remove the marinating chicken from the fridge to bring to room temperature 2 hours before you start cooking.

Make the rice as described on page 196.

Fry the chopped garlic in smoking-hot sunflower oil in a large heavy pan or wok for a few seconds, then add the chicken pieces and all the marinade. Stir and toss.

Add the fish sauce, stir and cover with a lid. Bubble fiercely for 5-6 minutes, take off the lid and add the shallots. Stir, lower the heat and simmer until the chicken is just cooked, about 10 minutes.

Serve in bowls with the plain boiled fragrant rice garnished with whole coriander leaves.

FOR 4

8 chicken thighs
1 garlic clove, smashed and chopped
3 tbsp sunflower oil
2 tbsp Thai fish sauce
170 g/6 oz shallots, diced
whole coriander leaves [cilantro], to garnish

FOR THE MARINADE:
1 lemon grass stalk
4 tbsp boiling water
1 garlic clove
4 cm/1 1/2 in piece of root ginger, peeled and grated
225 g/8 oz [1 cup] canned tomatoes, drained and blitzed to a purée in the food processor
1 tbsp palm sugar
1 tbsp turmeric
2 small fresh, hot red chillies, deseeded and shredded
1 tsp salt
1 tsp pepper

FOR THE FRAGRANT RICE:
350 g/12 oz [2 cups] Thai fragrant rice
6 whole cardamom pods

Chicken with Cabbage Dolmades and Balsamic Sauce

San Francisco has 52 hills, of which Russian Hill – named after some sailors who were buried there – is one of the highest. Russians came to California early and there is a still a big Russian colony in San Francisco. Today the city has one of the largest Russian communities of any in the USA. Incidentally, when in San Francisco do not attempt to jump your hire-car off the top of even the lowest hill. Unlike in the movies, this cracks the sump.

This dish of stuffed cabbage is about as Russian as you can get unless you are Polish, in which case it is very Polish. Think of the balsamic vinegar as a present brought to a Russian cook who seizes upon its culinary inspiration and uses it to give a sweet-and-sour edge to the sauce without making it remotely astringent.

Any large-leaf cabbage of the Savoy type will do, or you could adapt the recipe to use 8 fresh, frozen or canned grape-vine leaves. This dish is based on one by chef Martin Webb of Quaglino's in London. He's not Russian or Polish, but an Australian citizen from Lancashire, England. You can't get more Californian than that.

FOR 4

1 free-range grain-fed chicken, weighing about 1.25 kg / 2 1/2 lb
olive oil, for brushing
30 g / 1 oz [2 tbsp] butter
1/4 nutmeg
salt and pepper

FOR THE CABBAGE DOLMADES:

1 Savoy cabbage
1 red onion
30 g / 1 oz [2 tbsp] butter, plus more for greasing
450 g / 1 lb pork mince [ground pork]
2 tbsp chopped flat-leaf parsley
225 g / 8 oz [1 1/3 cup] cooked long-grain rice
300 ml / 1/2 pt [1 1/4 cups] Chicken Stock (page 24)
salt and pepper

FOR THE SAUCE:

115 g / 4 oz shallots
2 garlic cloves
55 g / 2 oz [2/3 cup] mushrooms
30 g / 1 oz [2 tbsp] butter
150 ml / 1/4 pt [2/3 cup] dry sherry
3 1/2 tbsp balsamic vinegar
575 ml / 1 pt [2 1/3 cups] Chicken Stock (page 24)

Trim the cabbage, selecting the 8 largest leaves for wrappers. Cut out the stems and blanch the leaves briefly in a basket dipped in rapidly boiling salted water. Refresh in cold water, drain and reserve. Cut the remaining leaves into a chiffonnade.

Peel and dice the onion and sweat in the butter until soft and translucent. Put in a mixing bowl with the pork mince, chopped parsley and cooked rice. Season with salt and pepper and mix thoroughly with your hands.

Preheat the oven to 180°C/350°F/gas4 and butter a gratin dish.

Spread out a leaf, put on an egg-sized ball of stuffing, wrap the leaf over from each side, then roll into a neat sausage. Place in the buttered gratin dish, seam side down. Repeat with the remaining 7 leaves. Pour chicken stock around to halfway up the packages. Bake in the oven for 30 minutes and then remove. Increase the oven setting to 250°C/475°F/gas9.

Brush the chicken all over with olive oil and season with salt and pepper. Place breast down on a rack and roast for 30 minutes. Turn breast side up and lower the temperature to 200°C/400°F/gas6 and continue to cook for 20 minutes. Remove and allow to rest for 15 minutes.

While the chicken is cooking, make the sauce: peel and finely chop the shallots and garlic. Slice the mushrooms, then chop them. Sweat together in the butter until soft. Turn up the heat and deglaze with the sherry and vinegar.

Cook down to a residue, then add the stock and reduce by half, skimming frequently. Reserve.

Lower the oven back to 180°C/350°F/gas4 and return the cabbage dolmades for 10 minutes. Reheat the balsamic sauce. Blanch the julienne of cabbage leaves for 2 minutes in rapidly boiling salted water. Drain and return to the pan with 30g/1oz [2 tbsp] butter and some grated nutmeg and black pepper. Toss.

Carve the chicken breasts, legs and thighs from the bird, cutting each breast in 4. Put some cabbage in the middle of each of 4 warmed plates. Put 2 slices of breast and a leg or thigh on top and 2 cabbage dolmades on either side. Coat these with 2-3 tablespoons of sauce.

Albondigas with Olive and Wild Mushroom Sauce

FOR 4

285g/10oz chicken breasts
225g/8oz minced pork [ground pork]
100g/3¹/₂oz shallots, finely chopped
1 tbsp fresh white breadcrumbs
white of 1 egg
¹/₂ tbsp paprika
1 tsp dried oregano
285g/10oz [1²/₃ cups] long-grain rice
salt and pepper
sunflower oil, for frying
small bunch of chives, to garnish

These meatballs are made from a mixture of chicken and pork and are sauced with an intensely flavoured mixture of wild mushrooms and pitted black olives. Serve with steamed rice or buttered tagliatelle.

The sauce is a velouté, that is one which is based on a flour-and-butter roux. Outside of Cajun cooking, this is pretty much frowned on in restaurants these days and for all the wrong reasons. Far from being heavy or less subtle than a cream-thickened sauce, velouté has an honourable place in the kitchen. It goes wrong when it is cooked insufficiently to remove the raw flour taste. In this case it is finished with a little crème fraîche, which gives it a lovely silky consistency.

Start the sauce: pour 300ml/¹/₂pt [1¹/₄ cups] of very hot water over the mushrooms and leave to rehydrate for 1 hour. Drain in a sieve set in a bowl, reserving the liquid. Rinse the mushrooms under the tap, rubbing with your fingers to make sure there are no small stones, grit or twigs. These mushrooms were picked in a wood, so such foreign objects are not unknown. Strain the soaking liquid through muslin or cheesecloth or a washed (fragrance removed) J-cloth into a saucepan. Add the white wine and reserve.

Skin the chicken breasts and cut into cubes. Put through a mincer [meat grinder] or pulse-chop briefly in a food processor. Mix in a bowl with the pork, breadcrumbs, egg and spices, mashing to a coherent mass with a fork. Season, pull off a small piece and fry in a hot pan. Taste this: it is the only way to judge

FOR THE OLIVE AND WILD
MUSHROOM SAUCE:

55 g / 2 oz dried porcini or
   forestière mix
2 glasses of dry white wine
15 g / 1/2 oz [1 tbsp] butter
15 g / 1/2 oz [1 1/2 tbsp] flour
1 onion, finely chopped
1 garlic clove, finely chopped
12 pitted black olives
2 tbsp chopped flat-leaf parsley
3 tbsp crème fraîche

the seasoning. Add more salt and pepper if you think it needs it and mash in again to distribute evenly. Divide into walnut-sized pieces and roll into balls on a floured surface. Reserve on a lightly floured tray or plate.

Chop the mushrooms coarsely, discarding any dodgy-looking stems. Bring the white wine and mushroom soaking liquid to a boil, lower the heat and simmer for 10 minutes.

In another pan, melt the butter and stir in the flour to make a roux. Cook, stirring, for a minute, then stir in the hot liquid. Add the mushrooms, onion and garlic and cook over the lowest heat for 15 minutes, stirring. Chop the olives and stir in with the chopped parsley.

While the sauce is cooking, steam the rice in a rice steamer or cook in lots of rapidly boiling salted water for 8-10 minutes. Drain, put into a hot dish, fluff with a fork and keep warm.

After the sauce has been simmering for 10 minutes, heat a frying pan. When very hot, add the sunflower oil and the albondigas. Turn down the heat and fry gently, turning until nicely browned and cooked through, about 5-6 minutes.

Stir the crème fraîche into the sauce. Add the meatballs and stir together. Serve in bowls, garnished with chives snipped into 3 cm / 1 1/4 in lengths.

Talking Turkey, Meatloaf and Trimmings

If you want to taste a great roasted turkey go to Greenblatt's on Sunset Boulevard, where they serve it cold 365 days a year. Hollywood and Beverly Hills inhabitants are big consumers of turkey, for its low-fat moist white meat makes the perfect West-Coast sandwich. Greenblatt's version, however, being made up of wafer-thin slices piled high enough to give you lockjaw, is not for the faint-hearted.

Turkey is very much a part of the American delicatessen tradition. The rest of the nation talks turkey at Thanksgiving, which is more universally celebrated as a national holiday than Christmas in the USA. The turkey ritually consumed for lunch is potent symbolically since it was an indigenous bird enjoyed by the Pilgrim Fathers as part of the natural bounty of the new country, and integral to that first November feast of benediction the annual holiday recalls.

1 oven-ready turkey, ideally
   weighing about 4.5 kg / 10 lb
575 ml / 1 pt [2¹/₃ cups] Chicken
   Stock (page 24)
225 g / 8 oz unsmoked streaky
   bacon [unsmoked thick-
   sliced bacon]
150 ml / ¼ pt [²/₃ cup] olive oil
piece of butter or little cream
   (optional)
flat-leaf parsley, to garnish

FOR THE MEATLOAF:
170 g / 6 oz pancetta, in a piece
2 tbsp olive oil
285 g / 10 oz onions
3 garlic cloves
1 tbsp chopped tarragon
3 tsp dried oregano
¹/₂ nutmeg
2 tbsp Worcestershire sauce
3 eggs
450 g / 1 lb minced loin of pork
   [ground lean pork]
450 g / 1 lb premium pork
   sausagemeat
5 tbsp dry sherry
2 tsp salt
1 tsp pepper
170 g / 6 oz chicken livers
3 bay leaves
115 g / 4 oz thinly sliced Parma
   ham [prosciutto]

People the world over look upon these turkey-centred occasions with mixed feelings. They tend to confuse the size of the bird with generosity of spirit and come unglued when the moment of truth arrives and they have to cook a turkey the size of an ostrich. Since this happens but once a year for the majority, all lessons learned from the last turkey roast have been forgotten. How long and at what temperature? How to get the potatoes crisp without and floury within? What do you mean by 'giblet gravy'? And afterwards, staring at the remains and wondering how to dress them up and serve them afresh without family mutiny.

'Plan ahead' and 'keep everything simple' are the tactical watchwords to ensure that you will enjoy a traditional dinner along with everybody else. The critical thing is not to try to do too much on the day, but to apply the restaurant approach of mise en place, which means pretty much everything can be prepared in advance. This relieves pressure on the cook, gets things to the table on time and allows a more relaxed atmosphere to develop in the hours before lunch or dinner, surely more preferable than an aura of impending doom.

Familiar does not have to equate with dreary or monotonous, so introduce a note of vitality by making slight changes to the usual accompaniments, which in the States always include cranberry sauce and candied vegetables. Most importantly, improve the quality of everybody's life with the smallest turkey that is just enough to feed however many will sit at table. That giant brute with its pendulous breasts is a penance and brings with it the curse of leftover meat stretching grimly into the distant future. A 4.5 kg / 10 lb bird will easily feed 12 people.

Do not stuff the bird, but cook the forcemeat separately as a meatloaf, which can be easily sliced for serving. Any leftovers make great sandwiches. It is also a fine dish in its own right, with a little gravy and mashed potatoes.

Serve your Thanksgiving turkey and meatloaf with crisp roast potatoes, cranberry compote and caramelized carrots. A simple clear gravy of reduced chicken stock completes a truly celebratory plate of food.

Make the forcemeat 2 days before you want to cook it. This is convenient from a time point of view but also benefits the loaf, allowing the flavours to develop. Cut the pancetta into 5 mm / ¼ in dice and fry gently in the olive oil until its fat starts to run and the bacon darkens noticeably in colour towards brown. Peel and dice the onions into similarly sized dice and add to the pan. Continue to cook until soft and translucent. Add the garlic cloves, smashed and chopped. Fry and stir for a minute, then remove from the heat.

In a large bowl, put the tarragon, oregano, grated nutmeg, Worcestershire sauce and eggs. Beat together, then add the pork, sausagemeat, pancetta, onions, sherry, salt and pepper. Mix thoroughly with a fork.

450 g/ 1 lb [4¹/2 cups] fresh
  cranberries
grated zest of 1 orange
grated zest and juice of 1 lemon
1 sharp eating apple, peeled,
  cored and chopped
170 g/ 6 oz caster sugar
  [³/4 cup + 2 tbsp granulated
  sugar]

Pick over the chicken livers, cutting off and discarding any tubes, fat or green bits. Heat a dry frying pan until smoking hot, season the livers with a little salt and pepper and sauté vigorously for 60 seconds. Transfer to a cold plate and reserve.

Put 3 bay leaves down the middle of the bottom of a terrine or large non-stick loaf pan. Line this with the Parma ham, leaving some overhanging the sides which can be folded back to cover the top. Fill with half the forcemeat, packing down with a fork. Arrange the livers down the centre and cover with the remaining forcemeat. Smooth the surface level and bring the ham overhangs up over the top. Cover with plastic film and refrigerate.

Make the cranberry compote (you can make this several days in advance and keep covered in the fridge): put all the ingredients together in a saucepan and stew over a low heat for 30-45 minutes, then cool.

Your bird may not have giblets and even if it does, make a strong chicken stock (page 24) in advance (it will keep for a week in fridge or freeze as cubes). You use chicken wings, which are very cheap, added to the carcass of a cooked chicken.

Work your fingers under the skin of the turkey to detach and pull away from the breast meat, being careful not to tear holes in the skin. Push in the bacon to make a layer between the meat and the skin. This will help keep the breast moist during roasting. Return to the fridge or larder.

Calculate the cooking time for the turkey, which will be cooked using a combination of roasting at high heat followed by low heat. The bigger the bird, the fewer minutes per 450 g/ 1 lb:

• a 3.5-5.5 kg/ 8-12 lb bird will need 45 minutes at 220°C/425°F/gas7 followed by 1¹/2-2 hours at 160°C/325°F/gas3.

• a 5.5-6.8 kg/ 12-15 lb bird needs 45 minutes at the high heat followed by 2-2¹/2 hours at the lower.

• if you have a whopper of around 6.8-9 kg/ 15-20 lb, the same 45 minutes at the high heat then 2¹/2-3 hours at the lower temperature.

Work back from your estimated serving time and allow at least 20 minutes for the first course (which will more or less be the resting time for the cooked turkey). Write down your in and out times while drinking, muttering and cursing the imminent arrival of relatives, or forget overnight and do the calculations all over again the next morning.

Remove the bird from the refrigerator at least 2 hours before you start cooking it, brush it generously with olive oil and season with salt and pepper.

If you have giblets, put them in the roasting pan along with 300 ml/ ¹/2 pt [1 ¹/4 cups] of white wine and 575 ml/ 1 pt [2¹/3 cups] of water. This, with the drippings from the roasting bird and your previously prepared stock, will make the gravy.

Cover the bird loosely with foil and put on a rack in the roasting pan.

Position as high up the oven as space will allow, but with at least 2.5 cm / 1 in clearance above the bird to allow circulation of air.

Assuming you are sensible and are cooking a 4.5 kg/ 10 lb bird, preheat the oven to 220°C/425°F/gas 7 and roast for 45-50 minutes. Remove the foil, baste and lower the heat to 160°C/325°F/gas 3. Baste from time to time. Put the forcemeat into the oven below the turkey about 1 hour before the bird is due to come out of the oven.

Add some of the roasting juices to your prepared concentrated chicken stock and put in a pan to reduce over a medium heat.

As the first course is being served, remove the forcemeat loaf and turn off the oven. Allow the turkey to rest in the switched-off oven with the door open for about 30 minutes. Carve the bird, turn out the forcemeat and slice.

Taste the gravy and season if necessary. If you like, whisk in a bit of butter or add a little cream.

Unless being very grand, it is much easier to put the turkey and meatloaf on plates in the kitchen, offering the vegetables in serving dishes at the table. Just make sure your plates are hot. If oven space has made this difficult, put them in the sink and pour boiling water over them.

Garnish the turkey with a few leaves of flat-leaf parsley. Pass the gravy and cranberry compote in jugs or sauce-boats at the table.

Roast Squab with Saffron Mashed Potatoes

Squab are the best reared birds you can eat and very different in flavour and texture from their wild wood-pigeon cousins. Where the wood-pigeon is tough and lean, the squab is plump and succulent. Birds range in dressed weight from 350 g/ 12 oz to 500 g/ 1 lb 2 oz and one average-sized bird makes a generous single serving.

Squab are really doves that have been bred for the table. They have always been thought special in France and are now very popular in California and Australia. Apparently they are not produced commercially in Britain because the climate is too damp and leads to some kind of terminal infestation to which they are prone. Most squab are thus still imported to

Britain from France – where they are called pigeonneaux, as opposed to palombes or wood-pigeon – and are very expensive with plucked and cleaned birds currently selling wholesale in London at around £12 per kilo. Slightly cheaper Italian birds are starting to make an appearance.

Ask your butcher to check out the meat market. He will almost certainly have to buy a box at a time, so if he is not prepared to take that risk, set up a Squab Club with your friends, then you can buy whatever the minimum number is and the butcher will have no excuse to say no.

The best way to cook squab is straightforward, high-temperature roasting. Don't throw away the carcasses as they will make beautiful stock.

FOR 4

4 dressed squab, each weighing
   about 400 g / 14 oz
4 tbsp olive oil
1/2 glass of red wine
575 ml / 1 pt [2 1/3 cups] well-
   flavoured Chicken Stock (page
   24)
salt and pepper
bunch of chives, to garnish

FOR THE SAFFRON MASHED
POTATOES:
900 g / 2 lb floury potatoes
12-16 strands of saffron
5 tbsp double cream [heavy cream]
85 g / 3 oz [6 tbsp] butter

Remove the squab from the fridge 1 hour before cooking to allow to come to room temperature.

Preheat the oven to 250°C/475°F/gas9. Brush the birds all over with olive oil and season well with salt and pepper. Put on a rack, breast sides down and roast for 10 minutes. Turn breasts up and cook for a further 3-5 minutes. Remove and allow to rest in a warm place for 5-8 minutes.

As the birds go into the oven, add the wine to the chicken stock in a pan and reduce at a rapid boil. You want to end up with just a few tablespoons of intensely flavoured reduction. Keep warm.

You want the potatoes to be done 5 minutes after the birds come from the oven, since mashed potatoes are best when eaten immediately after they are mashed. You should therefore start cooking them when you switch on the oven. Peel the potatoes, put in a pan and cover with cold water. Add 1 tablespoon of salt and bring to the boil. Reduce the heat to give a gentle bubble and cook until just done, about 20 minutes.

Halfway through this time, bring the cream to a simmer in a small pan with the saffron threads and 55 g / 2 oz [4 tbsp] of the butter. Remove from the heat and allow to steep and colour.

Mash the potatoes dry with a potato masher. Never use a machine like a food processor or mixer, which causes the starch to exude from the potatoes and makes them go sticky and pasty. When smooth, beat in the gently reheated saffron liquid with a wooden spoon. Taste and season.

Serve a whole bird on each plate; or, if asbestos-handed, leave to rest for 5 minutes, then carve off the breasts, legs and thighs and arrange on warmed plates. (Use the carcasses for stock.)

Whisk 15 g / 1/2 oz [1 tbsp] butter into the reduction and spoon this over the meat. Put a big scoop of saffron mash on each plate, dotting the top with a small bit of the remaining butter. Snip over a few 3 cm / 1 1/4 in lengths of chive to garnish.

Warm Pigeon Salad with Borlotti Beans and Sugar-snaps

Wood pigeons have virtually no fat and, with the exception of the breast meat, are accordingly tough and dry when simply roasted. They have a good flavour and are cheap enough to allow you to use only the breast meat in a dish. The carcasses can then be used to make very good stock. Borlotti are those lovely Italian beans, purplish brown and speckled like a farmyard hen's egg. Cooked in chicken stock they have a brilliant meaty flavour.

FOR 4

4 wood pigeons
170 g / 6 oz [1 cup] dried borlotti beans
1 bay leaf
3 tbsp olive oil
170 g / 6 oz mange-touts [snow peas] or sugar-snap peas
1 red onion, diced
4 Little Gem lettuces [Romaine hearts]
5 tbsp Chilli Balsamic Vinaigrette (page 36)
salt and pepper

FOR THE BEAN DRESSING:
1 garlic clove
150 ml / 1/4 pt [2/3 cup] Greek-style or other thick plain yogurt
small bunch of chives, snipped

The day before, put the beans to soak in plenty of cold water.

Next day, bring to the boil, drain in a colander, rinse in cold water and return to the pan. Cover with cold water by 2.5 cm / 1 in. Add a bay leaf, bring to the boil and immediately lower the heat to a simmer. Cook for 1–1 1/2 hours until tender, seasoning with salt and pepper only towards the end of the cooking time. Remove and leave to cool in the liquid.

Cut the breasts from the pigeons and put into a bowl with the olive oil, 1 teaspoon of salt and 1/2 teaspoon of coarsely milled pepper. Toss to coat.

Trim the peas and blanch for 2 minutes in rapidly boiling salted water. Refresh in cold water and reserve.

Put a heavy dry frying pan over a medium heat until smoking-hot. Lay the breasts in it, skin side down, for 30 seconds. Turn and sear the other sides. Repeat on both sides, giving a total cooking time of 2 minutes. They should be very pink. Remove and keep warm. Drain off any cooking juices and reserve.

Make the bean dressing: smash and chop the garlic. Put into a bowl with the yogurt, reserved pan juices and salt and pepper. Whisk until well mixed. Add the snipped chives and stir in. Toss the peas and the borlotti beans with the red onion in the yogurt dressing. Taste and adjust seasoning.

Cut the lettuces lengthwise into quarters and toss in the balsamic vinaigrette.

Arrange 4 lettuce quarters on each plate radiating outwards and mound the beans in the middle. Cut each breast across into 2 and arrange on top of the beans. Mill some coarse pepper on top to finish.

Roast Guinea Fowl with Potato and Parsnip Purée

Guinea fowl are really farmed game, sharing qualities of chicken, squab and pheasant. They have quite a strong flavour, not as strong as game but more pronounced than chicken. Being virtually fat-free, they need sensitive and finely timed cooking if they are not to be too dry. They do not take a lot of roasting and 30-35 minutes in a 250°C/475°F/gas9 oven will be enough time for a 1 kg/2¼ lb bird. A 10-15 minute rest after coming out of the oven before carving will give an even distribution of juices in the meat and a uniformly tender and moist result. One guinea fowl will serve 2 people generously, 3 without a fight, 4 with bitter recrimination...

The parsnip is a taproot like a turnip, but has a sweeter taste and is in fact a relative of the carrot. Its earliest human consumption is recorded by the Ancient Greeks and it was a basic food of the poor throughout Europe in the Middle Ages before it was superseded by the potato in the sixteenth century. It then became more widely used as animal fodder, an association which has given it a poor image to this day. Parsnips should always be parboiled until virtually cooked before being finished in a secondary cooking, which may be roasting in dripping in the oven or on the hob with butter or cream. You can also accentuate their natural sweetness by sprinkling with sugar and caramelizing them as Americans do to accompany Thanksgiving turkey.

FOR 4

2 guinea fowl, each weighing about 1.15 kg/2½ lb
4 garlic cloves
1 tbsp rosemary leaves
4 tbsp olive oil
salt and pepper
small bunch of chives, to garnish

FOR THE MUSHROOM SAUCE:

55 g/2 oz dried wild mushrooms
2 shallots, finely chopped
2 garlic cloves, finely chopped
2 tbsp olive oil
100 ml/3½ fl oz [7 tbsp] gin
200 ml/7 fl oz [⅞ cup] Chicken stock (page 24)
150 ml/¼ pt [⅔ cup] crème fraîche
55 g/2 oz [4 tbsp] softened Parsley, Garlic and Red Chilli Butter (page 42)

FOR THE POTATO AND PARSNIP PURÉE:

900 g/2 lb parsnips
450 g/1 lb potatoes
55 g/2 oz [4 tbsp] butter
2 tbsp extra-virgin olive oil
2 tbsp crème fraîche
¼ nutmeg, grated

First prepare the mushrooms for the sauce: pour 300 ml/½ pt [1¼ cups] boiling water over them and leave to rehydrate for 30 minutes. Put into a colander and wash under running water, rubbing gently to remove any grit or stones. Reserve.

Preheat the oven to 250°C/475°F/gas 9.

Put 2 garlic cloves and some rosemary inside each bird. Brush the birds all over with olive oil and season generously. Transfer to a rack over a roasting tray, set breast down, and cook for 20 minutes. Turn breast side up, spoon over the pan juices and return to the oven for a further 10-15 minutes.

While the birds are roasting, make the sauce: sweat the shallots with the garlic in the oil. Turn up the heat, add the gin and ignite. Flame carefully and shake the pan, then add the stock and mushrooms and reduce by half. Add the crème fraîche. Bring to the boil and finish by whisking in the flavoured butter.

At the same time, peel the parsnips and potatoes. Cut them into chunks and cook in boiling salted water for about 20 minutes. They will take the same time to cook. Drain, return to the pan and stir over a low heat to get all the excess moisture out. Mash with a potato masher. Don't put them in a food processor, which will make them gluey. With a wooden spoon, beat in the butter, olive oil and crème fraîche. Add the grated nutmeg. Taste and season with salt and pepper.

Remove the bird from the oven and let it rest for 10 minutes before carving off the legs, thighs and breasts.

Serve with a scoop of the purée and with the mushroom sauce spooned over and around the meat. Scatter a few snipped chives over to garnish.

Grilled Lemon Poussin

Throughout southern California you will find citrus groves. For those of us who grew up in less clement lands, there is something magical about being able to pick a lemon from a tree, to find limes being sold by the roadside for pennies and to use their juice liberally in our cooking as well as in drinks. Lemon juice makes a great marinade and is the key which unlocks delicious barbecued chicken. Here we use poussins, the ideal barbecue bird. This is also an excellent way of cooking squab.

Poultry shears make the spatchcocking very easy and are useful for other serious bits of butchery. As you crunch through a joint with the greatest of ease try not to think of it being your thumb. Zip-lock bags maximize the effective-ness of the marinade. I now find it hard to imagine cooking without them.·

The day before: cut down either side of the birds' backbones and open each bird out. Remove this central strip and use for stock. Flatten the bird by putting it cut side down and slamming down with the heel of your hand on the breast.

FOR 4

4 poussins [squab chickens]
2 garlic cloves
4 lemons
4 tbsp sunflower oil
2 tbsp Worcestershire sauce
2 tsp dried hot chilli flakes
3 tbsp olive oil
salt and pepper
2 bunches of watercress, to serve

Smash and chop the garlic and put into a food processor with the juice of 2 of the lemons, the sunflower oil, Worcestershire sauce and chilli flakes. Whizz briefly to homogenize and pour half into one zip-lock and half into the other. Put 2 birds in each bag and zip shut. Turn and shake to coat, then refrigerate for 24 hours, turning the bags whenever you go to the fridge. Remove 2 hours before you want to cook them.

Just before cooking, put 1 teaspoon of salt, 1 teaspoon of black pepper, the olive oil and the marinade from the bags into the food processor and whizz to blend. Pass through a fine sieve. This is now your basting liquid.

You can grill the birds under an overhead grill [broiler] or on a charcoal grill. If the latter, start the birds at least 15 cm / 6 in away from the coals. You don't want to char the skin too soon or you will end up with a dry and bitter exterior before the interior flesh is cooked. Grill, turning and basting frequently. They take about 15 minutes and will emerge with a beautifully burnished and crisp skin. Serve on warmed plates, with half a bunch of watercress and half a lemon on each. This is mostly finger food, so finger bowls will be appreciated.

Chicken Fajitas

The first time I ate chicken fajitas was at Chuey's, a pit barbecue café in Carpinteria. This is a basic, no-frills establishment – plastic chairs, metal tables and paper plates. Even the Margarita pitchers are made of plastic. Inside you order from a counter and off to your left is a huge floor-level barbecue with the chickens turning on long spits. Memory does funny things, but I never remember chicken tasting better, sitting out there in the sun and watching my wife throw back her head and laugh with the sheer joy of it all, her sunglasses reflecting the image of a giant white truck sliding by down the empty street.

What makes fajitas appealing is the number of different elements on the table that allow you to pick and choose the filling for your tortilla: spicy stir-fried chicken, refried beans and guacamole, with a bowl of sour cream or crème fraîche, some more hot chillies for those who like them and a tomato, red onion and coriander salad. People make their own fajitas, rolling the tortillas around their chosen food and eating them with their fingers. A pitcher or two of Margaritas will turn an impromptu meal into a party.

In California, food markets have large sections dedicated to tortillas, and we are at last starting to see soft wheat-flour tortillas in supermarkets here. However, if the ones I have tried are anything to go by, make them yourself because they are easy to produce, have to taste better than the ones British supermarkets are offering and can be made ahead of time and frozen.

FOR 4

4 skinless chicken breasts
   [breast halves]

2 onions

4 garlic cloves

2 red sweet peppers

1 fresh habanero (Scotch
   bonnet) or other very hot chilli

4 tbsp sunflower oil

1 tbsp cumin seeds

1 tbsp coriander seeds

1 tsp salt

1 tsp black pepper

handful of coriander leaves
   [cilantro], to garnish

TO SERVE:

8 large Wheat-flour Tortillas
   (page 57)

Refried Black Beans (page 32)

Guacamole (page 68),

sour cream or crème fraîche

more hot chillies, (optional)

tomato, red onion and coriander
   [cilantro] salad

Cut the vegetables into strips, discarding the seeds and pith from the peppers and chilli. Sweat over a low heat in the oil for 5 minutes, or until soft and the onions are translucent.

While they are softening, put the cumin, coriander seeds, salt and pepper into a dry heavy iron pan over a very low heat and toast them for 2-3 minutes, stirring. Grind to a powder.

Sprinkle the frying vegetables with the spices, then turn up the heat. Cut the chicken into strips and add to the pan, tossing and turning to cook. This takes very little time, no more than 3 or 4 minutes. Scatter over coriander leaves over before bringing to the table.

Fry-and-steam Duck and Courgettes

We start out doing things in a certain way because somebody tells us to. We receive wisdom and only with time do we acquire the skills and the knowledge to judge whether we have been handed a valuable truth or a worthless habit.

The duck in this recipe is a case in point. Duck leg and thigh joints may be roasted in the oven, pan-fried or poached in fat – confit. We have been told often enough that when you are pan-frying you do so without a lid because if you put one on, you will be steaming rather than frying. But surely, that is not an either/or condition. Is it not frying in contact with the pan while steaming at the same time? Might this not produce an interesting effect? So I tried it, removing the lid for the last 10 minutes to allow the skin to crisp. The result is moist and tender, but don't just take my word for it.

FOR 4

4 leg and thigh duck pieces
1 tsp dried oregano
2 tbsp Kikkoman soy sauce
450 g / 1 lb courgettes [zucchini]
1 tbsp olive oil
2 tbsp Quick Tomato Sauce
  (page 34)
salt and pepper
bunch of chives, to garnish

Remove the duck pieces from the fridge 2 hours before you start cooking them. Rub $\frac{1}{4}$ tsp salt, $\frac{1}{2}$ tsp coarsely ground pepper and $\frac{1}{4}$ tsp dried oregano into each. Leave to absorb the flavours on a tray.

Lay the pieces skin side down in a frying pan large enough to hold them in a single layer without touching, or use 2 pans. You will need tight-fitting lids. Turn the heat on at medium and when you hear the fat starting to sizzle, turn down to low and put on the lid. Turn after 10 minutes and again after a further 10 minutes. Brush the upper skin side with the soy sauce.

Trim the courgettes, cut them in half if they are large and then across at an angle of 45 degrees into 1.5 cm / $\frac{5}{8}$ in slices. Film the bottom of a saucepan with olive oil and then put in the courgette slices. Turn with the tomato sauce to coat. Put on the lid and reserve.

Remove the lid from the duck and cook uncovered, skin side down, for a final 10 minutes. The idea is to have the flesh pink around the bone. Transfer to a rack, skin side up, and allow to rest in a warm place.

Put the heat on high under the courgettes. When steam starts to escape, turn down the heat, shake the pan vigorously and cook, shaking from time to time, for 12 minutes.

Serve a mound of courgettes next to each duck portion. Scatter over 2 cm / $\frac{3}{4}$ in lengths of chives and serve immediately.

Glazed Magret of Duck
with Masoor Dal

Duck breasts are delicious when cooked still pink, but with the skin beautifully crisp. I no longer think duck should be very rare but, with the exception of Peking roast duck, it should never be well-done. You want it to be moist and tender. Pan-frying is probably the best way to cook magrets. The subcutaneous fat keeps the meat juicy, while the pan gives you plenty of control to ensure the skin is crisped without being burnt. Duck magrets cooked this way are also brilliant in Chinese pancakes with shredded spring onions [scallions], cucumber and hoi-sin sauce.

Red lentils, masoor, are in reality pink in colour and turn yellow when cooked. There are many kinds of split peas and beans that are used to make Indian dal, which can be served with lots of liquid to give a soupy consistency or have the liquid reduced to deliver a drier finish. In this version, two flavouring stages are used. Fresh ginger, garlic and lime leaves are boiled with the lentils, while the spices and onions are cooked separately and added to the dal only just prior to serving.

FOR 4

2 large magrets of duck, each weighing about 350g/12oz
150ml/¼pt [²/₃ cup] Chicken Stock (page 24)
handful of fresh coriander leaves [cilantro], to garnish

FOR THE MARINADE:
3 tbsp Kikkoman soy sauce
1 tbsp Worcestershire sauce
1 tbsp lemon juice
1 tbsp caster sugar [US granulated sugar]
salt and pepper

The day before, put the magrets in a zip-lock bag with all the marinade ingredients and refrigerate overnight. Remove from the fridge 2 hours before you cook them, turning the bag over when you take it out to redistribute the marinade around the duck.

Wash the lentils in a sieve under running cold water. Put them in a pan and cover with 1.75 litres/3 pt [7½ cups] of cold water. Add the garlic, ginger and the lime leaves. Bring to the boil, skim, lower the heat and simmer, stirring from time to time until the lentils purée. Depending on the age of the lentils this will take from 40 to 50 minutes. At all times keep the surface covered with water, topping up the level if they start to dry out. When you deem them to be nearly done, add salt to taste.

Peel the onions and cut into thin slices. Put the sunflower oil in a pan and fry the onions over a medium heat until golden brown. While they are cooking, toast the coriander, cumin and mustard seeds in a small dry frying pan over a low heat. Grind in a coffee grinder. Stir into the onions and fry gently for 2 minutes.

225 g / 8 oz [1 heaped cup] lentils

3 garlic cloves, smashed and
    chopped

5 cm / 2 in piece of root ginger,
    peeled and cut into fine strips

2 Kaffir lime leaves

450 g / 1 lb onions

4 tbsp sunflower oil

2 tsp coriander seeds

2 tsp cumin seeds

1 tsp black mustard seeds

Stir this spiced onion mixture into the dal, remove the pan from the heat and put a lid on it. Leave to stand for 4 minutes before serving.

About 10 minutes before you judge the lentils will be done, remove the magrets from the marinade and pat dry. This is not some sort of precise crystal-ball gazing about the time but just the idea that in cooking everything happens backwards from the moment when your guests are ready to be fed or, more realistically, when you want them to eat.

Put the marinade in a pan with the chicken stock, bring to the boil, lower the heat and simmer to reduce by half.

Put a frying pan over a medium heat and immediately lay the magrets in, skin side down. When they start to sizzle, turn down the heat to low. Turn after 10 minutes, then turn every 5 minutes until done. They will take about 25 minutes at this low temperature.

When cooked, transfer to a wire rack, skin side up and leave to rest for 5 minutes before carving, skin side down, at an angle into 1 cm / ½ in thick slices.

Mound the dal in large warmed soup plates. Arrange the slices of duck overlapping on top. Spoon a little of the marinade sauce over the meat and scatter generously with whole coriander leaves.

Chicken Breast Quesadilla
with Avocado Pepper Salad

This is a very attractive way of presenting what would otherwise be a delicious salad, but just a salad nonetheless. Quesadilla is a pretty name, and the combination of flavours – the bite of the chilli and the fresh herb-citrus dressing – is special.

FOR 4

4 chicken breasts

2 large, ripe avocados

1 buffalo mozzarella cheese

2 yellow sweet peppers,
   roasted and peeled (page 26)

4-6 large Wheat-flour Tortillas
   (page 57)

1 red onion, diced

1 garlic clove, smashed and
   chopped

olive oil, for brushing

salt and pepper

handful of basil, to garnish

FOR THE HERB-CITRUS DRESSING:

4 plum or vine-ripened tomatoes

2 fresh Anaheim-type
   (medium-hot) green chillies

juice of 1 lemon

125 ml / 4 fl oz [^{1}/2 cup] extra-
   virgin olive oil

handful of coriander [cilantro]

handful of flat-leaf parsley

Brush the chicken breasts with a little olive oil and season with salt and pepper. Cook in a non-stick pan over a medium heat for 12-15 minutes, starting skin side down and turning at regular intervals until done. Transfer to a cutting board, skin side up, and reserve.

While the chicken is cooking, prepare the vegetables for the dressing: blanch the tomatoes in boiling water for 30 seconds, refresh in cold water and peel. Cut into quarters, remove the seeds and pulp, then cut the flesh into tiny dice. Remove seeds from the chillies and cut them into julienne strips.

Prepare the salad ingredients: Cut the avocados in halves and remove the stones. Peel and cut the flesh into 1 cm / ^{1}/2 in slices. Drain the mozzarella and cut it into 5 mm / ^{1}/4 in slices. Cut the sweet peppers into strips. Cut the chicken into thin strips.

Make a lemon-herb dressing by mixing the lemon juice with salt and pepper, then whisking in the oil. Chop half the parsley leaves and half the coriander leaves and stir in. Stir in the tomato dice and chilli strips.

Using a pastry cutter or a saucer to guide your knife, cut 8 discs with a diameter of about 10 cm / 4 in from the tortillas.

Put 1 tortilla disc on each plate and layer the ingredients on top, starting with the chicken, then the sweet pepper, then the mozzarella, some onion and garlic and finally the avocado. Pour a spoonful of the dressing over each, then put the second tortilla disc on top. Spoon the remaining dressing around the plates and sprinkle the remaining whole coriander and parsley leaves over all. Finally, tear the basil leaves and put on top of the quesadilla.

Shredded Duck Tostada with Roasted Jalapeño Crème Fraîche Sauce

Tostadas are usually made with corn tortillas but since I can never quite get away from the thought that they taste strangely of hessian sacks, let's use wheat-flour tortillas instead.

FOR 4

2 duck breasts [breast halves]
4 oven-dried tomato halves
    (page 26)
1 tbsp sherry vinegar or white
    wine vinegar
2 tbsp olive oil
juice of 1 lime
225 g / 8 oz [2 cups] Cheddar
    cheese, grated
4 Wheat-flour Tortillas (page 57)
salt and pepper
handful of coriander leaves
    [cilantro], to garnish

FOR THE JALAPEÑO CRÈME FRAÎCHE
SAUCE:

2 fresh jalapeño-type (very hot)
    chillies, cut into julienne strips
    (discard the seeds if you like or
    include for more fire)
150 ml / 1/4 pt [2/3 cup] dry sherry
4 tbsp chopped shallots (3-4)
2 garlic cloves, finely chopped
350 ml / 12 fl oz [1 1/2 cups] Chicken
    Stock (page 24) or duck stock
300 ml / 1/2 pt [1 1/4 cups] crème
    fraîche

First prepare the chillies for the sauce: put a non-stick pan over a low heat and roast the chilli strips in it, stirring with a wooden spoon, for 2-3 minutes. Remove and reserve.

Season the duck breasts and lay in the pan, fat side down. Cook for 5 minutes and turn. Give them 4 minutes and turn to the fat side again for 2 minutes, turning for the last time for a final minute. Transfer to a cutting board, fat side up and leave to rest. They should be rare in the middle.

While the duck is cooking, make the jalapeño crème fraîche sauce: put the sherry, shallots and garlic in a pan and reduce over a high heat until almost all the liquid has evaporated. Add the stock and reduce by half. Add the crème fraîche and the chilli. Lower the heat, season with a little salt and pepper and leave to simmer. You want it to reduce by half again. Stir from time to time.

Preheat the oven to 190°C/375°F/gas5.

Dice the tomatoes and put into a bowl with the vinegar, olive oil and lime juice. Stir and season lightly. Turn the duck breasts fat side down and carve into the thinnest slices you can manage. Arrange the tortillas on a baking sheet, mound the duck on each and sprinkle over the cheese. Spoon the tomato mixture over the tops and bake for 10 minutes or until the cheese melts. Remove and transfer to serving plates.

Spoon the jalapeño crème fraîche sauce over and around the tostadas and scatter whole coriander leaves over before serving immediately.

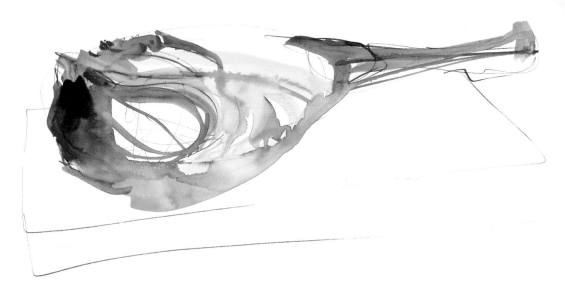

Pancetta-stuffed Leg of Lamb with Polenta Chips and Deep-fried Onions

In many people resides a prejudice that cold meat is somehow inferior to meat served hot, a misconception that derives from the idea of leftovers. The Chinese have always known better and never serve roasted meats hot, but at room temperature. When meat is cooked to be served thus it is not carved until just before it is brought to the table. The result is much more moist, since all juices have been retained within the meat. The cook benefits from cooking and serving a leg of lamb this way for it is much easier to carve cold, while the contrast of cool meat and hot accompaniments is always pleasing.

Stuffing usually implies a boned piece of meat but in this case deep and narrow incisions are made at intervals down to the bone and the resulting channels are then filled with a mixture of pancetta, herbs and anchovies. When the leg is carved, these present as a marbled effect in the slices.

When cooking this dish for people in California I never tell them it includes anchovies because so many unfathomably hate them. This may be because they were exposed to poor-quality anchovies on pizzas when they were young. One described them as 'fish with fur', a repulsive thought indeed. Once cooked, nobody would know that the intriguing salt flavour which enriches the lamb was ever anything to do with a fish.

The lamb may be cooked the day before and refrigerated overnight, but please take it out of the fridge at least an hour before carving and serving to allow it to come to room temperature.

2 kg / 4 1/2 lb leg of lamb
140 g / 5 oz pancetta
350 g / 12 oz [3 cups] polenta
2 garlic cloves
55 g / 2 oz canned anchovy fillets
handful of flat-leaf parsley
3 tbsp olive oil
450 g / 1 lb onions
pepper
sunflower oil, for deep-frying
small bunch of chives, to garnish

Well ahead of time, make up the polenta according to the instructions on the packet and pour into a container which will allow it to set to a depth of 1 cm / 1/2 in. Leave to set in a cool place.

Preheat the oven to 250°C/475°F/gas9.

Dice the pancetta in 5 mm / 1/4 in cubes. Smash and coarsely chop the garlic. Put these with the anchovy fillets and flat-leaf parsley in a food processor and blitz briefly to pull all the ingredients together.

With a long thin knife, make incisions at regular 5 cm / 2 in intervals where the meat is thickest, pushing right down to touch the bone. Push a finger in to open them out so that they are large enough to be able to push the stuffing mixture into the holes. Brush the finished leg all over with the olive oil and season generously with pepper. No salt is needed on the surface as the salt of the anchovies and pancetta is sufficient.

Place on a rack in a roasting pan and brown for 15 minutes, then lower the temperature to 220°C/425°F/gas7 and cook for a further 45 minutes (10 minutes per 450 g / 1 lb), delivering a pink-to-medium-rare finish. The meat may be cooked for a further 10 minutes if you like a more medium result. Remember that the meat is not going to be carved until completely cooled and that it will continue cooking for 15 minutes after it comes from the oven.

About 20 minutes before you want to serve: preheat oil for deep-frying to 190°C/375°F.

Cut the polenta into 1.5cm/3/4 in batons. Cut the onions into 5 mm / 1/4 in thick slices and separate these into rings.

Deep-fry the onion rings first until soft and just starting to brown. Remove and reserve. Fry the polenta chips until browned and crisped, removing them to paper towels to drain. While they are draining, return the onions to fry briefly until crisp. Drain on paper towels.

Carve the cold lamb into 1 cm / 1/2 in thick slices. Put 2 or 3 slices on each plate around the edges and mound polenta chips in the middle, scattering crisp onions over the top. Finish with snipped chives.

Spiced Rack of Lamb with Sautéed Turnips

Racks of lamb are at their best with new season's meat. The spicy crust offsets the sweetness of the meat, while the sautéed turnips are a splendid vegetable to have with any roast. Alternatively, roast the turnips.

FOR 4

2 racks of lamb (to give 3
   cutlets or chops per person)
2 tsp coriander seeds
2 tsp cumin seeds
1 tsp black peppercorns
3 tbsp extra-virgin olive oil
575 ml / 1 pt [2¹/₃ cups]
   Chicken Stock (page 24)
1 glass of red wine
30 g / 1 oz [2 tbsp] Parsley, Garlic
   and Red Chilli Butter (page 42)
salt and pepper

FOR THE SAUTÉED TURNIPS:
675 g / 1¹/₂ lb small white turnips
4 tbsp olive oil
55 g / 2 oz [4 tbsp] butter
2 shallots
1 garlic clove
2 tbsp chopped flat-leaf parsley,
   plus some whole leaves for
   garnish
small bunch of chives

Preheat the oven to 250°C/475°F/gas9.

Put the coriander seeds, cumin and peppercorns in a dry frying pan and toast over a low heat for 2-3 minutes, stirring. Transfer to a coffee grinder and blitz to a coarse powder. This should still have discernible bits in it.

Carefully cut a 1 cm / ¹/₂ in lattice pattern into the fat of the lamb, then brush the racks all over with olive oil. Rub the spice mixture into the meat, pressing it into the cuts. Put to roast for 15-18 minutes, fat side up, on a rack. Remove and allow to rest for 8 minutes, which will give you a medium-rare finish.

While the lamb is cooking, peel the turnips and cut across into 1 cm / ¹/₂ in slices, then cut these into uniform dice. Blanch in rapidly boiling salted water for 3 minutes and drain.

Also, put the stock and wine in a saucepan, bring to the boil and reduce by about half. Keep warm.

While the turnip dice are blanching, peel and dice the shallots. Smash and chop the garlic.

Put the olive oil and butter in a frying pan over a medium heat and sauté the turnips and shallots, tossing and shaking the pan until they are a pale golden colour and cooked through but not a mush. Season with salt and pepper. Stir in the garlic together with the chopped parsley and chives cut into 5 mm / ¹/₄ in lengths.

Whisk the flavoured butter into the reduced stock mixture. Carve the lamb into cutlets and arrange 3 overlapping on each of 4 warmed plates. Mound the turnips next to them, spoon the gravy over the meat and scatter whole leaves of parsley over the turnips.

Spiced Lamb Shanks with Dirty Rice and Crisp Onion Garnish

Not so long ago the only time you ever ate lamb shanks was in a Greek or Turkish restaurant. Now these small individual pieces cut from the shin of the leg are to be found on most menus and buying them is consequently more expensive than it used to be. Allow one per person.

Dirty rice is a Cajun dish, Cajuns being the Acadian French who moved to the bayous of Louisiana from Nova Scotia in the 1750s. Cajun cooking is characteristically spicy, uniquely uses sassafras (filé) powder and emphasizes long-cooked roux for flavouring as well as thickening stews. For a while in the 'Eighties Cajun food was very smart stuff everywhere, then people noticed what its principal exponent Paul Prudhomme looked like – as in huge – and did a double-take. Dirty rice is one of the dishes that deserves longer legs and it happens to be perfect with this lamb. The name comes from the dark flecks of gizzard meat. Some ethnic butchers sell gizzards, but you can get a similar effect by first poaching lamb hearts until tender, then cutting them into small pieces. My mother cooked lamb hearts for her psychopathic Border Terrier, Liza. I used to steal bits when I was little but you had to be careful because as soon as you went near her bowl she bit you.

Crisp onions add a sweet caramelized crunch that works as a perfect counterpoint with many potato, noodle and rice dishes. They feature a lot in South-east Asian dishes but work just as well with mashed potatoes. A lot of raw onions cook down to a relatively small amount, but then they simply burst with a sweet intense flavour. You can cook them in one continuous process in a frying pan, but doing them in two stages, with an initial deep-frying, speeds up an otherwise very slow procedure. The only downside is that the onions taint the oil in which they are fried so you must either drain it off through muslin or cheesecloth and reserve for the next batch or throw it away. Orange flower doughnuts, for example, would not benefit from being cooked in it.

FOR 4

4 lamb shanks

5 tbsp olive oil

1 onion

2 carrots

2 garlic cloves

$^1\!/_2$ bottle of dry white wine

575 ml / 1 pt [$2^1\!/_3$ cups] lamb stock
   or Chicken Stock (page 24)

whole coriander leaves
   [cilantro], to garnish

Roasted Tomato Chilli Sauce
   (page 33), to serve

FOR THE MARINADE:

4 tsp ground ginger

4 tsp black pepper

4 tsp turmeric

2 garlic cloves

handful of coriander leaves
   [cilantro]

2 tsp salt

First make the marinade: put all the dry spices into a dry heavy pan and toast for 2-3 minutes over a low heat. Smash and finely chop the garlic cloves and finely chop the coriander. Add the spice mix and salt and work to a paste. Rub this into the lamb and put to marinate at room temperature for 3-4 hours.

Start the onion garnish: preheat oil for deep-frying to 180°C/350°F. Peel the onions and cut across in 5 mm / $^1\!/_4$ in slices, then separate into rings. Fry in a basket, taking care when you first plunge them into the hot oil as the high water content of the onions will cause the level to surge upwards with an angry hissing and popping. Fry for about 5 minutes, stirring to redistribute the

350g / 12oz [2 cups] long-
    grain rice
115g / 4oz minced pork [¹/₂ cup
    ground pork]
1 lamb's heart or 225g / 8oz
    chicken gizzards
2 bay leaves
2 tsp hot cayenne pepper
2 tsp paprika
1 tsp ground cumin
1 tsp dried oregano
1 tsp dry mustard
1 onion, diced
3 celery stalks, thinly sliced
1 green sweet pepper, diced
2 garlic cloves, smashed and
    chopped
55g / 2oz [4 tbsp] butter
about 1.1 litres / 2pt [5 cups]
    Chicken Stock (page 24)
1¹/₂ tsp salt
1¹/₂ tsp black pepper

FOR THE CRISP ONION AND PINE NUT
GARNISH:
675g / 1¹/₂ lb onions
1 tbsp pine nuts
sunflower oil, for deep-frying

onions at regular intervals. As soon as the edges start to brown, transfer to paper towels and drain. These can now be held for up to 4 hours before finishing in a non-stick pan.

Put 2 tablespoons of the olive oil into a frying pan over a medium heat and seal the shanks gently, turning them carefully with tongs. The idea is just to brown them and you need to be careful not to burn them as the spice and garlic coating will blacken and go bitter if you use too high a heat. Reserve.

Peel the onion and carrots and cut into a mirepoix, i.e. very small dice. Smash and chop the garlic. In a heavy pot with a tight-fitting lid that is just large enough to hold the shanks standing upright, sweat the onion and carrot over a low heat until soft, then stir in the garlic and cook for 2 minutes.

Put the lamb shanks on top and pour around the wine and stock. Bring to the boil, immediately lower the temperature, put on the lid and cook at a bare simmer for about 1¹/₂ hours, or until tender. It may take only an hour to reach this stage, so check and do not assume it will take the longer time.

About 25 minutes before the lamb will be ready, prepare the dirty rice: in a large saucepan or casserole dish with a lid and over a high heat, fry the pork and chopped heart or gizzards in oil briefly. Reduce the heat to medium and add the dried herbs, spices and mustard. Cook, stirring, for 60 seconds. Add the onion, celery, green pepper and the garlic. Add the butter and cook for 5-8 minutes, stirring. Stir in the rice and pour on the chicken stock. Bring to the boil, lower the heat and put on the lid. Cook for 7 minutes. Remove from the heat and leave to stand for 8 minutes.

While the rice is standing, finish the onion garnish: add the cooked onions to a large dry frying pan over a low-to-medium heat and cook, stirring constantly, until crisp and uniformly golden brown. Add the pine nuts for the last 2-3 minutes. Season with the salt and pepper and transfer to fresh paper towels. They can be stored like this in an airtight container for up to a week but will not be as nice as when served immediately.

Remove the lamb shanks from the pot and keep warm while you finish the sauce by reducing the liquid in the pot at a fast boil until you have about 450ml / ³/₄ pt [2 cups]. Put this with the vegetables in a food processor, blitz briefly to purée, then pass through a sieve, pressing with the back of a spoon.

Put 1 shank on each plate with the sauce spooned around and over it and serve with dirty rice and a spoonful of the chilli tomato sauce at room temperature as a relish. Scatter over the onions and garnish with whole coriander leaves.

Barbecued Pork Ribs

California and barbecues are inseparable, but the West Coast charcoal grill is different in character to what is meant by the word in other states. As you head south through the Midwest you cross an invisible line that takes you into pit-barbecue country. Several states – including Arkansas, Missouri, Kentucky and Carolina – would lay claim to barbecue as uniquely their own. Tennessee definitely has a barbecue culture and Memphis, on the banks of the mighty Mississippi River, gets about as down-home as a person could tolerate and come out still speaking English.

Each May the barbecue is celebrated in a contest where more than 170 teams with names like Pork Forkers, Super Swine Sizzlers, Pig Diamonds and Hogaholics compete for the title of World Champion in three categories: whole hog, shoulder and ribs. Several of the winning recipes involve marinades which shamelessly use commercial products like Razorback Barbecue Sauce and Liquid Smoke. Others have more natural ingredients. All combine sweet-and-sour with spicy and aromatic.

Southern barbecue is slow-cooked and part-smoked, something you can achieve at home if you have one of those barbecues with a lid that turns it into an oven. In fact the kind of marinades and basting sauces that are part of the Southern barbecue work just as well with chicken and ribs cooked over the open fire and make a pleasant change from all that barely seared this and healthy that, with its chiffonnade of basil. You chiffonnade basil in Memphis and they'd likely shoot you.

Put the ribs or chicken in zip-lock bags and add the mixed marinade ingredients. Zip shut and refrigerate overnight. Remove from the refrigerator 3 hours before you want to cook, turning the bags so the other side is covered.

Preheat a charcoal grill or overhead grill [broiler]. Remove the ribs or chicken from the bag. Pat dry and grill on a rack a good 15 cm / 6 in from the fire, turning frequently and brushing with the marinade as you go along. Both ribs and poussins will take between 20 and 25 minutes. This kind of barbecue should always be done to the point where the meat will pull off the bone with your fingers. If you need to use a knife it isn't barbecue.

Serve with some crisp rolls, Superior Slaw (page 167) and a simple crisp green salad.

FOR 4

2 racks of pork baby back ribs or 4 poussins [squab chickens], spatchcocked (see page 178)

FOR THE MARINADE:

150 ml / 1/4 pt [2/3 cup] white wine vinegar

3 tbsp Worcestershire Sauce

2 tbsp Kikkoman soy sauce

2 tbsp tomato ketchup

2 tbsp lemon juice

1 tbsp Colman's mustard powder

1 tbsp caster sugar [US granulated sugar]

4 tsp Salsa Picante (page 39) or Tabasco sauce

1 tsp dried oregano

2 tsp cracked black pepper

Peppered Pork Chops with Shiitake and Shallots

Pork chops are quite tricky things to cook, especially if they are rather thin and lean. They should be cut 2 cm / ¾ in thick and a good 2 cm / ¾ in fat around the edge is desirable. The best way to cook them is with initial searing over a high heat, followed by a comparatively lengthy frying over a low heat. Marinating overnight both imbues flavour and tenderizes the meat.

Shiitake mushrooms are cultivated but have a good meaty flavour. Boost this further with the addition of a few dried wild mushrooms. Big banana shallots are the best, but any shallots will do.

FOR 4

4 pork chops on the bone,
each weighing about
350 g / 12 oz
55 g / 2 oz [4 tbsp] Lime, Orange
and Mint Butter (page 42)
salt and pepper
olive oil, for brushing

FOR THE MARINADE:
2 tbsp Kikkoman soy sauce
2 tbsp Worcestershire sauce
2 tbsp lemon juice
2 tbsp Chilli Oil (page 40)
2 tsp Salsa Picante (page 39)
or Tabasco sauce

FOR THE MUSHROOMS:
225 g / 8 oz fresh shiitake
mushrooms
30 g / 1 oz forestière mix of dried
mushrooms
150 ml / ¼ pt [²/3 cup]
Chicken Stock (page 24)
100 ml / 3½ fl oz [7 tbsp] dry sherry
55 g / 2 oz [4 tbsp] butter

FOR THE SHALLOTS:
350 g / 12 oz banana shallots
3 tbsp olive oil
pinch of dried oregano

Put all the marinade ingredients in a blender or food processor and blitz until homogenized. Put the chops in a zip-lock bag with the marinade, seal and refrigerate overnight. Take out of the refrigerator 2 hours before you want to cook and turn the bag over to redistribute the marinade.

Bring the stock, sherry and 100 ml / 3½ fl oz [7 tbsp] water to a simmer, add the dried mushrooms and remove from the heat. Stir and leave for 30 minutes to rehydrate. Drain in a fine sieve set in a bowl, reserving the liquid. Rinse the mushrooms under a tap, rubbing gently to get rid of any grit.

Peel the shallots. Put in a pan, cover with water and bring to the boil. Drain in a sieve and rinse under cold running water. Pat dry. Put a non-stick pan over a medium heat. Cut the shallots in half lengthwise, put in a bowl with the olive oil and oregano and toss to coat. Lay in the pan, cut side down. Shake occasionally. You want to caramelize the cut surface slowly.

Put the butter to melt over a low heat in a pan. Slice the shiitake into 1 cm / ½ in slices and the wild mushrooms into roughly 1 cm / ½ in dice. Add both to the pan and sweat gently, stirring from time to time, for 3 minutes.

Turn up the heat and add the mushroom soaking liquid, passing through a muslin- or cheesecloth-lined sieve to make sure there is no grit. Bubble through, lower the heat to minimum and keep warm.

Drain the chops and pat dry. Brush with olive oil and season with salt and pepper. Put a heavy frying pan large enough to hold the chops in one layer (or 2 pans) over a moderate heat. When smoking-hot, lay the chops in and sear for a minute on either side. Turn down the heat to low and cook for 15-20 minutes, turning frequently.

Put a chop on each warmed plate. Put a mound of shallots next to it, cut side up. Spoon the mushrooms on the other side and spoon the sauce over and around the chop. Put a slice of the Lime, Orange and Mint butter on top of each of the chops.

Roast Loin of Pork with Drunken Apricots and Apple Relish

Responding to fears about cholesterol, pork has been bred leaner and leaner in recent years, so that large-scale producers are now able to claim that it is one of the lowest-fat sources of animal protein available to us. As a consequence, it is a beast to cook because it has no natural basting material and, therefore, an inevitable tendency to dryness. A few pigs are again being bred as fat as medieval husbandry intended and if you seek out an organic butcher you may well find he can supply you with properly bred and raised pork which has a decent lubricating cover and a fabulous flavour. If not, there are farmers who will supply by mail order.

We will assume for the sake of this recipe that your loin comes from such a producer. Loin is a lean cut anyway so, while it is not essential, it will cook better if you wrap it in caul fat, which you can read about in Spiced Sausages en Crépinettes on page 194. The caul also allows you to wrap herbs and spices on to the meat so they stay there during cooking.

The drunken apricots are something I always have in the store cupboard and are made by putting dried apricots in jars, adding sugar, covering them with a suitable spirit and leaving for at least a month. Pitu or any South-American aguardiente is very good for this purpose. At one point there happened to be several bottles of this sinister cane spirit lurking in my cellar. It tasted foul in the glass but combined with the apricots in a satisfactory fashion. White rum also does the job. In fact, any spirituous liquor helps an apricot go higher. The syrup left over makes a great addition to fruit salads.

Serve the pork with a simple gravy, the apricots cooked with caramelized onion, the apple relish and mashed potatoes.

FOR 4

1 centre-cut boneless pork
   loin, weighing about 550 g/
   1 1/4 lb
4 tbsp olive oil
2 sheets of caul fat
2 sprigs of thyme
450 g/ 1 lb onions
2 garlic cloves
20 drunken apricots (see
   above)
150 ml / 1/4 pt [2/3 cup] red wine
550 g/ 1 1/4 lb potatoes
55 g/ 2 oz [4 tbsp] unsalted butter
1 heaped tbsp crème fraîche
   or double cream [heavy cream]
1 tbsp chopped flat-leaf parsley
575 ml/ 1 pt [2 1/3 cups] Chicken
   Stock (page 24)
1 bay leaf
1 star anise
salt and pepper

First make the relish: cut the unpeeled apples into quarters and then into 1 cm/ 1/2 in dice. Cut the red onion(s) into the same size dice. Dice the celery and finely chop the leaves. Mix together with the sultanas. Sprinkle on the sugar, season with salt and pepper and pour over the extra-virgin oil and cider vinegar. Stir, cover with plastic film and leave to develop in flavour for 2 hours. Stir again before serving.

Preheat the oven to 220°C/425°F/gas7.

Brush the loin with a little oil and season liberally with salt and coarsely ground pepper. Spread out 1 sheet of caul and put the second on top to cover any holes. Put the thyme at one edge, sit pork on top and roll up tightly.

Put on a rack in a roasting pan and put in the oven. Cook for 45 minutes. Remove and leave to rest for 15 minutes in a warm place.

FOR THE APPLE RELISH:

140g/5oz [1 1/4 cups] Granny
    Smiths
140g/5oz [3/4 cup] red onions
140g/5oz [1 1/4 cups] inner stalks
    of celery with their leaves
55g/2oz sultanas [1/3 cup golden
    raisins]
2 tsp caster sugar [US
    granulated sugar]
5 tbsp extra-virgin olive oil
5 tbsp cider vinegar

While the pork is cooking, slice the onions and garlic thinly and fry gently in the olive oil, stirring from time to time. After 30 minutes, turn up the heat a little and fry until golden brown. At this point add the apricots, 2 tablespoons of their syrup and 2 tablespoons of the red wine. Lower the heat and continue cooking over the lowest possible heat until the apricots starts to break down. Remove from the heat and keep warm.

Meanwhile, peel the potatoes and boil in lightly salted water until tender, about 20 minutes. Drain, return to the hot pan and shake to dry. Mash dry with a potato masher, then beat in 30g/1oz [2 tbsp] butter and 1 tablespoon of crème fraîche with a wooden spoon. Stir in the chopped parsley. Taste and adjust the seasoning if needed.

Put the remaining red wine with the stock, bay leaf and star anise in a pan and boil to reduce by half. Pour the fat from the roasting pan into a double spout gravy jug, adding the meat juices to the reduced stock. (If you don't have one of these neat devices, pour off most of the fat from the pan into a bowl and then spoon and scrape what remains into the stock). Finish by whisking in 30g/1oz [2 tbsp] butter.

Slice the loin in 5mm/1/4in thick slices, put 2 or 3 on each warmed plate and spoon a little of the gravy over. Put a scoop of potato to one side and a spoonful of the drunken apricots and onions on the other. Offer the apple relish in a bowl for people to help themselves at the table.

Spiced Sausages en Crépinette with Flageolet Purée

You may be fortunate enough to live within shopping distance of an Italian food shop which makes its own peppered pork sausages. These are filled with coarsely chopped pork, Parma ham and diced pancetta. It is fun, however, to make your own. The ones I bought in California were rather sweet and all seemed to contain fennel, which is fine in merguez but not quite so nice in pork sausages.

As always, its just a matter of personal preference and the wine, too, is optional. This mixture makes great sausages, but if you don't want to stuff sausage skins, take the caul route and make sausage cakes. Dead easy and they taste just as nice.

450 g / 1 lb belly of pork [fresh
    pork side]
225 g / 8 oz chicken thighs
225 g / 8 oz pancetta
3 tbsp sherry
30 g / 1 oz [3 tbsp] black
    peppercorns
2 garlic cloves
3 sheets of caul fat
salt
1 lemon, quartered
    lengthwise, to serve

FOR THE FLAGEOLET PURÉE:
350 g / 12 oz [2 cups] dried
    flageolets
1 onion
2 garlic cloves
1 bay leaf
1 fresh serrano-type (hot) red chilli
juice of 1 lemon
handful of flat-leaf parsley
5 tbsp extra-virgin olive oil, plus
    more for dressing
salt and pepper

About 3-4 days ahead: put all the meat through a mincer [meat grinder]. If you don't have one, cut the different meats into uniform 1 cm / ½ in dice and pulse-chop briefly in 4 batches. Put into a bowl and stir in the sherry.

Grind the peppercorns briefly in a coffee grinder. The result should be mignonette, i.e. coarse ground, not a powder. Smash and chop the garlic finely. Stir it and the pepper into the sausage meat. Add 1 teaspoon of salt and mix in carefully. Take a walnut-sized piece of the mixture and fry in a pan over a medium heat, turning until cooked. Remove, leave to cool and taste. Add more salt to the bowl if you think it needs it. Cover with plastic film and refrigerate for 24 hours.

Next day: divide the mixture into 8 and roll into balls. Double wrap in caul fat. Arrange in one layer on a plate, cover with plastic film and refrigerate for 2-3 days. The maturation period allows the flavours to develop, something from which all sausages benefit.

The day before serving: put the beans for the purée to soak in lots of cold water overnight.

Next day: bring the beans to the boil and boil hard for a few minutes, then throw away the water (an anti-flatulence manoeuvre you can omit next time you have a dinner guest who must chair an important meeting in the City early the next morning). Cover with fresh water by 3 cm / 1¼ in. Chop the onion and 1 garlic clove and add to the pot with the bay leaf, chilli and about ½ tsp ground black pepper. Bring to the boil, lower the heat and simmer until done. Season with salt about 15 minutes before you think they will be finished. Turn off the heat and leave in the pot while you fry the crépinettes.

Cook them in a dry non-stick pan over a low heat, turning several times until well browned.

Drain the beans, reserving the cooking liquid. Discard the bay leaf and chilli and put into a food processor with the lemon juice, the remaining garlic clove, peeled and finely chopped, and the parsley, coarsely chopped, reserving a few whole leaves. Blitz to a purée, then add the olive oil through the feeder tube. Add just enough cooking liquid to achieve a smooth and creamy finish. Taste and adjust the seasoning.

Put 2 crépinettes on each plate with a mound of flageolet purée. Dress the purée with a little more oil, scatter the reserved parsley leaves on top and put a wedge of lemon on each plate.

Crispy Beef with Spinach and Japanese Dressing

Crispy beef is very Cantonese and sweet-tasting. The spinach has a splendid Japanese-style dressing, quite sour and sharp. The two play a great East-meets-East balancing game. If we were talking high technology it would be US-embargoed.

This is a good way of making a small amount of beef serve four people. A bowl of steamed glutinous rice on the side is appropriate. An electric rice steamer is an inexpensive piece of kit, but a great space-saver on the hob and a time-saver too. It cooks rice to perfection every time and then keeps it hot and ready to eat for several hours. The technique for cooking glutinous rice using an ordinary saucepan and measured water is foolproof if you don't take the lid off until just before you serve it.

First make the marinade: peel the ginger, grate on to a piece of muslin or cheesecloth and squeeze the juice into a bowl. Add all the other marinade ingredients and whisk until smooth. Cut the beef into 1 cm / 1/2 in strips, put into the marinade and toss to coat. Cover the bowl with plastic film and refrigerate overnight.

Cook the rice in the steamer following the manufacturer's instructions or follow this method: put the precisely measured rice with exactly 400 ml / 14 fl oz [1 3/4 cups] water in a saucepan with a tight-fitting lid and bring to the boil. As soon as it does, lower the heat to it lowest level and cook for 15 minutes. Turn off the heat and leave with the lid on for a further 15 minutes. At no time remove the lid until the moment of service.

Make the Japanese mustard dressing and reserve. Put a pan of salted water on to boil. Preheat oil for deep-frying to 190°C/375°F. Peel the second piece of ginger and cut into julienne strips.

Lay the beef strips on a tray. Scatter with the sesame seeds and the black pepper, then dredge in a seasoned mixture of the two flours. Lay on a clean tray. Deep-fry the beef in batches for 2 minutes each, transferring to mounded paper towels to drain as they are cooked. Keep warm.

Blanch the spinach in the boiling water for 30-45 seconds. Drain, add to the dressing and toss.

Mound the spinach in 4 warmed bowls, arrange the beef strips on top and garnish with ginger julienne and 3 cm / 1 1/4 in lengths of chives. Put the rice on the table in a large bowl for people to help themselves.

Ingredients

FOR 4

450 g / 1 lb best sirloin steak
500 g / 1 lb 2 oz [2 1/2 cups] glutinous (sushi) rice
6 cm / 2 1/2 in piece of root ginger
1 tbsp sesame seeds
1 tsp black pepper
3 tbsp flour
1 tbsp cornflour [cornstarch]
450 g / 1 lb spinach
small bunch of chives
sunflower oil, for deep-frying
salt and pepper

FOR THE MARINADE:

6 cm / 2 1/2 in piece of root ginger
1 egg
2 tbsp Kikkoman soy sauce
1 tbsp dry sherry
1 garlic clove
1 tbsp Thai fish sauce
1 tbsp muscovado or other moist brown sugar
1 tbsp cornflour [cornstarch]

FOR THE JAPANESE MUSTARD DRESSING:

2 tsp Colman's mustard powder
3 tbsp Kikkoman soy sauce
juice of 1/2 lemon
1 tsp olive oil

Beef Stew with Walnuts and Coriander

A straw poll suggests that even within the United States, people don't think of California as cattle country. As you drive north on 101 with the ocean on your left and rolling hills to your right, however, you will see plenty of cattle ranches and even, if you look very hard, the odd bison. Well, there is one to my certain knowledge, but that is in the Santa Ynez Valley and since it is immediately next to an ostrich farm and only a few yards from a breeder of miniature horses the size of poodles, you would be forgiven for thinking you were under the influence of hallucinogenic drugs when you first sight it.

While ox-cheek has become fashionable for stewing and braising, shin remains my favourite stewing cut, the muscles being interleaved with connective tissue which breaks down during cooking to produce a rich sauce. Always buy it in a piece so you can cut the meat into 175-200 g / 6 1/2-7 oz portions, which will be about the size of a postcard and 3-4 cm / 1 1/4 - 1 1/2 in thick. These reduce in size while stewing but make a very presentable portion on the plate. The only time they should be cut smaller is when they are to be used in a pie or a pudding.

The wine of choice for both cooking the dish and drinking with it is a big California Cabernet Sauvignon bursting with fruit. While chefs have a tendency to marinate the meat in wine and then use it in large quantities in the cooking, my preference is to forego the wine marinade, using only a quarter of a bottle to flavour rather than dominate, with the poaching liquid being mostly a well-flavoured chicken stock.

I never use veal stock, finding the intensity and richness it imparts unpalatable, quite apart from misgivings about veal per se. Every chef I know disagrees, but then they judge the sauce with a teaspoon and in the kitchen. Frankly I don't want something which if dropped on the table would glue the plate to the cloth or that makes you feel, after the second mouthful, like a terrier with a toffee.

Unusually the sauce is finished with ground walnuts and coriander. Walnuts are another California crop and using them in this way is an old Provençal trick. Coriander, always called cilantro in the USA, is the predominant herb of the Southwest. If you actually dislike it, and there are many who do, substitute flat-leaf parsley. The bacon of choice is pancetta, but any decent streaky bacon [thick-sliced bacon] will work. Serve with mashed potatoes, soft polenta or boiled long-grain rice.

FOR 6

1 kg / 2¼ lb shin of beef [beef
    hind shank]
115 g / 4 oz pancetta
2 tbsp olive oil
450 g / 1 lb onions
3 garlic cloves
55 g / 2 oz [7 tbsp] flour
2 tsp dried oregano
4 tbsp sunflower oil
200 ml / 7 fl oz [⅞ cup] big
    fruity red wine, preferably
    Cabernet Sauvignon
2 celery stalks
1 cinnamon stick
2 Kaffir lime leaves
1 fresh hot red chilli
2.2 litres / 3¾ pt [10 cups] Chicken
    Stock (page 24)
3 tbsp Worcestershire sauce
900 g / 2 lb canned tomatoes
1 bay leaf
115 g / 4 oz [1 cup] walnut pieces
large handful of coriander [cilantro]
salt and pepper

Cut the pancetta into lardon strips and put with the olive oil in a casserole dish over a low heat. Fry slowly, stirring from time to time. When the fat has run and the bacon starts to crisp, cut the onions into rings and add. Continue to cook until the onions have softened and become translucent. Smash and chop the garlic and stir it in.

Put the flour in a bowl with the oregano, 1 teaspoon of salt and ½ teaspoon coarsely milled pepper. Trim off any obvious fat from the meat; cut into 6 postcard-sized portions and dredge in the flour.

Put the sunflower oil in a pan and brown the meat vigorously to get a strong colour. Don't overcrowd the pan as this leads to steaming.

Transfer the browned meat to the casserole, turn the heat up under the pan and pour in the wine. Add the remaining flour and turn with a spoon. Deglaze the pan, scraping up any stuck bits to incorporate them, and add to the casserole.

Tie the celery, cinnamon, lime leaves and chilli into a bouquet garni and add. Pour over the stock. Add the Worcestershire sauce, tomatoes and bay leaf. Bring to the boil, skim, lower the heat and simmer gently uncovered for 1½-2 hours, or until you judge the meat to be done. Contrary to popular belief, and with the exception of ox cheek, stewing cuts do not benefit from endless hours on the stove. There comes a point when all the fat and connective tissue cooks out, leaving a fibrous and flaky residue which is dry and unpleasant. Taste a piece after 1½ hours. It should still have a certain spring to its step and when cut with a sharp knife will not flake. If it does you have taken it too far.

Remove the bouquet garni and discard. The dish can be taken to this point the day before, in which case always reheat very gently. To finish, put the walnuts and coriander (reserving a few whole leaves for garnish) in a food processor and blitz briefly to a crumb. Stir into the stew and warm through for 2-3 minutes, but no longer.

Serve in soup plates scattered with whole coriander leaves.

Flank Steak Fire Chilli

Should the classic chilli con carne have beans integral to its creation or should it be served with beans as an optional side dish? I think the latter, as they are frowned upon in that great American competition, the chilli cook off, and there is something pure and central about keeping it a no-nonsense, honest-to-God meat dish. The idea of a Linda McCartney tofu chilli is enough to make any self-respecting cowboy spit and reach for his gun.

You support and enhance the beef with side dishes – rather like a rijsttafel – allowing people to combine what they like on their plate. Little dishes of shredded spring onions [scallions], diced red onion, crème fraîche with chives, shaved Parmesan or Cheddar cheese, green olives, sliced hot green chillies and a big plate of refried beans make the chilli special. (Shaved Parmesan may be considered effete around the campfire, but it is a great deal nicer than grated Monterey Jack.) A stack of warm wheat-flour tortillas is also a good idea for mopping up the sauce or to use for rolling all the bits and pieces into burritos.

Chilli is almost certainly based on an early Conquistador Mexican dish of pork and chillies. Today there is no one recipe for chilli. All you can say is that it contains beef – or a mixture of beef and pork – chillies and cumin, and after that you go where your fancy and palate lead you. Lime leaves and cinnamon would probably be grounds for lynching in Texas, but in California you can be as weird as you like. How much fire you put in is also a matter of personal preference, but it wouldn't be chilli if it wasn't hot.

Chilli is always best made the day before and allowed to stand overnight at room temperature for the flavours to develop fully.

FOR 4

1 kg / 2¼ lb flank steak
1 tbsp cumin seeds
1 tbsp coriander seeds
2 tsp black peppercorns
225 g / 8 oz smoked streaky bacon [smoked thick-sliced bacon]
30 g / 1 oz [2 tbsp] lard or beef dripping
450 g / 1 lb onions
3 garlic cloves
4 fresh hot green chillies
4 tbsp sunflower oil
½ tbsp hot chilli powder
450 g / 1 lb canned tomatoes
2 Kaffir lime leaves
4 tbsp tomato ketchup
1 tbsp dried oregano
1 cinnamon stick
700 ml / 1¼ pt [3 cups] Mexican dark lager, such as Dos Equis, or strong beer
salt

TO SERVE:
Refried Black Beans (page 32)
rings of red onion
250 ml / 8 fl oz [1 cup] crème fraîche with 1 bunch of chives chopped and stirred in
tomato and red onion salad
250 g / 8 oz Reggiano Parmesan, shaved
2 fresh hot green chillies, shredded
black olives

Toast the cumin, coriander and peppercorns in a dry pan over a low heat for 2-3 minutes, stirring, until they give off their aroma. Grind in a coffee grinder and reserve.

Cut the flank steak into thin slices, then cut these into dice about the size of your little fingernail. Reserve.

Cut the bacon into lardon strips, then fry in the lard or dripping in a frying pan until brown. Transfer to a casserole. Dice the onions and fry gently with the fat and oil until soft and translucent. Do not let them brown. Smash and chop the garlic and stir in. Remove the stem from the chillies and shred, then stir in with their seeds. Add the spices and cook all together for 2 minutes, stirring. Transfer to the casserole and continue to cook over the lowest heat.

Heat a dry frying pan until smoking hot. Add the oil, throw in the meat and chilli powder and sauté vigorously to brown. Transfer to the casserole.

Whizz the tomatoes and their juice in a food processor and add to the meat along with the lime leaves, tomato ketchup, oregano and cinnamon stick. Season with salt, pour over the beer and add cold water just to cover. Stir, bring to the boil, lower the heat and simmer for 4 hours, adding water from time to time to keep it moist.

Warm through before serving, accompanied by all or some of the suggested side dishes.

Chopped Steak with a Gratin of Potatoes and Red Onions

You can put your chopped steak in a bun and call it a burger, but this is a very nice alternative way of serving it. Hamburgers are made from good-quality minced beef which should not be too lean. About 15% fat will give you the best result. It is always a good idea to choose the cut you want and have the butcher mince it for you. A good weight for a beef patty is 200 g / 7 oz. As a general rule, only salt and pepper are mixed in with the beef, with all the other things — raw onion, mustard and pickles or relish — being served separately for people to add them as they like. Natural heretics like to add Worcestershire sauce to the mixture but you decide whether the idea appeals.

There are so many variations on the gratin theme which is most famously expressed through that rich and buttery French classic, Dauphinoise. This version has a lighter feel, though one could not pretend it is a diet dish. The combination of red onion and crème fraîche genuinely gives a different flavour to an old favourite. You need only a small portion and it partners any roast or grilled meat dish to perfection. An interesting effect of mixing crème fraîche and milk is that the combination does not have the same tendency to curdle as frequently happens when cream is used, and as a consequence it can be cooked at a higher temperature.

Use a mandolin to slice the potatoes to a thickness of 3 mm / 1/8 in but, if using a Japanese Benriner (the ultimate mandolin and as sharp as a scalpel), do not as I did — caution your children never to use it without the safety grip between you and the blade, ignore your own excellent advice as soon as they have left the room and promptly slice a gash into your thumb deep enough to need stitching.

Preheat the oven to 200°C/400°F/gas6. Peel the potatoes and slice across into 3 mm / 1/8 in thick ovals using a mandolin or a sharp knife, but not the slicing disc on a food processor, which has too violent an action for this task. Peel the onion and cut in half and then into quarters. Slice these across into

1 kg / 2 1/4 lb minced beef [ground beef]
1 tbsp Worcestershire sauce
salt and pepper
1 red onion, to serve
olive oil, for brushing

FOR THE GRATIN:
900 g / 2 lb waxy potatoes
1 red onion
4 spring onions [scallions]
225 ml / 8 fl oz [1 cup] crème fraîche
1/4 nutmeg
150 ml / 1/4 pt [2/3 cup] half-fat milk
butter, for greasing

3 mm / $^1\!/_8$ in thick strips. Trim the spring onions and cut at an angle into 3 mm / $^1\!/_8$ in strips.

Butter a rectangular dish (about 25 × 12.5 × $^1\!/_2$ cm / 10 × 5 × 1 in) and lay potato slices to cover the bottom. Season with salt and pepper, strew with red onion and put small dollops of crème fraîche at intervals on the surface. Put on a second layer of potato slices, pressing down. Scatter on the spring onions, repeat with the crème fraîche and again season with salt and pepper. Put on another layer of potato, then the remaining red onion and a final layer of potato. Season with salt, pepper and grated nutmeg and spoon on the remaining crème fraîche. Don't try and cover it evenly. The crème will become liquid in the oven. Pour over the milk and push down the potatoes to compact them. Put the dish on a tray and bake for 45–50 minutes, when the top will be bubbling and golden brown.

Season the minced beef with salt, pepper and the Worcestershire sauce. Divide into 6 and form them into hamburger patties with your hands, moulding them into firm and coherent shapes. If you handle them too much you will get a tougher result, but if you don't squeeze them together enough then they will tend to fall apart.

Preheat a heavy dry frying pan over a medium heat. Brush the burgers with olive oil and cook for 2$^1\!/_2$ minutes on each side for medium-rare. Transfer to warmed plates, put a thin slice of red onion on top of each steak and mound the gratin to one side.

Grilled Peppered Sirloin and Baby Hasselbacks with Elephant Garlic and Chrysanthemum Onions

A properly aged sirloin steak – brushed with olive oil and seasoned with mignonette pepper – is seared on the ridged grill and served with crisp skinned hasselback potatoes, elephant garlic and roasted onions. The steaks come to the table moistened with Parsley, Garlic and Red Chilli Butter (page 42).

The potato accompaniment was something that developed after Alastair Little introduced me to the original hasselback – named after the Stockholm restaurant which invented it – a potato peeled and sliced almost all the way through at 5 mm / $^1\!/_4$ in intervals before being roasted in butter or oil. Those small mature potatoes like Belle de Fontenay or Charlottes that the supermarkets sell at huge profit are the ones that triggered the dish. They are the potatoes which used to be riddled out from the big guys in case somebody

4 sirloin steaks, each weighing
about 225 g / 8 oz
55 g / 2 oz [4 tbsp] Parsley, Garlic
and Red Chilli Butter (page 42)
2 tbsp olive oil
salt and coarsely ground black
pepper

FOR THE ROASTED VEGETABLES:
4 onions
100 ml / 3¹/₂ fl oz [7 tbsp] olive
oil, plus more for brushing
550 g / 1¹/₄ lb small potatoes
2 heads of elephant garlic

complained, until some bright spark thought of boxing them up and selling them at a premium. They obviously lend themselves to being sliced the same way as larger potatoes but are roasted in olive oil unpeeled together with whole unpeeled elephant garlic cloves.

Eat baby hasselbacks with other dishes instead of ordinary roast potatoes. Most people find them addictive. They are also good as part of a mezze or as a hot nibble to go with drinks.

Elephant garlic is not easy to find, but use the plump moist cloves of new season's garlic when it makes its brief appearance in the shops. Ordinary garlic works too, though it is not quite so delicate. All garlic roasted in its skin is sweet-tasting and not nearly as strong as the uninitiated suspect, emerging from the skin after roasting as soft as a purée.

As they cook, onions cut this way open like flowers. If you squint at them from the corner of your eye they look a bit chrysanthemum-like. Maybe.

Preheat the oven to 200°C/400°F/gas6.

Take the onions and cut off the top and bottom neatly. Run all the way around the onion at its widest point with a small sharp knife in a shallow cut and peel away the outer layer from the top half. Now when you sit the onion on its flat base you have a white top and a brown-skinned lower half. Make a series of parallel cuts across the onion down to where the skin begins – about 4 cuts for a smallish onion, up to 8 for a larger one. Cut again 4 or 8 times at right angles to the first cut so you now have a grid when you look down from above. Brush all over with olive oil, season with salt and pepper and put snugly in a suitable ovenproof dish with a couple of tablespoons of water. Cover with

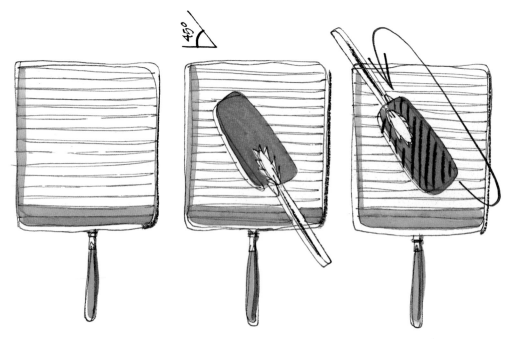

foil and roast at for 40 minutes. Remove the foil and baste with olive oil after 15 minutes, then again after a further 15 minutes. The onions will be cooked after about an hour.

Pick over the potatoes and cut out any eyes or scrape off any bits of earth the market failed to wash off for you. Using a small knife, cut down the potato in parallel cuts almost all the way through. There are special hasselback boards you can buy to speed this process and ensure you don't cut them all the way through but they aren't really necessary. Mix 2-3 tablespoons of the oil with 1 teaspoon of salt and $^1/_2$ teaspoon of coarsely milled pepper, then toss the potatoes in it to coat evenly. Put them in an ovenproof dish just large enough to hold them in a single layer and roast for about 45 minutes, i.e. add them to the oven 15 minutes after the onions have gone in. Increase the oven temperature to 220°C/425°F/gas7.

About 25 minutes before the potatoes will be ready, break the cloves off the heads of garlic and toss in the bowl with the remaining oil. Add to the potatoes and shake the roasting pan. Continue to cook until the cloves are just done and the potatoes are crisp and have fanned open along the cut lines. Grind over more pepper before bringing to the table in the roasting dish in which they were cooked.

About 10 minutes before you want to serve: preheat a ridged grill pan until smoking hot. Brush the steaks with olive oil, then press pepper and salt into both sides. Lay the steaks on at an angle of 45 degrees to the ridges. Turn three times to give a neat cross-hatch (or quadrillage). Cook for 2 minutes a side for rare, $2^1/_2$ minutes each side for medium.

Put a disc of the flavoured butter on each steak before serving.

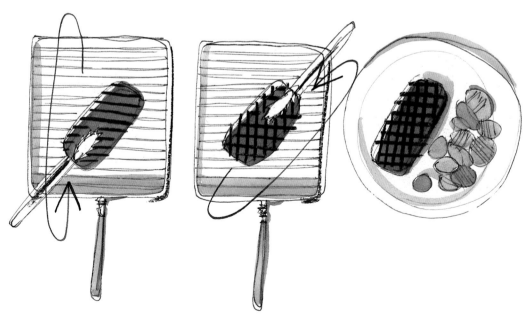

Seared Fillet Steak with Noodles in Broth

Grilled steak is not usually paired with chicken broth and Oriental noodles, but this is a combination that works most emphatically.

You can still find great steakhouses in California, like The Hitching Post on East Highway 246, half a mile east of Buellton on 101, a sober, split-timber building dedicated to simple treatments of the best locally raised aged beef. The cowboys who frequent the bar, Stetsons firmly in place, would not tolerate anything so namby-pamby and deviant as this dish. Chef-proprietor Frank Ostini knows his market and it's all meat, bar the odd fried or baked potato. Frank also grows his own grapes and produces a very drinkable house Pinot Noir. I hope he would not disapprove of this treatment too much, for it makes a little good steak go a very long way. The dish is finished with ginger and spring onions cut into the finest julienne you can manage and scattered on as a raw contrasting garnish.

You are going to be cutting the steaks into strips, so when buying specify the thin end of the fillet [tenderloin], which is slightly cheaper than the premium-priced thicker part.

FOR 4

350 g / 12 oz beef fillet [tenderloin] cut from the thin end
1 garlic clove
2 tbsp Kikkoman soy sauce, plus more for dressing
5 cm / 2 in piece of root ginger
8 spring onions [scallions]
1 red onion
1 tbsp olive oil
1.1 litres / 2 pt [5 cups] Chicken Stock (page 24)
250 g / 8 1/2 oz egg thread noodles
salt and pepper

The day before: smash and finely chop the garlic. Put with the steak in a zip-lock bag. Add the soy, seal and leave overnight in the fridge.

Next day: remove the steaks from the fridge 1 hour before you plan to cook. Peel the ginger and cut lengthwise into wafer-thin slices, then cut these into paper-thin strips. Top and tail the spring onions and cut into fine strips. Peel the red onion and dice.

Sauté the diced red onion over a low heat, stirring from time to time. When translucent and softened, remove from heat.

Put a pan of salted water on to boil. Put the stock in a pan and bring to a simmer. Preheat the ridged grill pan over a medium heat until smoking hot.

Pat the steak dry, then grill, laying at an angle of 45 degrees to the ridges for 1 minute, turning to cook the other side for 1 minute at the same angle then repeating at an angle of 45 degrees in the opposite direction to achieve a neat cross-hatch or quadrillage (see pages 202-3). This way the edges of the cut steak will have neat stripes but this is not essential. Indeed, you can cook the steaks in a heavy frying pan for this dish if you prefer. Transfer to a warm place to rest while you cook the noodles.

Blanch the noodles following the packet instructions, drain and return to the pan. Add the red onion dice and toss, then pile into 4 soup bowls. Pour a ladle of broth over each.

Cut the steak into strips at an angle of 30 degrees and arrange over the noodles. Strew the julienne of ginger and spring onion over and dribble a little soy on the meat.

Grilled Strip Sirloin Bruschetta and Mixed Salad

These are very superior steak sandwiches. Get your butcher to cut large steaks of about 285-350 g / 10-12 oz each, so one steak will serve two. Bruschetta are just toasts of good bread, rubbed with raw garlic and then drizzled with olive oil, but people have been trained now to think of toast as an inferior product.

FOR 4

2 strip sirloin steaks, each weighing about 285-350 g / 10-12 oz
1 tbsp sunflower oil
4 thick slices of good crusty bread
1 garlic clove
4 tbsp extra-virgin olive oil
salt and pepper

FOR THE SALAD:

1 large bag of mixed salad leaves
4 tbsp extra-virgin olive oil
1 tbsp lemon juice
salt and pepper

Remove the steaks from the fridge at least 30 minutes before you plan to cook them. Brush them with a little sunflower oil and press coarsely ground pepper and sea salt into the surfaces.

Preheat a deep ridged grill pan over the highest heat for 5 minutes, then lay the steaks on at an angle of 45 degrees to the ridges. This will produce a lot of acrid smoke. To achieve a neat cross-hatch effect or *quadrillage* when using a grill pan, lay the steaks at an angle of 45 degrees to the lines of the ridges, turning the first time to the same angle then repeat with the steaks laid in the opposite direction. This means each surface will come into contact with the pan twice. For rare steaks: grill for 60 seconds 4 times, that is a total of 2 minutes a side. Leave the steaks to stand for 5 minutes, then slice them thickly at an angle.

While the steaks are cooking, toast the slices of bread under the grill [broiler]. Rub with raw garlic and drizzle with olive oil. Make a dressing for the salad by mixing the oil and lemon juice with some seasoning. Toss the leaves in it just before serving.

Arrange the slices of steak on the bruschetta, with a mound of salad to the side of each of them.

Desserts for me are simple statements...

... that have one predominant flavour. I actively dislike the current restaurant fashion for incredibly elaborate endings. This happens when the chef has taken his eye off the ball and is showing off. From the cook's point of view, desserts should ideally be capable of prior preparation, which is why things like home-made ice-creams, sorbets and tarts always feature on my menus. You don't need to have dozens of puddings in your repertoire. About 10 or 12 will ensure you never serve guests the same thing twice.

Prune and Apricot Tart with Sugared Mascarpone

In the USA dried fruit tarts are one of the oldest dessert traditions of Thanksgiving, dating back to a time when fruit could only be preserved for winter eating on a large scale by drying it. Today California is one of the world's largest producers of dried fruits, notably prunes, apricots, sultanas [golden raisins] and currants — all of which can be used in this tart, which is characterized by a crisp candied base and a golden glazed puff pastry lid. Dried fruits are not necessarily inferior to fresh if they are first marinated in alcohol before being baked.

Served warm, with a scoop of clotted cream, vanilla ice-cream or sugared Mascarpone as here, this is a delicious way to finish any celebratory meal. It is a very easy dessert to make and nobody will complain if you use frozen puff pastry. The tart is best eaten while still warm but is also good cold.

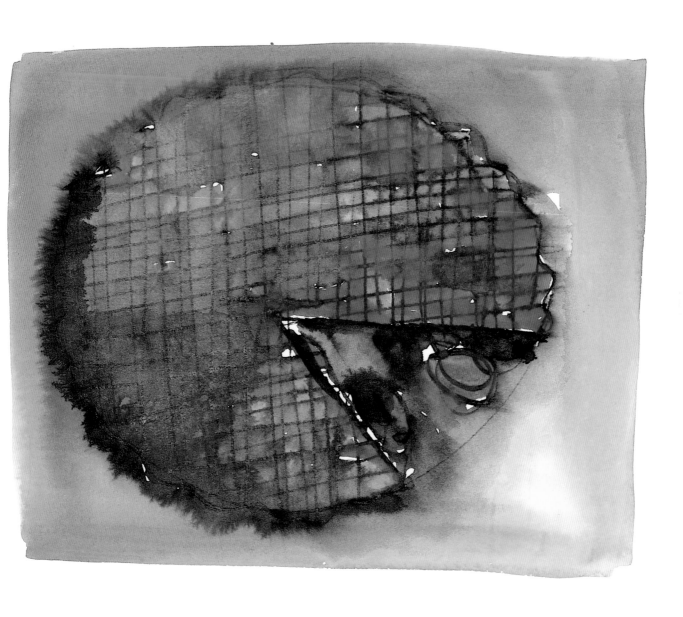

450 g / 1 lb stoned [pitted] prunes

450 g / 1 lb dried apricots

225 g / 8 oz sultanas [golden raisins]

115 g / 4 oz [¹/₂ cup] caster sugar

575 ml / 1 pt [2¹/₂ cups] dry or medium dry cider

150 ml / ¹/₄ pt [²/₃ cup] cooking brandy or rum

450 g / 1 lb sweet shortcrust pastry (page 60)

450 g / 1 lb frozen puff pastry, defrosted

1 egg yolk

2 tbsp double [heavy] cream

225 g / 8 oz Mascarpone

If you have no drunken prunes or sultanas macerating in jars of alcohol, put all the dried fruit in a bowl and pour over the cider and brandy or rum. Stir in 55g/2oz [¹/₄ cup] sugar, cover and leave for 48 hours, stirring from time to time.

If all the liquid has not been absorbed, transfer to a pan and simmer gently until it has evaporated. Remove from the heat and leave to cool.

Preheat the oven to 190°C/375°F/gas5. Roll out the shortcrust pastry, scattering a little of the sugar on as you roll, and use to line a 27 cm / 10³/₄ in tart tin with a detachable base, folding overhanging pastry back to give a double thickness to the sides. Line this with foil, fill with beans and bake blind for 15 minutes. Remove the foil and continue cooking until the base is crisp and golden brown (about 5-7 minutes). Remove from the oven and leave to cool. Then fill with the fruit.

While the shortcrust pastry base is cooling, roll out the puff pastry and cut a circle to fit the top. With a scalpel or the point of a very sharp knife, incise a fine cross-hatch pattern into the surface of the puff pastry disc, taking care not to cut all the way through. Brush the rim of the base with a little of the glaze made by mixing the egg and cream and press the puff pastry lid securely on top all round. Make a small hole in the centre to allow steam to escape and brush the lid with the remaining glaze. Increase the oven temperature to 200°C/400°F/gas6.

Bake for 20-30 minutes, until the crust is well risen and a deep golden-brown. Go for that French finish where the edges almost blacken... anaemic pastry is horrid. Leave in the tin on a rack to cool until warm before serving, cut in slices with spoonfuls of Mascarpone on the side. Shake a little sugar over the cheese.

Chocolate Chip Steamed Pudding with Hot Chocolate Custard Sauce

Chocolate chips are very American. Indeed, chocolate chip cookies are the stuff over which expats come over all weepy and go on about the joy of eating them, after school, washed down with ice-cold milk. Whatever turns you on.

Steamed puddings make lovely desserts. They can be very light and subtle. This one has chocolate chips folded into the batter. The better the quality of chocolate, the better the pudding.

140 g / 5 oz plain chocolate
  [semisweet chocolate]

2 tbsp milk

170 g / 6 oz [³/₄ cup] butter

170 g / 6 oz caster sugar [³/₄ cup
  + 2 tbsp granulated sugar]

4 drops of vanilla essence
  [vanilla extract]

3 eggs

170 g / 6 oz plain flour [1 ¼ cups
  all-purpose flour]

1 tsp baking powder

FOR THE CHOCOLATE CUSTARD
SAUCE:

225 g / 8 oz plain chocolate
  [semisweet chocolate]

300 ml / ½ pt [1 ¼ cups] milk

3 egg yolks

55 g / 2 oz caster sugar [¼ cup
  granulated sugar]

3 drops of vanilla essence
  [vanilla extract]

1 tbsp rum or whisky

Put water on to boil in a large saucepan (which has a tight-fitting lid) in which the pudding basin will sit on top of a rack, trivet or inverted plate or inside a Chinese steamer. Always do this before mixing the pudding which should be put to cook the instant it is in the bowl. The water should come just below halfway up the bowl.

Grate 85 g / 3 oz of the chocolate and put into a bowl with the milk. Set over the pan of simmering water to melt.

Cream the butter and sugar until white and fluffy, then beat in the melted chocolate. Add the vanilla essence.

Whisk the eggs and beat them in. Sift in the flour and baking powder and fold in to make a thick batter which has a dropping consistency.

Shave the remaining chocolate into small pieces and stir in. Butter a pudding basin or other dome-shaped heatproof mould, then pour and scrape in the mixture.

Steam for 2 hours. The water should be simmering, not boiling hard. From time to time, replenish with more boiling water to stop it boiling dry.

Make the chocolate sauce: in a bowl set over simmering water, melt the chocolate, whisking the milk in when it is liquid. Whisk the egg yolks and sugar in a bowl and pour the hot milk chocolate in, whisking. Return to the bowl, add the vanilla essence and liquor and cook, stirring until thick and smooth.

Turn out the pudding and cut it into slices. Put into warmed bowls with the chocolate sauce poured around.

Orange Flower Doughnuts

In California the haves eat very little, the have-nots too much of the wrong things. A standard nutritional pattern the world over, you might say, but the extremes are more obvious. At the top of the ladder you have people completely obsessed with good health and longevity. In fact, pretty soon there are going to be an awful lot of very fit, perfectly toned, zero-cholesterolled Californians dying very fit and perfectly toned because even they can't live forever. 'Hey, Lord, this just ain't fair. My callipered fat assessment was only 1 cm yesterday and I did an hour on the Stairmaster every day and went to the gym four times a week. I can't be dead.' The Lord smiles gently as he indicates the other entrance down the hallway to Eternity's Rôtisserie. 'Son, you're 86 years old. Was that any way to behave? Now get your trim butt to Hell where you belong.'

On the bottom rungs you have the whale people. These are to be found at amusement parks like Disneyland and Six Flags Magic Mountain. You didn't think they made shorts the size of flying spinnakers? Check these people out. They are so fat it is a wonder they can move, and as they waddle between the rides they eat. In America fast food is called fast because of the speed with which it is consumed, and everywhere at the parks the smell of old frying oil hangs in the air so thick you can taste it.

Fit people never eat deep-fried food because they see the whale people and think 'one bag of donuts and I'm going to be there with them, buying my Levi's at the Gross n'Giant store'. That is until you make them these Orange Flower doughnuts. It is the orange flower that does it. Something that exotic-sounding and sophisticated has to be good news. And it is.

The cleaner the frying oil the better. If you strain it through muslin or cheesecloth between uses it will be recyclable five or six times, replenishing when needed. This does not apply if you fry anything in breadcrumbs because some inevitably detach from the food and burn during prolonged frying, tainting the oil irreparably. I always use sunflower oil, though any good-quality vegetable oil works as well. Mixed-source vegetable oils are to be avoided. They often contain palm oil, which actually has more cholesterol than beef dripping or lard. You really need an electric mixer with a dough hook to make this dough. It is too sticky otherwise and you would need to be a weight-lifter on steroids to knead it by hand.

6 oz / 1¼ oz sachet of instant
    easy-blend yeast
2 tbsp warm water
6 eggs
225 g / 8 oz [1 cup + 2 tbsp] sugar
3 tbsp orange flower water
675 g / 1½ lb plain flour [6 cups
    all-purpose flour]
55 g / 2 oz [4 tbsp] softened butter
sunflower oil, for deep-frying
icing [confectioner's] sugar, to dust
good-quality apricot jam, to serve

Fry about four at a time, never overcrowding the pan. Heat the oil to maximum – 190 °C/375°F – before putting the beignet into it. The temperature will drop immediately. Check with a thermometer. If it falls below 180°C/350°F, then the food will not seal on the outside but absorb oil excessively.

Put the yeast and warm water in the bowl of the food mixer and stir in. Add the eggs, sugar and orange flower water and switch on the dough hook at low. Add the flour and work at low speed for 8 minutes. Increase the speed to medium, add the softened butter and continue to work for 2 minutes.

Transfer the dough to an oiled bowl, cover with plastic film and leave to rise for 2 hours.

Turn out on to a floured surface and knead. Cut into 12 pieces and shape into balls. Cover with a cloth and leave to rise again for 30 minutes.

Deep-fry in batches of 4 at 190°C/375°F (see above) until golden and expanded. Dust with icing sugar and serve while still warm, with a spoonful of apricot jam.

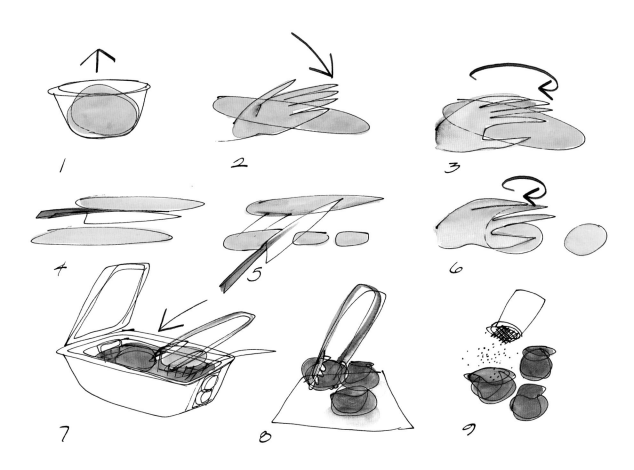

1

2

3

4

5

6

7

8

9

Grape Tart

FOR 8

350g/12oz seedless green grapes
350g/12oz seedless black grapes
   one 23cm/9in sweet shortcrust
   tart shell, baked blind (see pages
   58-60)
icing sugar [confectioner's]
   sugar, for dusting

FOR THE PASTRY CREAM:
6 egg yolks
115g/4oz [$^1/_2$ cup + 1 tbsp]
   vanilla sugar
30g/1oz cornflour [3$^1/_2$ tbsp
   cornstarch]
300ml/$^1/_2$pt [1$^1/_4$ cups] full-fat
   milk
150ml/$^1/_4$pt single cream [$^2/_3$
   cup light cream]
2 tbsp rum or brandy

Once an expensive treat for the most special occasions or to be eaten with relish by visitors beside a hospital bed, dessert grapes like Black Hamburg and Siegerrebe are grown in limited quantities under glass in Britain but are also imported all year round on a huge scale, mostly from California. There are many different varieties in both seeded and seedless forms, with different flavours, sizes and toughness of skin. Muscat grapes – with their extraordinary floral fragrance and sweet intensity – are arguably the finest.

The skin colour really makes no discernible difference to the taste of a dessert grape and is more a matter of cosmetic preference than an indicator of its quality. It is nice if serving grapes on their own as a dessert to have both green and black, precisely because of the colour contrast. A small sharp pair of scissors on the dish on which they are brought to the table is not an affectation but a simple courtesy, allowing people to snip the amount they want and leave the bunch with some visual integrity. Pulling off individual grapes leaves an unsightly mess.

Make the pastry cream: whisk the egg yolks with the vanilla sugar to a stiffish ribbon consistency. If you do not have any vanilla sugar, add a teaspoon of vanilla essence [vanilla extract] to ordinary caster sugar [US granulated sugar]. Whisk in the cornflour, beating hard to make sure there are no lumps. Then, while continuing to whisk, pour in the milk in a thin stream until you have a smooth texture, followed by the cream.

Put in a saucepan and stir constantly over a low heat until the custard thickens. Add the liquor and continue stirring and cooking for a couple of minutes. Pour and scrape into the pastry case, smoothing to even the surface, and leave to cool and set.

Scald the grapes for 5 seconds in boiling water, refresh in cold water and peel. If you neither have the time nor inclination, use them unskinned, in which case don't scald. Arrange in the custard to fill the tart, pressing down so that half of each grape shows above the surface. Dust the top with icing sugar [confectioners' sugar]. This tart looks pretty and tastes special and, as an added bonus, is unsuitable for a hospital visit.

Peach and Blueberry Crumble

FOR 6-8

450 g / 1 lb [3 cups] blueberries

1.35 kg / 3 lb ripe peaches

2 tbsp flour

1 tbsp caster sugar [US
   granulated sugar]

2 tbsp brandy

FOR THE TOPPING:

115 g / 4 oz plain flour [^{3}/4 cup +
   1 tbsp all-purpose flour]

100 g / 3½ oz demerara sugar
   [^{1}/2 cup raw brown sugar]

1 tbsp caster sugar [US granulated
   sugar]

100 g / 3½ oz [7 tbsp] butter,
   chilled and cut into small
   dice, plus more for greasing

FOR THE LEMON CREAM:

^{1}/2 lemon

575 ml / 1 pt double cream
   [2^1/3 cups heavy cream]

4 tsp icing sugar [confectioners'
   sugar]

Peaches and blueberries are two of my favourite individual fruits and also work splendidly together. The most recent American trend in desserts has been to create ever more complex visual forms on the plate and not always to the benefit of the ingredients. Once a fork has been pushed into the New World pâtissier's work of art, it looks a ravaged mess. If you cook for taste and get that right, the food will invariably look right too, for food should look like itself and taste of itself if it is to be pure in effect.

Here there is nothing to get between the cooked fruit and the person eating it and the last mouthful will look as good on the plate as the first. I like to think Alice Waters would approve of this serendipitous combination which emulates her own peach crisp.

First make the topping: put the flour and sugars into a food processor and whizz briefly, then add the butter and process again until the mixture crumbs.

Preheat the oven to 190°C/375°F/gas 5 and butter a 2.25 litre / 4 pt [2½ qt] gratin dish.

Rinse and pick over the blueberries, discarding any that have burst. Cut the peaches into quarters, then peel and slice each quarter into 3. Put them into a bowl and toss with the flour and sugar to coat.

Put the blueberries into the prepared dish, then arrange the peach slices overlapping on top of them. Dribble the brandy over and sprinkle on the crumble topping.

Bake for 30-40 minutes, when the topping will be golden brown and the fruit thick and bubbling. Leave for 10 minutes before serving.

Meanwhile, grate the zest from the lemon. Whip the cream until it forms soft peaks, then fold in the lemon zest and icing sugar.

Serve the crumble with a big spoon of this lemon cream on the side.

Strawberry Shortcake

FOR 6-8

225 g / 8 oz self-raising flour [1²/₃
   cups self-rising flour]
pinch of salt
30 g / 1 oz caster sugar [2¹/₂ tbsp
   granulated sugar]
85 g / 3 oz [6 tbsp] unsalted butter,
   chilled and cut into 1 cm / ¹/₂ n
   cubes
grated zest of 1 lemon
2 egg yolks
300 ml / ¹/₂ pt [1 ¹/₄ cups] milk

TO FINISH:
450 g / 1 lb strawberries
300 ml 1 ¹/₂ pt double cream [1 ¹/₄
   cups heavy cream]
30 g / 1 oz caster sugar [2¹/₂ tbsp
   granulated sugar]
icing sugar [confectioners' sugar], for
   dusting

The short in the title is from shortening, the American word for the fat element in pastry or cakes. The traditional American way of serving shortcake is to split it while still warm from the oven and spread with butter before adding the strawberries and pouring over thick cream. This version leaves out the butter spread, serves the shortcake cold and whips the cream.

English midsummer strawberries have an unbeatable flavour, but this need not preclude serving imported Californian berries in a shortcake with whipped cream, a delightful combination at any time of the year.

Preheat the oven to 220°C/425°F/gas7 and line a non-stick 20 cm / 8 in cake pan.

Sift the flour into a food processor with a pinch of salt and the sugar. Add the butter and process briefly until you have a crumb texture. Add the lemon zest and egg yolks and process briefly again to combine. With the machine running at full speed, add the milk in a stream through the feeder tube until you have a thick batter-like dough.

Scrape the batter into it the prepared pan and bake for 20 minutes, until risen and golden brown. Check it is done by inserting a skewer: if it comes out dry and hot to the touch it is ready; if still moist, continue baking for a few more minutes before turning out on to a cake rack to cool.

Cut the strawberries in half vertically, and whip the cream with the sugar until it just stiffens. Be careful not to take it too far or it will separate.

Using a serrated knife, cut the shortcake in half horizontally.

Spread whipped cream on the bottom half and cover with halved strawberries. Gently put on the top half, spread the top with the remaining cream and cover neatly with more strawberries. Finally, dust with a little icing sugar.

Lime Cheesecake with Blueberry Compote

Wherever you go in the USA you will find cheesecakes. Indeed, it is not unusual to find a dozen or more different ones to choose from. Usually the base is a sweet crumb crust, and while this is very nice I prefer the cake served in an almond pastry shell and with mascarpone as well as cream cheese. Typically a cheesecake is a thick affair. This is presented as a tart, the top covered in an intensely flavoured compote of blueberries. The strength of the limes cuts the richness of the cream cheese very effectively.

First make the compote: put 200 g / 7 oz [1 1/3 cups] of the blueberries in a pan with the sugar and 100 ml / 3 1/2 fl oz [7 tbsp] water. Bring to the boil, lower the heat and simmer until the blueberries are soft and start to break down (about 12-15 minutes). Remove the compote from the heat, stir in the remaining blueberries and reserve.

Preheat the oven to 180°C/350°F/gas4.

Wash the limes carefully and dry them. Then grate off the zest and reserve. Juice the limes and the lemon and reserve also.

In an electric food mixer, beat the eggs and sugar until light and white. Continuing to beat, adding the cream cheese and mascarpone. When smoothly incorporated, add the zest of the limes and the citrus juices.

Put the tart shell on a baking tray and pour in the cheese mixture. Smooth the top and bake for 30 minutes, or until set. Remove and allow to cool.

Spread the blueberry compote on top of the cool cheesecake and refrigerate for about 1 hour before serving.

FOR 6-8

one 23 cm / 9 in almond tart
    shell, baked blind (pages 58-60)
4 limes
1 lemon
4 eggs
200 g / 7 oz caster sugar [1 cup
    granulated sugar]
285 g / 10 oz [1 1/4 cups] cream
    cheese
115 g / 4 oz [1/2 cup]
    mascarpone cheese

FOR THE BLUEBERRY COMPOTE:
285 g / 10 oz [2 cups] blueberries
85 g / 3 oz caster sugar [7 tbsp
    granulated sugar]

Citrus Curd Tart with Candied Orange Peel

Curd tarts are very easy to prepare and make popular desserts. This one combines orange, lemon and lime juices, and the top is finished with strips of orange peel which are cooked in sugar syrup until they candy.

Scrub the fruit in hot soapy water, rinse well and pat dry with a cloth. Grate the zest from the lemons and limes and reserve. Cut the peel from both oranges in continuous thin strips, taking care not to lift too much pith. Juice all the fruit and reserve.

Melt the butter over a low heat. Whisk the eggs together with the caster sugar and the citrus juices. Add to the pan with the grated zest. Cook, stirring, until the mixture thickens to a thick custard, about 15 minutes. Pour and scrape into the tart shell.

Put the remaining granulated sugar and 5 tablespoons of water in a small pan and bring to the boil. Add the orange peel strips and cook until all the liquid has evaporated, leaving the strips candied. Pile in the centre of the tart and leave to cool, then refrigerate for at least 1 hour.

FOR 6-8

3 lemons
3 limes
2 oranges
55 g / 2 oz [4 tbsp] unsalted butter
8 eggs
225 g / 8 oz caster sugar [1 cup
    + 2 tbsp granulated sugar]
one 23 cm / 9 in sweet shortcrust
    tart shell, baked blind (pages
    58-60)
2 tbsp granulated sugar

Sweet Fig Pizza with Goats' Cheese

The basic bread dough on page 52 welcomes dessert interpretations. Try this for a quick and easy tart with a difference and serve it warm with a piece of mild goats' cheese on the side.

FOR 6-8

225 g / 8 oz pizza dough (page 54)
2 tsp polenta flour or cornmeal
12 ripe figs
4 tbsp dark brown sugar
4 tbsp extra-virgin olive oil
icing sugar [confectioners'
    sugar], to dust

Press the dough into a 25 cm / 10 in tart pan with a detachable base.

Scatter the base first with the polenta. Cut the figs lengthwise into quarters and press them into the surface. Cover with a cloth and leave to rise at room temperature for 1 hour.

Preheat the oven to 220°C/425°F/gas7.

Scatter the brown sugar over the top of the pizza, then dribble on the olive oil and bake for 15 minutes.

Dust with icing sugar, remove from the pan and cut into eight wedges. If the idea of cheese with this does not appeal, then clotted cream or a scoop of vanilla ice-cream is equally delicious.

Lime Polenta Cake with Raspberry Coulis

FOR 6-8

115 g / 4 oz plain flour [¾ cup +
    1 tbsp all-purpose flour]
1½ tsp baking powder
½ tsp salt
115 g / 4 oz [1 cup] instant polenta
225 g / 8 oz caster sugar [1 cup
    + 2 tbsp granulated sugar]
2 size-1 [US jumbo] eggs, plus
    whites of 3 more size-1 eggs
55 g / 2 oz [4 tbsp] butter, softened,
    plus more for greasing
3½ tbsp olive oil
grated zest and juice of 3 limes
150 ml / ¼ pt [⅔ cup] crème fraîche
clotted or whipped cream, to
    serve (optional)

California's vineyards are noted for their fine food as well as great wines. Annual tastings are frequently conducted as open-air fiestas, with regular buyers gathering for a day made special by the cooking as well as the joy of tasting the new vintage. The idea for this cake comes from John Ash of Fetzer, one of the biggest wineries, who makes his with lemon rather than lime and serves it with a rosemary syrup. Eat it the same day you bake it.

You can use instant Valsugana-type polenta, or experiment with a mixture of cornmeal and traditional coarse polenta, using a higher percentage of flour than polenta. A proportion of 75% to 25% will work well.

Preheat the oven to 180°C/350°F/gas4 and grease a 20 cm / 8 in non-stick cake pan with a little butter.

Sift the flour, baking powder and salt into a bowl, then stir in the polenta. With an electric whisk, beat the sugar, eggs and egg whites until white and stiff. Add the softened butter, olive oil, lime zest and juice and the crème fraîche, continuing to beat until smooth and fully amalgamated.

FOR THE RASPBERRY COULIS:
450 g / 1 lb [2 pt] raspberries
1 tablespoon lemon juice
sugar syrup (below), to taste

Lightly fold in the polenta mixture, scooping and turning the bowl. Do not stir in too vigorously or the end result will be heavy. Pour and scrape into the greased pan and level the top with a narrow metal spatula.

Place on a baking sheet and bake for 30 minutes, or until a skewer inserted into the middle comes out warm and dry. Do not overcook or the cake will be dry and crumble when cut. Turn out on a rack and allow to cool.

Make the raspberry coulis: put the raspberries in a food processor and blitz to a purée with the lemon juice and sugar syrup to taste.

Spoon this coulis on to serving plates. Cut the cake into wedges and set a wedge to one side of each plate. Add a scoop of cream if you like.

Blood Orange Granita

Granita is an Italian granular sorbet which specifically is not made in a churn because it is supposed to have discernible chunks of ice in it. This mixture will obviously freeze as a sorbet if you use a churn. The amount of sugar syrup you use will depend on how tart the oranges are. It is anyway usual to add some lemon juice to cut the sugar. While blood oranges are specified because of their stunning colour and depth of flavour, any juicy sweet orange will do, but beware those ones like footballs that have a thick spongy rind and an excessively pithy flesh.

*MAKES ABOUT 1.1 LITRES /
2 PT [1 QT]*

*12 juicy oranges, preferably
blood oranges*
*170 g / 6 oz caster sugar [³/₄
cup + 2 tbsp granulated sugar]*
juice of 1 lemon
mint leaves, to decorate

Make a syrup by putting the caster sugar in a heavy-based saucepan and adding the juice of the lemon and 100 ml / 3 ¹/₂ fl oz [7 tbsp] water. Stir to dissolve over a low heat, then increase heat to medium and bring to the boil. Boil for 3 minutes and leave to cool.

Scrub the oranges thoroughly in hot soapy water, rinse well and pat dry. Grate the zest off the oranges and add to the syrup. Squeeze the oranges and add their juice to the syrup mixture with 125 ml / 4 fl oz [¹/₂ cup] cold water. Stir all together and pour into a dish which will go into the freezer.

Freeze, removing from the freezer every 15 minutes and stirring, turning the mixture thoroughly as its starts to freeze. Then repeat every 10 minutes, until it is too stiff to turn. You should have a nice granular texture.

Remove from the freezer 10 minutes before serving and scoop out portions to bring to the table in chilled glasses, decorated with a couple of mint leaves.

Campari and Grapefruit Sorbet

Campari and grapefruit juice is a very pretty summery drink, only improved by the addition of a large slug of Stolichnaya. Leave out the vodka and turn it into this fresh-tasting sorbet, which you need to churn and freeze in an ice-cream maker. Add an egg white and achieve a texture that is intriguingly somewhere between an ice-cream and a sorbet.

MAKES ABOUT 1.1 LITRES / 2 PT
[1 QT]

100 ml / 3 1/2 fl oz [7 tbsp] Campari
750 ml / 27 fl oz [3 cups] fresh
  grapefruit juice
115 g / 4 oz caster sugar [1/2 cup
  + 1 tbsp granulated sugar]

Put the sugar in a saucepan with 125 ml / 4 fl oz [1/2 cup] water and bring to the boil. Stir until you have a clear syrup. Leave to cool until warm, then add the Campari and grapefruit juice.

Freeze in an ice-cream maker. Alternatively, make it into a granita: pour into a shallow metal tray and put in the freezer. Remove every 15 minutes and stir and turn with a fork to break up the ice as it starts to form. Keep on doing this for 3 or 4 hours, or until you have a fairly uniform crystal size and the mixture is firm without being frozen solid.

Vanilla Ice-cream with Butterscotch Sauce

Cold creamy ice and hot butterscotch sauce. There is no dessert to match it and nothing could be simpler. The sauce can be made up to a week in advance and kept in the fridge. Fresh ice-cream is always best eaten as soon after it has been frozen as possible which, realistically, let us call the next day. People think that frozen things don't deteriorate, but they do. In the case of ice-cream, it rapidly gets a freezer taste.

A classic vanilla ice-cream, heavily scented with vanilla pods, will always be one of the finest ice-creams. When you have used the vanilla pods, wash and dry them and store in a jar of sugar to infuse it with their scent. Use the sugar for the next batch of ice-cream.

The idea of using semi-whipped cream comes from Andrew Peaston, a chef in Perth, Australia, I tested the recipe in Santa Barbara.

Split the vanilla pods and scrape out the seeds with the edge of a teaspoon. Put the pods and seeds in a pan with the milk and slowly bring to the boil. While this is heating, whisk the sugar and egg yolks in a glass or stainless steel bowl until almost white. As soon as the milk boils, pour it on to the yolks, whisking until incorporated.

4 vanilla pods [vanilla beans] or
   good-quality vanilla essence
   [vanilla extract] to taste
575 ml / 1 pt [2¹/₃ cups] full-fat milk
225 g / 8 oz caster sugar [1 cup
   + 2 tbsp granulated sugar]
8 egg yolks
300 ml / ¹/₂ pt single cream [1¹/₄
   cups light cream]

FOR THE BUTTERSCOTCH SAUCE:
225 g / 8 oz caster sugar [1 cup
   + 2 tbsp granulated sugar]
300 ml / ¹/₂ pt single cream [1¹/₄
   cups light cream]
115 g / 4 oz [¹/₂ cup] unsalted
   butter, diced

Place the bowl on top of a pan of boiling water and stir constantly with a wooden spoon until the custard starts to thicken and coat the back of the spoon. Remove from the heat and strain through a fine sieve into a clean bowl. Leave to cool.

Whip the cream until it just starts to thicken and then fold it into the custard. Pour into an ice-cream maker and churn until just frozen. Spoon into a plastic container with a lid and put in the freezer, removing 3-4 minutes before serving.

Make the butterscotch sauce: put the sugar and 100 ml / 3¹/₂ fl oz [7 tbsp] water in a heavy pan and bring to the boil. Lower the heat and use a thermometer to take the caramel to 180°C/350°F, when it will be a deep golden brown. Remove the pan from the heat and gradually add the cream, starting with a spoonful at a time as the mixture will foam up when the cold cream hits the incandescent toffee.

When all the cream has been incorporated, gradually stir in diced unsalted butter to give a smooth creamy sauce. Use immediately or cool and refrigerate for up to a week. Reheat gently, only returning to a boil after the butterscotch is heated through.

Serve the ice-cream with the sauce spooned over it.

Vanilla Ice Praline Tart

Everything you do in the kitchen should avoid duplication of effort. On one level this is planning, the mise en place of the restaurant, but on another it is seeing opportunities to ring the changes on a particular base element. In this book we see this in the flavoured butters, roasted tomatoes and sweet peppers, different mayonnaises and sauces. Vanilla ice-cream is also a case in point. Here a standard almond pastry shell is baked blind, filled with vanilla ice-cream and topped with praline. Serve it with the warm butterscotch sauce. Same ingredients, different combination, unique effect.

FOR 6-8

850 ml / 1¹/₂ pt [just under 1 qt]
   Vanilla Ice-cream (above),
   slightly softened
one 23 cm / 9 in almond tart
   shell, baked blind (pages 58-60)
Butterscotch Sauce (above), warmed,
   to serve

FOR THE PRALINE:
225 g / 8 oz caster sugar [1 cup +
   2 tbsp granulated sugar]
170 g / 6 oz [1¹/₄ cups] blanched
   almonds

First make the praline: in a saucepan, dissolve the sugar in 100 ml / 3¹/₂ fl oz [7 tbsp] water over a medium heat, stirring with a wooden spoon until the syrup boils. Then reduce the heat and continue to cook uncovered and without stirring until it is a pale caramel colour.

Tip in the almonds and swirl the pan to coat them, then pour and scrape on to a buttered baking sheet and leave until cold and set. Break this up into pieces, put into a food processor and blitz to crush to a uniform coarse texture. This praline will keep in an airtight container for up to 3 weeks.

Fill the tart shell with the vanilla ice-cream, freeze again briefly and top with the praline. Serve it with the warm butterscotch sauce.

Frozen Strawberry Yogurt

California was one of the first places to embrace frozen yogurt as a healthier alternative to traditional high-fat ice-cream. When making frozen yogurt it helps to have a food processor and an ice-cream maker, but it is possible to freeze it in a tray in the freezer.

You can make ices without an egg-based custard, but they tend not to hold together well on the plate. The custard does not have to be thick, nor to contain the number of egg yolks found in cardiac-arrest ice-creams. However, you can enrich this frozen yogurt by adding 300 ml / ½ pt [1 ¼ cups] of lightly whipped cream halfway through churning should you wish to clamber on the hi-fat, lo-fat fence.

This is one dish where canned strawberries actually work better than fresh.

575 ml / 1 pt [2⅓ cups] plain yogurt
450 g / 1 lb canned strawberries, including juice
30 g / 1 oz cornflour [3½ tbsp cornstarch]
little milk
2 egg yolks
55 g / 2 oz caster sugar [¼ cup granulated sugar]
juice of 1 lemon
mint leaves, to decorate

First stabilize the yogurt: mix the cornflour to a paste with a little milk. Put the yogurt in a pan over a low heat and whisk in the cornflour mixture. Bring to the boil, lower the heat and simmer for 8-10 minutes.

Beat the egg yolks and sugar to a pale fluffy cream. Whisk in the stabilized yogurt and return to the pan over the lowest heat, cooking gently until it thickens slightly.

In a food processor, blitz the strawberries with their syrup and the lemon juice to a smooth purée. With the machine still running, add the yogurt custard through the feeder tube.

Scrape into an ice-cream maker and churn until set. If you do not have a machine to do the job, pour into trays. Wrap in plastic film and freeze until set. After 30 minutes remove and stir with a fork, then repeat 1 hour later and so on. It will take between 3 and 6 hours to complete the process.

Serve decorated with mint leaves.

Index